My Wide World

Jim McKay

Macmillan Publishing Co., Inc.
New York
Collier Macmillan Publishers
London

My  Wide World

Macmillan Publishing Co., Inc.
866 Third Avenue, New York, N.Y. 10022
Collier-Macmillan Canada Ltd., Toronto, Ontario

Library of Congress Catalog Card Number: 73–2754

First Printing 1973

Printed in the United States of America

The strain from *On the Banks of the Wabash* in the chorus used by kind permission of Maurice Richmond Music Co. Inc. Copyright MCMXVII by Shapiro, Bernstein & Co. Inc. Copyright Renewed MCMXLIV and Assigned. Used by permission.
From "To an Athlete Dying Young" from "A Shropshire Lad"— Authorised Edition—from *The Collected Poems of A. E. Housman.* Copyright 1939, 1940, © 1965 by Holt, Rinehart and Winston, Inc. Copyright © 1967, © 1968 by Robert E. Symons. Reprinted by permission of Holt, Rinehart and Winston, Inc., and by permission of The Society of Authors as the literary representative of the Estate of A. E. Housman; and Jonathan Cape Ltd., publishers of A. E. Housman's *Collected Poems.*

*This book is dedicated
To Margaret, Mary, and Seàn,
Who lived these events with me, and put them all in
perspective by making home the main place
in my wide world*

Acknowledgements

In addition to my wife, my daughter, and my son, to whom this book is dedicated, there are a number of people who have deserved my thanks through the years. These are some of them, and each knows why. Edwin P. Young, assistant to the publisher, *The Providence Journal*. Robert Cochrane, WMAR-TV, Baltimore. The late Richard Swift. Hugh Beach. Roone Arledge. William O. Sires, M.D. Mr. and Mrs. Joseph F. McManus, my mother and father. Mrs. W. M. Oeste, my sister.

Rick Giacalone of the ABC photo department and my associates at ABC Sports have all been extremely kind and helpful.

Contents

Introduction

"Well," I said to my wife, Margaret, "It's time to move the car from one side of the street to the other."

"All right," she said, then, "Oh, on the way back, would you mind stopping at the laundry room and picking up the sheets? I left them in the dryer this afternoon."

This was in the 1950s at our apartment in the building at 750 Park Avenue in New York. It was eleven o'clock and we had just finished watching Ed Murrow's TV program, "Person to Person." In case you are too young to remember it, this was one of the most popular shows of its time, on which Ed Murrow sat in a studio and talked, live, to people who conducted him on a tour of their home.

I had to move the car because of a maddening new law that had just been passed in New York. It stated, in effect, that if you wanted to park your car on the street in Manhattan, you would have to move it from one side of the street to the other every night. To find another place often took as long as twenty minutes.

As I walked to our car, a light blue Pontiac convertible, around the corner on 73d Street, I saw the large CBS mobile unit sitting at the side door of an apartment building. Obviously, one of the "Person to Person" interviews had been held inside and the crew was starting to break things down.

I was working at CBS then. The associate director, a friend, strolled out of the building and lit a cigarette.

"Who lives in there?" I asked him. "Which part of the show was this?"

"Dag Hammerskjöld," he said. "Come on in and take a look at the apartment and say hello to him."

"No, I can't do that. I look like a bum and I don't want to bother him."

The A.D. insisted, so inside we went and there was the Secretary General of the United Nations, holding out his hand, smiling, and offering me a drink when I told him I had seen the show.

"Was it good?" he asked. We were now sitting in armchairs—he in his handsome English-cut suit, I in my old sweater and wearing no tie.

I told him it was very good and we discussed the segment in detail, which required another Dewar's White Label on the rocks with a twist before we finished.

Then we said good night and he thanked me for coming by.

I moved the car (taking another twenty minutes to find a place), walked back to the apartment house, and down to the laundry. I picked up the sheets, took the elevator to the second floor, and clumsily knocked on the front door, my arms full of white linen.

It was only then that I realized I had been gone a long time, more than an hour, and Margaret might be worried. She was.

"Honey, where in the world have you been?" she asked.

"If I told you," I said, "you'd never believe me."

It's been like that on a larger scale for most of the past twelve and a half years, the time during which I have been the host of ABC's Wide World of Sports.

I've left home frequently, not to go around the corner, but around the world; and often, on my return, when Margaret or the kids ask me what happened on a trip, I use the same line: "If I told you, you'd never believe me."

To tell the whole twelve-and-a-half-year story would take more time than either you or I have.

What I will do instead is to tell you the story of one man's summer of 1972, from late April until early September, from Indianapolis to Munich, from racing to golf to the Olympics, from Mark Donohue and Lee Trevino to Dave Wottle and Olga Korbut, from the beauty of Pebble Beach to the terror of Building 31 in the Olympic Village.

Along the way, I'll recall some of the other things that have happened in the twelve and a half years, during which we at Wide World of Sports have covered more than 100 sports in thirty-five countries and forty-five states.

We have visited Lenin Stadium in Moscow, Wembley Stadium in London, The Melbourne Cricket Grounds, Croke Park in Dublin, and the Olympic stadia in Mexico City and Munich.

Many of our events have taken place in natural settings, like ski racing in the Alps, the Rockies, and the mountains of Chile; the races for the America's Cup in the waters of the Atlantic off Newport, Rhode Island; the finish of the Baja 1,000 road race on a lonely, dark stretch of primitive highway outside La Paz, Mexico, at the far end of Baja California.

We have seen men race, and sometimes die, on the automobile race courses of the world. We've seen them in the Indianapolis 500, that confusing blend of Hoosier hoopla, hot dogs, beer, 300,000 people, magnificent racing machines, thousands of balloons rising against a Memorial Day sky, brave drivers, and sudden death. We've seen them in the 24 hours of LeMans, that annual French experience that is almost as exhausting for the spectators as it is for the drivers.

In covering the events, we have stayed in an eleventh century chateau in France, Claridge's in London, and tiny Southern motels that feature paper bath mats and steak fried in batter.

Our travels have brought rewards—five Emmy awards from the Television Academy for Wide World, a Peabody "for furthering international understanding," and the top prize in "News and Sports Outside Broadcasts" at the Cannes Television Festival. Two individual Emmys have come my way, and, in 1973, a George Polk Memorial Award as the outstanding television news reporter of 1972.

It has been a long, exciting, tiring, and rewarding journey.

Still, in all the years, there was never anything quite like that summer of 1972.

My Wide World

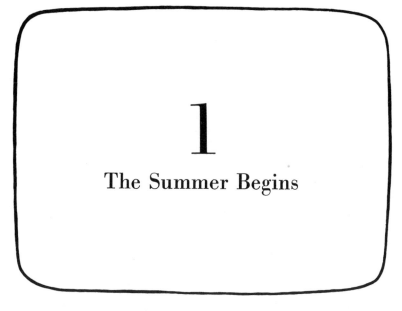

1

The Summer Begins

The road to Munich and the games of the Twentieth Olympiad began for me on this day, illogically enough, with a trip to Los Angeles.

Actually, there is a logic to the wanderings of ABC Sports, but it is a logic that leads down many side roads and byways and involves unending changes of plan. It is, for that reason, a disconcerting place to work in many ways. No one likes uncertainty in his life on a regular basis. No one is fond of the phone call that comes as you are walking out the door on a brief holiday, the phone call that tells you it is all changed, that suddenly there is a foot race or a ski race or a road race that demands your immediate presence in Eugene, Oregon; Val d'Isere, France; or Monte Carlo, Monaco.

Sometimes the location is considerably less glamorous, such as

1

Darlington, South Carolina; or Islip, Long Island, New York. Still, there is an excitement to this kind of life that most men find appealing, somewhere under the surface irritations.

We went to Los Angeles, for example, on a last minute change of plan that originally called for a trip to Terre Haute, Indiana, for a sprint car automobile race.

If you've never been a guest of honor in Terre Haute, you've never been a guest of honor at all. They are a very friendly group of Hoosiers, and when Wide World of Sports visits, they give us the modern-day mid-American version of a Roman triumph. This latter-day equivalent of palm fronds spread in your way consists of a welcome on the electric sign in front of every motel in town.

I would miss the Terre Haute welcome in 1972.

The reason for the change of plans this time was a presentation to be made by Roone Arledge, president of ABC Sports, and others from our department, to officials of ABC's affiliated stations, gathered in annual convention.

This was the day that the Apollo 16 astronauts splashed down safely and that Edmund Muskie withdrew from further competition in the presidential primaries. It's a time of swift change, all right. On the plane coming out, I had read some lines written by the songwriter Paul Simon, which said that all the world's people are either stoned or waiting for elections, drowned or swimming the wrong way.

Simon's lines contrasted sharply with something else I read on the way out, a profile of Bobby Jones by Herbert Warren Wind in *The New Yorker*. Jones had died shortly before, after many years of slowly declining health and painful ailments, and Wind wrote: "As a young man, he was able to stand up to just about the best that life can offer, and later he stood up with equal grace to just about the worst."

And he had a quote from Jones himself, just a day or two before his death. "If this is all there is to it," he said, "it sure is peaceful."

The entire life of Bob Jones—courtly, gentlemanly in the face of pain and tragedy—seems like something from another century of sport. Yet, he had seemed still a part of the current sporting scene when I first began covering major golf tournaments in the mid-1950s.

It's different now, and the changes have been swift. The life style of every young golfer or football player has changed each year that the purses increased on the golf tour or interleague warfare sent the pro football price tags soaring.

Everything is different, and bigger. Better? Maybe the travels of the next few months can give us some idea.

SPEEDWAY, INDIANA—FRIDAY, APRIL 28

We talked to the affiliates and hopefully got them excited about our Olympics coverage. It will take up their entire nighttime network schedule on week nights during late August and September, plus many more hours on the weekends, 61½ hours altogether.

I'm in the Speedway Motel near Indianapolis now, just after midnight, Indiana time. It's a real contrast to last night's hotel. That was the Century Plaza in Los Angeles, that big curving edifice that serves as the centerpiece for Century City, the world's fanciest shopping center.

There is something unsettling about the Century Plaza. It can't seem to make up its mind what it wants to be. The doorman is dressed as an English beefeater, for example, while the bellmen are made up as Chinese coolies.

The Speedway Motel, on the other hand, knows exactly what it is. It is an ordinary, middle-range American motel eleven months a year. Most rooms have two beds with thin brown bedspreads. The coat hangers have circular hooks, so you can't steal them off the pole. The TV set is bolted to its stand. Only one item gives away the motel's real reason for existence—a lamp in each room, the base of which is made to resemble a checkered flag, the sign of victory in automobile racing.

The Speedway Motel is located just outside turn two of the Indianapolis Motor Speedway. It is owned by Tony Hulman, who owns the racetrack, and in the month of May, it is the home of the racing establishment. For that one month, it is the toughest hotel in the country to get a room in.

When I arrived this evening, it was almost midnight. The elderly gentleman who greeted me was casual and friendly, sorting through a pile of reservation forms until he came across mine.

"Welcome back, Mr. McKay," he said. "Have a nice month with us." It was check-in time for the traumatic month of May at Indy. From the bar, at the very moment I walked in, one could hear the pianist playing the nostalgic melody of "Back Home Again in Indiana."

SATURDAY, APRIL 29

We are here not for a Wide World, but to put together a seven-minute segment for a "Monday Night Sports" show. This is a test series of three programs on which Howard Cosell and I are serving as commentators, exploring sport in greater depth than we have a chance to do normally.

This is the first weekend of practice for the 500, the only event I know of where the competitors spend one month on the scene practicing for a single afternoon's activity. Today, we documented the first man to get his car on the track. It was Denny Zimmerman of Connecticut.

"Well," said Denny, "we have two firsts down and two to go. We were the first car entered for the race and now we're first on the track. All we have to do from here is be the fastest qualifier and win the race."

We also went out to the neatly arranged garage at 1805 West 15th Street where the so-called Super Team put together by Parnelli Jones has its staging area.

The Super Team consists of Al Unser, winner of the previous two Indianapolis 500's; Mario Andretti, another former winner; and Joe Leonard, the many-time national motorcycle champion who won the 1971 USAC season-long championship.

We filmed different angles of their strange-looking new cars, with dihedral wings jutting out from the monocoque bodies at a forty-five-degree angle. George Bignotti explained them to us.

George is a man who has bridged the gap from the old days of guesswork and intuition to the modern racing scene of computers and high-priced engineers.

When I asked him if his title was team manager, George said, "I guess so, but I'd rather be called chief mechanic."

Today, April 29, 1972, is the eleventh anniversary of Wide World of Sports.

April 22, 1961, was one of those chilly, dank, soggy afternoons that Philadelphia often presents in late April. We were in old Franklin Field, home stadium of the University of Pennsylvania and the Philadelphia Eagles, and also the time-honored location of the Penn Relays.

The first production of ABC's Wide World of Sports was to feature the Penn Relays from there, interspersed with the Drake Relays from Des Moines, Iowa; both events were live. Roone Arledge sat in the New York control room coordinating things. Beside him was his young production assistant, Chuck Howard.

Expert commentators in Philadelphia with me were Reverend Bob Richards, "The Vaulting Vicar" they called him, and Jesse Abramson, long-time resident track nut for the New York Herald Tribune. ("Track nut," by the way, is not a term of opprobrium. It is the way track devotees and experts proudly label themselves.) Bill Flemming and Jim Simpson were the commentators in Des Moines.

Considering the weather and the lumpy old cinder track at Penn, and the normal difficulties of a first show, things went well. Only now, however, and for the first time to anyone, do I confess that on that day I called my first live track and field race. I had done many sports, but never a live track meet.

America did not rise and applaud our efforts. In fact, most people seemed not to have watched the show at all.

APRIL 30, 1972

Here is a very specific example of the kind of thing that makes ABC Sports a complicated operation.

While we were shooting on film here yesterday, our big video-tape mobile unit was to record the sprint car race in nearby

Terre Haute, then break down and move to Indy to work with us today.

But it rained in Terre Haute yesterday, requiring a few changes: Keith Jackson, scheduled for commentary on the sprint car race, had to be in Los Angeles today to call a basketball playoff game for ABC. This meant that Bill Flemming, who thought he had the weekend to spend with his family in Bloomfield Hills, Michigan, had to jump into his personal airplane and fly to Terre Haute for the race, now scheduled for today.

The engineering situation was even more complicated: A panic call was made to Chicago for another mobile unit, since the one in Terre Haute would now have to stay there. At midnight, a great hulking van was on its way down the interstate, getting to Indianapolis as fast as it could.

The crew, most of them men normally scheduled for inside studio operations, spent the night getting things put together, heavy cables strung out, heavier cameras put in place, and by morning were starting the complicated process of making everything work.

It took much longer than we had hoped. Cameras were finally ready, they said, at three o'clock in the afternoon.

I began to do a rather simple piece, where I stood beside A. J. Foyt's 1964 roadster, the last front-engined car to win the 500. In about a minute, I explained the differences between it and today's low-profile, rear-engine racer.

Just before I finished, producer Chet Forte stopped me. There was a problem with the camera. In all, I started the piece *twenty-three* times before everything was working satisfactorily. It wasn't really anybody's fault, just one result of a little cloud burst in Terre Haute yesterday. And it wasn't finished.

Half an hour later, Chet was sitting in the dark control room of the mobile unit, waiting for director Bernie Hoffman to return. Bernie had gone outside to try and speed things up by riding to one of the cameras in an electric golf cart.

Suddenly, Forte heard a small voice in the darkness: "Chet," it said, "I'm afraid I have to go to the hospital for a few minutes."

Hoffman, riding recklessly in his haste to get things done, had hit his shoulder on some sort of table standing in the pits and was streaming blood. While he went to the hospital for a few stitches, Forte took over the direction.

We wanted to do the closing of our piece out in the pit area, late in the day, with the sun beginning to set. With some difficulty, a long cable was dragged out there and a camera mounted on a tiny, flatbed electric cart. Just as we were about to begin, the camera went dead. Back behind the grandstand, a worker had come by, driving a big mechanical sweeper, cleaning up the day's debris. Blithely, he drove it straight over our cable, his big metal brushes chewing it to shreds.

"My God," said an engineer, "he's made linguine out of my cable!"

Another cable was pulled out, the engineers racing the descending sun. All was ready, and then the camera on the flatbed came loose and crashed to the cement pavement, all $80,000 worth of it. It would take a long time to fix it.

Another camera was rushed out. By now, the lighting was minimal for color television.

I was in place, ready to talk, when the stage manager ran over.

"Jim," he said, "Chet says there is no time to explain, but please just lean a little to your left while you do the piece. Please. We just have time to do the piece."

I did the closing, feeling ridiculous leaning to my left that way, and wondering why.

When we finished, I took the stage manager's headset and asked Forte what in the world it was all about.

The former Columbia University basketball All-America was laughing in his high-pitched way.

"Perfect, Jimmy," he said, "just perfect. Let me explain it to you. When they mounted the new camera on the truck, they put it on crooked, leaning to the right. I didn't know what to do with the light failing, so I had you lean to the left. You know, it made the whole thing balance out. It was perfect! Perfect!"

A few things still remained to be done. Associate Director

Roger Goodman would have to edit today's tape and I would have to return to the unit later that night to put on some additional commentary. (When we were in the middle of that, the generator started to run out of gas and someone had to go to a gas station and get some more.)

Somewhere around two or three in the morning, we would board a chartered Lear jet to return to New York. We would lose an hour in the process, since New York had gone on daylight saving time the night before and Indianapolis had not.

A rented limousine would meet me at LaGuardia Airport and take me home to Westport, Connecticut—fifty-five miles away.

After forty-five minutes of sleep, a shower, and a change of clothes, I would return to the city and the studio so that Cosell and I could join Roone Arledge and Chuck Howard to start putting together the program which was to go on the air that night.

NEW YORK—MONDAY, MAY 1

As I talk these notes into my tape recorder, I am standing on the sidewalk outside the ABC Studios on West 67th Street.

The "Monday Night Sports" program is over—after eleven hours in the studio. Some elements of the show were done live.

Our seven minute segment was finally cut to six, but it seemed to go well. I am exhausted, ready to take another rented limousine home to Connecticut. A good night's sleep is in order, because tomorrow we take the overnight flight to Munich with a group of some fifty television and sports writers from around the country. We have been asked to talk with them on the way over, so there will be no sleep on that one.

At this moment, the rented limousine stands at the curb, ready to whisk me to my home—except for one thing. It has a flat tire.

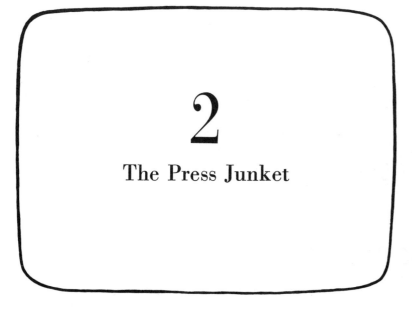

2

The Press Junket

The press junket is a hallowed ritual of network press departments. Chuck Howard says it always sounds like some kind of dessert to him. Actually, it is a gathering of newspaper writers, whisked to a specific location at the expense of the sponsoring network and exposed to some production that the network wishes to expose them to.

The sincere hope of the press department is that the writers—wined, dined, and informed—will return to their home typewriters and write something about the production involved. With luck, it will be something complimentary.

The press junket to Munich was to give the journalists a preview of the Olympic sites and the ABC facilities and, in the process, expose them to some Bavarian *Gemütlichkeit*.

9

A press junket is a complex affair. Weeks before they gathered at ticket counter 26 in John F. Kennedy Airport, New York, preparatory to boarding Lufthansa's flight 401 which departed at 6:45 P.M. for Frankfurt and Munich, the junketeers had received detailed instructions from ABC Press on what to pack, how to pack it, where the free bar would be in the Munich-Sheraton Hotel, helpful hints on shopping and sightseeing—and what to do if they missed the plane.

They also received an itinerary for the trip, some excerpts from which should give you the flavor of a TV junket in full flowering:

ABC PUBLIC RELATIONS—OLYMPIC PRESS TRIP

Tuesday, May 2

ABC's press guests will arrive at various times at JFK Airport and rendezvous at a private lounge at the Lufthansa terminal.

6:45 P.M.   Our group will depart on Lufthansa's flight 401. We will have a special section of a 747 aircraft and, en route, we plan to accomplish interviews with Messrs. Arledge, Barnathan, Howard, Schenkel, McKay, Mason, and the swimming and track and field sports commentators who will be aboard.

Wednesday, May 3

10:35 A.M.   Arrive in Munich. Met by various members of the press staff of the Olympic Organizing Committee and a German band which the OOC is arranging. We will encourage everyone to rest for a few hours at the newly completed Munich-Sheraton.

4:30 P.M.   Depart hotel for a Bavarian picnic in Ruhpolding, a small village in the breathtakingly beautiful Bavarian Alps. Because of the distance to this site (about seventy miles), we have asked the OOC to provide helicopters.

Thursday, May 4

10:00 A.M.   Leave hotel for walking tour of major venues at the

Oberwiesenfeld (the main Olympic site), encompassing the Olympic Stadium, indoor sports hall, swimming stadium, Olympic Village, press center and, if time permits, the cycling velodrome.

1:00 P.M.   Lunch in the tower restaurant at Oberwiesenfeld, 870 feet high, and providing a superb view of much of Bavaria.

6:30 P.M.   Depart for the Bavarian State Theater and whatever opera is playing. Late catered supper follows in the King's Room at the theater.

Friday, May 5

10:00 A.M.   Visit basketball stadium and Nymphenburg Palace, site of the equestrian events.

Noon   Lunch at Schleissheim Castle.

7:00 P.M.   Depart hotel in fifteen horse-drawn carriages for catered dinner under candlelight at Stuck Villa, an impressive mansion in the middle of town.

Saturday, May 6

9:00 A.M.   Tour through ABC Sports and BO & E [Broadcast Operations and Engineering] facilities . . . final briefing at European Broadcasting Union's hall . . .

Noon   Lunch at Methazer Beer Hall, a large, rambling restaurant which specializes in enormous steins of beer, enormous and various sausages, and a delightful "oom-pah" band . . . our press guests will be able to lead the band, a photo of which should delight them.

Sunday, May 7

11:10 A.M.   Leave on Lufthansa's flight 754, change in Frankfurt to a 747, arrive at JFK at 4:15 P.M., New York Time. We will have people and cars on hand to shuttle the press to connecting flights, to their homes in the New York area, or to Manhattan for an overnight stay for those going on to the coast the next day.

As you can imagine from the above, a press junket is extremely complicated and expensive to the sponsoring network. It is also something of a gamble.

There have been many successful press junkets, and there have been some total disasters. This one started uncertainly, but with what seemed to be a positive attitude on the part of all. We were assigned to one compartment of the mammoth 747, with seats strategically assigned by ABC's press department. The airline failed us on the dinner service. Somehow, we were served last of all, and by some error the dinner was served before the drinks. When dealing with press and television people, that is a bad move on the part of any airline. Still, we all talked to each other and did interviews all the way across the Atlantic, and from Frankfurt down to Munich.

Only one member of the party caused any disturbance during the flight. At a moment when some were napping in the semi-darkness, he awoke, sat bolt upright, and shouted, "Screw Moses!" several times, then tumbled back and snored through the night. (On advice of counsel, I decline to say whether the shouter was one of ours or one of theirs.)

Arrival in Munich was as impressive as promised. As we descended the steps of the plane, the Bavarian band struck up its welcome and girls in Bavarian costume rushed forward with flowers. Willi Daume, president of the Olympic Organizing Committee, was there. So was Hans (Jonny) Klein, press chief for the games of the Twentieth Olympiad.

On the second leg of the trip, from Frankfurt to Munich, I sat with Terence O'Flaherty, the San Francisco columnist. He told me a story, possibly apocryphal, of a conversation that took place after a soccer game the week before.

West Germany had defeated England in an international match, a major upset, and a German said to an Englishman with a smile of triumph, "Well, we finally beat you at your own game."

The Englishman replied, unsmilingly, "Mmmmm. Well, we beat you at yours twice."

It was a bitter little story and, as we were descending toward Munich, it made me wonder if the Germans could really pull off successfully what they were obviously trying to do—to present an Olympics of serenity, tranquillity, and brotherhood that would erase the memory of the so-called Nazi Olympics of 1936.

This was the admitted theme of the games. Even the uniforms of the security men had been specially designed by Courreges in a light motif—pale-blue blazers with white caps of the sort Ben Hogan used to wear. Nowhere would police or army uniforms be seen.

But would the world take the Munich Olympics on their own terms? Or would the old wounds still fester? Would the visitors be more aware of the nearness of Dachau or of the pale-blue blazers?

At this time all was friendly, the oom-pah band pumped away, hands were shaken, and flowers were distributed. In the center of it all, weary but smiling the rather boyish, bemused grin he adopts on such occasions, was Roone Pinkney Arledge, president of ABC Sports.

I leaned over and whispered in his ear, "Hey, Roone, it wasn't like this eleven years ago, was it?"

"It sure wasn't," he said. "It most certainly was not."

You have seen and heard the credit a thousand times if you are a television sports fan: "The executive producer is Roone Arledge." And so he is, and has been since Wide World of Sports began.

At the beginning, in fact, only three of us were regular members of the traveling group that went to Europe for events. In addition to Roone, there was, and is, Charles (Chuck) Howard, at the beginning a production assistant, now vice-president in charge of production.

It was very different at the beginning.

Wide World of Sports was to be a summer replacement series, twenty weeks in length, and so it was, leaving the air around Labor Day, 1961, but returning in January, 1962, and still running.

That first summer was critical and often discouraging.

I remember the 24 Hours of LeMans, the long, strange endurance contest over French country roads outside a provincial industrial city. It shares with the Indy 500 the title of "World's Most Famous Motor Race." We knew that, but not much more when we arrived there.

The three of us, along with director Bill Bennington, stayed up for some forty hours all told, on our feet for all but one hour, when we slept under glaring lights on hard seats in the IBM Computing Center.

Our credentials, for which we had stood in a dark, airless corridor at L'Automobile Club de l'Ouest for two hours along with the rest of the press, waiting our turn to be accredited, turned out to be all but useless. The passes allowed us in the pit area before the race, but shortly before the traditional start, we were summarily swept out along with the rest of the unprivileged.

For the next several hours, we scurried around the perimeter of the pits like rabbits sniffing and looking for holes in the chicken wire to get into a lettuce patch. The rabbits often are successful and so were we, but always with tension, waiting for the next gendarme to seize our arms and escort us to the pit exit.

During the night, it was cold and it rained.

Jacques Alexandre, a temperamental film cameraman working for us, finally stood under a naked light bulb in the pit of some car that had expired during the race, and with water dripping from his eyebrows, held up his credential dramatically.

"Do you know what this is worth, Monsieur Arledge?" he shouted. "Do you know?!!! It is worth zis!!!"

Then he tore the little piece of blue cardboard to shreds and flung it into the wet wind.

Things were very different at the beginning. No oom-pah bands, no flowers, no credentials.

At LeMans, we first met Phil Hill, the shy, emotional intellectual from Santa Monica, California, who was then at the peak of his driving skills. The only American ever to win the World Grand Prix Driving Championship, he teamed three times with Olivier Gendebein of Belgium to win at LeMans. No other pair has equaled that mark.

We learned, upon meeting Hill and Gendebien, how different men can be in personality, yet still join together in a magnificent team effort for the one interest they have very much in common. We learned that in the middle of the French night, at 2:30 in the morning.

Gendebien was out in the car, but Phil was going to take over on the next lap. In the glare of passing headlights, his face was gray and drawn as he pulled on his driving helmet and his gloves, wiped off his goggles, and moved to the pit counter. Deep in concentration, he was fearsome looking, and frankly, I was almost afraid to talk to him.

I asked him the time-worn racing question that is still in the front of every race-watcher's mind.

"What's it going to be like out there, Phil?"

He wheeled on me.

"What's it going to be like out there?" he repeated. "I'll tell you what it's going to be like out there! It's going to be terrible!"

"You can see that a fine rain is falling here. That means there is fog on the Mulsanne straight on the other side of the course, a straightaway more than three miles long. Fog, you understand?"

"I'll be going almost two hundred miles an hour over there. There are little French cars in this race going a hundred miles an hour slower than I am! Do you understand what I mean? I mean I could come upon one of those little French things in the fog without even seeing him, we could both die and never know what happened! That's what it's going to be like out there!!!"

The car came in, and Gendebien—handsome, suave, sophisticated, scion of a famous Belgian family—leaped over the side of the open-topped, red Ferrari racer, as was his wont. He seldom bothered to use the door.

Hill leaped in and blasted off into the messy night, tires screeching, tail of the car slithering a bit as he flew up the home straight toward the Dunlop Bridge.

Immediately, I went to Gendebien.

"Olivier," I said, "what was it like out there?"

He thought for a moment as he slipped on his checked, Rex Harrison-style tweed hat, then leaned against the wall.

"What was it lak?" (shrug of shoulders, mouth turns down at corners, one eyebrow raises). "It was like nussing."

"We are very far ahead again, the Ferrari is performing perfectly as always" (glance at complicated-looking racing wristwatch), "there are only thirteen and a half hours left in ze race. It is like . . ." (turning to me) "How do you say in America? It is like . . . driving to ze corner for a pack of cigarettes. Now, if you will excuse me . . ."

And he walked to the back of the pits.

There they were, then, the most famous racing partners of all time: Phil Hill, later to become a good friend and companion in commentary and in the drinking of fine wine (Chateau Haut-brion, 1937), and Olivier Gendebien, today as then charming, sophisticated, and European.

Two men drawn to the world's most dangerous sport, capable of working in unison like the finely tuned cylinders of their Ferrari, but as unlike in personality as two men can be.

It turned out to be as rainy at Ruhpolding in 1972 as it was at LeMans in 1961.

The Bavarian picnic scheduled for the junketeers had to be moved indoors, oom-pah band and all. The press still loved it. The cold cuts were delicious, the draft beer just fine, and the Germans couldn't have been more hospitable.

"Jonny" Klein, the press chief, in a dapper dark Bavarian suit and a string tie, stood on a chair to welcome us.

"We Germans," he called over the hub-bub of German and American accents, "are too stupid to improvise. Therefore, we must organize."

Everyone laughed at that.

"We hope that the Olympics will be organized well, and we hope you have a very good time while you are here."

Everybody seemed to have a good time, despite their lack of

sleep, despite the fact that the only rest room, in true picnic tradition, was an outdoor privy. The press walked through the rain to the small building when necessary and didn't mind at all.

The next morning, press and hosts took their first tour of the Olympic grounds, nearing completion on the Oberwiesenfeld. Long years ago, the Oberwiesenfeld had been a farmer's field, more recently a training ground for the armies of the king of Bavaria.

But since 1945, it had been an ugly, unhealed wound to the people of Munich. It was the dumping ground for the rubble of World War II, a reminder of the destruction wrought on the city by Allied bombers.

Now, it had been transformed into a world gathering place. Over the main track and field stadium, the swimming and gymnastics halls, the strange, controversial roof was spreading, an umbrellalike structure of individual, translucent, plastic panels. Originally, it was to have cost the equivalent of five million dollars. Finally, it would cost ten times that.

The press saw and made notes.

They saw that strange structure already known as Barnathan's Bungalow, named after ABC's small, dynamic vice-president of engineering, Julie Barnathan. The bungalow would house ABC's offices during the games, and was large enough to contain a cafeteria, graphic arts department, car dispatcher's office, and quite a few individual offices.

Originally, ABC had simply been assigned space in the television center across the street. A year or more before, Julie had indicated to the German hosts that we would need much more room.

"Very well," they had said. "Just draw us a picture of what you want and we will build it."

So, Julie sketched a low, one-story building and divided it roughly into the rooms that would be needed.

Six months later, the ABC group returned. Our building was there, completed, just as ordered. But it had no windows. Appreciatively, Barnathan thanked the Germans for their cooperation in putting up the structure, walked through it, and said it would be just fine. Then, diffidently, he pointed out that there was one strange thing about the bungalow, that it had no windows.

"Ah, but Mr. Barnathan," came the answer, "you didn't request any windows. Look, here is your original drawing."

Sure enough, the rough sketch did not specifically indicate windows. As Jonny Klein said at the picnic, Germans are not improvisers.

That night, many of us went to see *The Bartered Bride* at the Munich opera house, a beautiful structure completely rebuilt after having been leveled by bombs in the war.

The American press marveled at the opera house on the second night of the Olympics press junket. Some came for the music and others for the experience. As the audience returned to its seats for the second act, Blackie Sherrod, a Texas sports writer, was heard to murmur, "With my luck, this thing will go overtime!"

As the second act opened, some Bohemian peasants were frolicking on the green. A small group of them, stage right, were rolling bowling balls offstage, toward unseen pins.

"Good Lord," said another small voice in our row, "Eddie Elias is everywhere."

Eddie is the untiring Akron promoter who invented the Professional Bowlers Tour, long a Saturday afternoon staple on ABC.

"Yes," whispered another, "but the camera angles are terrible. You can't even see the pins."

I ducked the mammoth supper in the King's Room after the opera.

Instead, I took Don Freeman, the fine television writer of the San Diego *Union,* for his first visit to the Hofbrauhaus, that brawling monument to beer in downtown Munich. The little strolling band was playing "Lili Marlene," as we entered through the smoke. It was like a scene from a Kurt Weill–Bertold Brecht musical.

We had pig's knuckles and liters of beer in those great steins, and I introduced him to Frieda, the only waitress in the place who has ever carried sixteen steins of beer at one time.

Freeman, a painstaking reporter, had his little notebook out all the time.

"Is that a world record?" he asked.

"Of course," I said, "recognized by the F.I.B. That's the *Federation International de Bière*, the world sanctioning body."

3

Battle for the F.A. Cup

Munich is behind me now. I had to leave yesterday morning, missing the horse-drawn carriage ride to Stuck Villa, because there is a show to be done in London.

Munich seems far away.

I am in Wembley Stadium for England's greatest sporting occasion, the annual battle for the F.A. Cup. "F.A." stands for "Football Association" but the English game is soccer, of course, and the competing teams are professionals, survivors of a season-long knockout competition. Thousands of teams enter each year, from the top pros to small, amateur, and university teams. They are eliminated week by week, and in May, 100,000 fortunate souls enter Wembley, which to the British is Yankee Stadium, the Los Angeles Coliseum, and the Astrodome all rolled into one.

To the average soccer fan, seeing a Cup final in person is one of the events of a lifetime. Playing in one is the climax of an athlete's career.

The participants in this year's hundredth anniversary match are Arsenal and Leeds. Arsenal, the defending champion from the north of London and the home-town favorite, is led by long-haired Charlie George, who was born and reared within sound of the cheering Arsenal home field. Leeds, lean and hungry from the north of England, is invading the big city today in search of their first Cup victory in all those hundred years.

The match should be great, but we have been having our problems. Our producer, Doug Wilson, and the BBC director, Alec Weeks, have been disagreeing for two days. On the F.A. Cup match, we use the BBC's pictures. They assign us a few minutes of unilateral camera time to do our own openings and introductions. We augment their coverage often with film cameras.

On this occasion, we also have a completely portable videotape unit, which Wilson wanted to use on the sidelines. Weeks said no, the Wembley Stadium people said no, then yes, then no.

It is all terribly complicated and is resulting in bitterness between Wilson and Weeks, one of those things which happens under the pressure of television sports productions.

Doug, normally the most affable of men, is insisting on his camera. Weeks says no, and the stadium manager is threatening to bar Doug for life!

One of our film cameramen, Terry Gould, has been having his own problems. Terry, a large, sad-eyed, shaggy-haired Briton, is one of the best cameramen in the business. He is anything but athletic, but he has scaled stadium steps and mountain slopes in search of the proper shot from London to Kitzbühel.

This morning, Terry was about to enter the stadium when a pickpocket, a lad who looked like a character from Oliver Twist, slipped up and snatched his credential. Terry shouted for the police as he pursued the lad. A bobby immediately joined the chase and caught the boy. Gould thanked the officer profusely, then asked for his credential.

"I'm terribly sorry, sir," said the bobby, respectfully, "but I'm afraid we must keep the credential for evidence at the trial."

And so they did.

Terry Gould, brooding but resourceful, somehow got into the stadium *sans* credential.

The Queen of England has just arrived. It's almost game time.

Eleven years ago today, we did our first foreign event for Wide World. It was this same event, in the same place.

It was then that I noticed for the first time a certain amateur spirit, an innocence in a way, that exists among British and European athletes, even the toughest professionals. It is a spirit that often seems lost in our own professional sports. Except for the brief, ceremonial few minutes of champagne-dousing after the World Series, our pros seem to feel that an honest display of emotion is unprofessional, childish perhaps, out of date. It isn't that way at Wembley.

The star of that first game we saw here was Danny Blanchflower, a sandy-haired football magician from the north of Ireland who directed his teammates around the playing surface like Bobby Fischer deploying chessmen. Blanchflower also rallied his men on the Tottenham Hotspurs emotionally.

(Even the name, "Hotspurs," speaks of that turn-of-the-century, Frank Merriwell quality I'm talking about. Somehow, there's a romance about "Hotspurs" that you just don't get from nicknames like "Oilers," or "Dolphins.")

Danny Blanchflower's team won that game eleven years ago, and he sits beside me today as expert commentator for ABC. But the emotional star of the match for the Cup between Tottenham and Leicester City was a man named Len Chalmers of Leicester.

Chalmers was injured midway in the first half of the game, and from that point played for one more hour of playing time, with a broken leg. It was evident that he was in great pain, but the F.A. Cup was at stake and no substitutes were allowed in the game. A man with a broken leg hanging about down near the opponents' goalmouth was still more of a threat than nobody on the field at all. Who knows, went the reasoning, when a loose ball might appear, and Chalmers just might nudge it in with his good leg?

He didn't, but he played on. I was working on that day with Kenneth Wolstenholme, the BBC's top soccer commentator, and

*he continually referred to the injured back as "poor old Chal-
mers." To this day, Wide World viewers with excellent memories
ask me occasionally what ever happened to "poor old Chalmers."
He is a coach in the Second Division of the English league—but
"poor old Chalmers," a noble sporting figure, he will always be to
me.*

*When he finally left the game that day in 1961, a roar went up
from the throats of 100,000 Englishmen that enveloped the entire
neighborhood, all the way to John Bishop's "Green Man," a pub
on a hilltop overlooking the stadium, where we had filmed a
group of old soccer stars as they gathered before the game to
reminisce and drink pints of bitter, and where we went after the
game with our BBC colleagues.*

*We stood there (the English never sit to drink) long into the
night, talking of poor old Chalmers and Blanchflower and the
rest, getting a feeling for a foreign sport that we had never had
before.*

May 6, 1972, has turned out to be more emotional than May 6,
1961. Leeds has won the game on a goal by Alan Clarke. The
F.A. Cup will be taken back to that grimy northern industrial
city for the first time, after one hundred years of Cup finals.

It was a good, exciting match, but the moment of human
drama came right at the end. In the closing seconds, Mick Jones
of Leeds drove toward the Arsenal goal and, in the furious action
around the goalmouth, was hit and fell to the turf. Seconds later,
the game ended and his team had won.

In the excitement of the moment, his teammates failed to notice that he was still lying there, writhing in pain with what
turned out to be a broken elbow. They were leaping in delight,
running toward that long stairway that leads to the Royal Box,
where Queen Elizabeth stood, waiting to give the Cup and individual medals to the winning side.

The crowd watched two dramas simultaneously. The unknow-
ing players made the long climb up the victory stairs, waving to
the spectators. Down on the field, trainers were binding Jones's
injured arm to his side, preparing to load him on a stretcher.

Then, hearing the roar as the Cup was presented, the player turned his head and saw what was happening. He rose to one knee, waved off the trainers and uncertainly began to walk, then jog, across the field.

Another roar went up, this time recognizing the fact that Jones was not to be denied his moment of a lifetime no matter how much pain he was in. Somehow, he was going to climb those stairs.

He did, as his teammates turned and marveled.

Halfway up, a girl, tears running down her face, reached over the wooden barricade, pulled Jones's face toward her, and kissed him, gently.

The Queen gave Mick the medal, Prince Philip shook his hand and whispered something to him. The crowd, all 100,000 still in place, gave another special cheer for the plucky Jones.

One more thing remained, the traditional victory lap of the stadium by the winning team. The captain held up the Cup as he was hoisted to the shoulders of his teammates. They jogged along the running track, toward that end of Wembley where their supporters were gathered.

The real soccer fan is a working man who carefully saves his shillings to see as many games as he can. He buys the cheapest ticket, entitling him to stand, not sit. So the hottest fans gather to stand all day on the so-called "terraces," at one end of the field or the other, depending on which team they support.

The men of Leeds carried the Cup to their people, tens of thousands of them, who had spent the night on the long train ride down from the north and had now been standing for hours. Each time the captain raised the Cup, another roar filled the stadium.

Fifty yards away, Mick Jones collapsed onto a stretcher, a smile on his face, a medal in his hand, and was carried from the field.

OVER THE ATLANTIC—SUNDAY, MAY 7

I am in the tourist section of a 747, riding back to New York with Bob Goodrich, the production assistant on the F.A. Cup show. Doug Wilson, the producer, is unhappily heading for Monte Carlo, to handle the Grand Prix of Monaco automobile race. Normally, this would be a delight to the romantic Mr. Wilson, but today he is unhappy. He has, in fact, been banned from Wembley for life, although I have the feeling that the penalty won't stick.

Ronnie Hawkins, our associate director, is remaining in London to await the arrival of another Wide World crew, which will televise the Rugby League Cup from Wembley next week.

As Goodrich and I sip our wine at 37,000 feet, another plane is somewhere over the Atlantic bearing the happy members of the Olympics press junket.

When I arrive home, I will have covered more than 13,000 miles since I left for Los Angeles ten days ago.

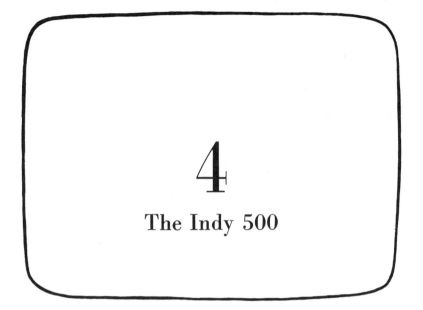

4

The Indy 500

It's a long way in space and mood from Wembley Stadium and the victory lap to the starting grid at the Indianapolis Motor Speedway.

Somewhere underneath, the race drivers of Indy feel strong emotion for their sport, just as the soccer players do, otherwise they wouldn't be here, at this moment of nostalgia that comes just before hours of great danger. But the race driver's profession demands total concentration and a seemingly calm exterior even now.

The varicolored balloons are still rising high into the Indiana sky, followed by the eyes of most of the 300,000 people who have gathered for the world's biggest one-day sports event. Some of the eyes are still a bit misty from the annual singing of "Back Home Again in Indiana."

May has been more traumatic than usual at Indy.

The first day of qualifying was rained out. Only A. J. Foyt got on the track, and he blew an engine. It was a bad break for us,

26

too, because we were doing a live qualifying segment on Wide World. I left the track to return to New York, getting an expeditious ride to the airport thanks to the Indianapolis Police Department. I was literally standing in the men's room, when I heard the page for me on the little loud speaker just above my head.

It was inevitable: a phone call from Don Ohlmeyer at the track, telling of a change of plans. Return to base. So it was Colonel Sanders Fried Chicken in Producer Dennis Lewin's room at the Speedway Motel, instead of dinner at home with the family.

The skies were threatening but the track was dry the next morning when driver Jim Malloy of Denver, in car number 16, took a sudden right turn into the wall coming out of turn three in practice. The car was destroyed and Malloy, in a deep coma, was airlifted to the hospital, his limbs broken, face and hands burned, internal injuries undetermined. On the following Wednesday, he died. He was the thirty-fifth driver to die on the Indianapolis Motor Speedway.

The threatening skies finally broke, rain delayed qualifying again, and a tornado touched down in Indianapolis just a couple of miles from the track. It was a day to make your palms sweaty. Everyone wished the sun would come out, or something.

Later in the day, qualifying finally started and Bobby Unser was the fastest qualifier, as expected, at over 195 miles per hour. It was about seventeen miles per hour faster than Peter Revson's pole-winning speed of last year. Unbelievable.

More rain, and an unusual move: six drivers who hadn't had a chance to get out because of the rain were told they could have their chance the following Saturday. So the battle for the pole, supposedly done on the first day of qualifying, finally took three days of trying, and over a week in total time.

Unser's time held up for the pole position the next weekend, with Revson and Mark Donohue second and third, rounding out the front row.

Like the playing of "My Old Kentucky Home" before the start of the Kentucky Derby, the ceremonial singing of "Back Home Again . . ." has been known to bring tears to the eyes of hardened racing mechanics and visiting English motor-racing fans who aren't exactly sure what Indiana is.

The sentimental words certainly speak of a time that has almost ceased to exist; the time of the American family farm, "the candlelight still shining bright through the sycamores" . . . "the new-mown hay" . . . "when I dream about the moonlight on the Wabash, then I long for my Indiana home."

It would have taken a master showman to invent the Indy 500 as it exists today, to bring together all the elements that evoke such contradictory emotions.

The first emotion of the day is a slowly growing excitement, an excitement that begins with the sight of an endless line of automobiles making its way through the darkness of very early morning toward the great racetrack. If you stay at the Speedway Motel, it is the sound of the automobiles and the sirens of the police cars keeping them in order that awakens you on race day.

The sun is still low in the east when the grandstand begins to fill. The main stand is a mile long, stretching from turn four through turn one, running the entire length of the famous home straightaway. Other stands are spotted around the course, a huge one behind turn three, for example, where the cars are often known to have problems with the swirling wind.

The anticipatory titillation of early morning matures into something else when the race cars are pushed onto the track, surrounded by the thousands of "press" who have somehow managed to acquire the coveted pin and piece of cardboard bearing the number "99" that gains admittance to the pit area.

The populace in the grandstand (some have paid as high as forty dollars list price for their tickets) peers at the crowd in the pits through binoculars. They scan the shining, low-slung racers in their bright hues of blue and orange and off-white and one purple car strangely called the Mystery Eagle. They pan the crowd, trying to glimpse Hoagy Carmichael or Phil Harris, both Hoosiers, or possibly an astronaut or the Smothers Brothers. Did somebody say Paul Newman might come this year?

There seem to be enough cameras in the pit area to strengthen the Japanese economy for years to come. Everyone there is in motion, bending over to inspect the cars, crouching to take pictures, leaping out of the way as another car is wheeled out to the peremptory cry from a mechanic, "Watch it!"

Only the drivers are still. Perhaps they are marshaling their energy for the long, hot grind. Maybe there is something more psychological about it. But they are very still before the race. They stand, endlessly polishing their goggles, talking rather aimlessly with friends and reporters.

For the next few hours, they are something different from the rest of us. In their Nomex, fire-retardant driving suits, complete with a tightly fitting hood that gives them the appearance of medieval knights, they are in a world closed to all others. They share a common knowledge of how inwardly terrifying it is to head into turn one with thirty-two other determined drivers, sitting in a beautiful piece of metal which, underneath, is a bathtub full of explosive racing fuel, surrounding you, capable of destroying you in one flaming moment against a wall or another car.

There is a special danger at Indy. It comes from the walls the drivers race between—a high outer wall on the driver's right, a low inner one on his left. At today's incredibly high speeds, a car out of control tends to bounce from one wall to the other crazily and unpredictably, and there is nowhere for the following cars to go. The possibility of mass pileups is ever present.

Just the other night at dinner, Scotland's Jackie Stewart, the World Grand Prix driving champion, was talking about the danger.

"I'm afraid people will think me a bit old-fashioned," he said, in his lilting Scottish burr, "but the cars here are now going too fast."

He went on to explain about the walls and the near-impossibility of avoiding the careening car in front. This from a man who twice nearly won the 500—but who refuses to race in it any more, primarily because of the danger.

Why is this more dangerous, I asked Jackie, than the Formula One circuit he still races? Walls or no walls, many more men have died in Formula One in recent years than at Indy. He feels that safety precautions (fire trucks, ambulances, etc.) generally are better organized at the Speedway. Thus, a driver has a better chance of surviving a crash here. But psychologically, Stewart knows more fear here. Formula One crashes tend to be one car affairs, and inwardly, each driver feels that the unfortunate man must have made a mistake that *he* would not make. At Indy, you know, for sure, that you could be involved in a fatal accident through no fault of your own.

The same night I had been talking with Jackie (who is here working with us as expert commentator), I had a drink in the bar with Parnelli Jones. Rufus Parnell Jones is from the old school of American drivers. In his driving days, during which he won at Indianapolis, he was a very quick man with his fists at post-race arguments. His hair was cut short and so was his temper. However, there has always been something of the romantic underneath Parnelli's hard-hat exterior.

Now that he is the owner of the three Super Team cars, along with partner Vel Miletich, Jones has modern-looking sideburns descending from his thinning sandy hair. And although his Indy driving days are done, he likes to take part in off-road races, driving dune buggies or four-wheel drive machines through the Nevada desert and over the desolate landscape of Baja California.

Parnelli disagrees with Stewart about the cars going too fast. Not at all, he says.

"In fact," he said, leaning forward, "these cars are more forgiving than the old front-engine roadsters were."

Why?

"The handling characteristics of the cars. The big wing on the back holds it to the road, the big, improved tires give it far better traction. The overall aerodynamics make these safer cars at 200 miles an hour than the roadsters were at 150."

Jones's use of the phrase "more forgiving" sounded more like a European road racer than a tough old Indy hand. I asked him if he had ever considered driving in Formula One.

"Yes," he said. "I drove for Colin Chapman one year here at the Speedway (Chapman is the English car designer; quiet, reserved, look-alike for David Niven) and Colin made me a definite offer to come to Europe and drive for him in Grand Prix."

"I almost did it, too."

Why not?

Parnelli Jones, race driver, smiled with one side of his mouth and looked down at his drink.

"It would have involved a lot of flying back and forth across the Atlantic," he said. "Would you believe that I'm not very fond of flying on those big commercial airplanes?"

The men who drive racing machines are indeed hard to fathom, from Phil Hill and Olivier Gendebien to Jackie Stewart to Parnelli Jones, to the men who now sit on the front row of this year's starting line:

On the pole—Bobby Unser, gum-chewing Indy veteran from New Mexico, eldest living son of the racing Unsers (Jerry, the eldest son, died at Indy some years ago). Unser, handsome in a sardonic, tough-jawed way, has won the big race once. His younger brother, Al, has won it the past two years running. But this time Bobby has the fastest machine here by far. Prepared by former driver Dan Gurney, the Eagle broke all records by qualifying at a speed of over 195 miles per hour. The car is white and is sponsored by Ozzie Olson of Michigan, president of Olsonite, the world's largest manufacturer of plastic toilet seats, and the Swedish Crucible Steel Company.

Front row, middle—Peter Revson, strikingly good-looking young bachelor. His father was one of the founders of the Revlon cosmetics empire. Peter went to Cornell, transferred to the University of Hawaii, and out there bought and raced his first car, a Morgan, a little English sports car with a wooden frame. Peter started on the sports car circuits and came to Indy with the Bruce McLaren organization from England. He drives one of their orange cars today.

Front row, outside—Mark Donohue. In his mid-thirties now, this Brown University engineering graduate looks ten years younger. He has a vulnerable look about him. Still, he is a favorite here, because of his driving skill and because of the navy blue race car he sits in. It was a McLaren, bought by team owner

Roger Penske, a former sports car driver, and improved in secret. The Penske operation is as meticulously groomed as Penske himself, a smooth-talking, knowledgeable automobile dealer from Bloomfield Hills, Michigan. In the trade, they call Penske "Captain Bligh," and Donohue, "Captain Nice."

The three men sit in their silent machines with helmets and goggles in place now—Unser, from a garage in Albuquerque; Revson, from the beaches of Hawaii and the swinging salons of New York and the continent; and Donohue, the scholar from the Halls of Ivy who has been sleeping on a cot in the team garage for much of the last month. Behind them, thirty other drivers—defending champion Al Unser, former winners Mario Andretti and A. J. Foyt, national driving champion Joe Leonard, hungry veterans like Gordon Johncock and Roger McCluskey, and eager rookies like Mike Hiss and Sam Posey.

A crowd of photographers has now gathered around track owner Tony Hulman. As an older man, Tony still carries himself with a straightness that goes back to his days as a Yale track man. The wealthy Hoosier loves this one moment in the spotlight each year, although he normally is a retiring, self-effacing man.

The words are world famous now! "Gentlemen," Tony said, "start your engines!!"

From silence, there was thunder, as thirty-three engines generating about 30,000 total horsepower, all started up at once.

Wait—make that thirty-*two* engines. One of them wouldn't start. It was A. J. Foyt!! The famous tough Texan, three-time Indy winner out for an unprecedented fourth triumph, a man who helps prepare his own car with a thoroughness that rivals Penske's, just couldn't get his automobile to start!

The most famous American driver of his time got out of the car, as frustrated as a commuter caught with a dead battery on a winter morning.

The other cars were off on their pace laps.

Shortly thereafter came a moment that still baffles many. The cars were coming out of turn four on their second pace lap in ragged formation. They did not look ready for a start.

Starter Pat Vidan, a hearty, muscular, health club operator, still held the yellow flag and, as the cars approached, he raised one finger of the other hand, indicating that they would take one more lap before the race began. Each driver indicated his understanding by raising one finger.

Suddenly, at the last possible moment, driver Sam Hanks pulled the pace car off the track, almost nipping the nose of Bobby Unser's car. Vidan dropped the yellow flag and hurriedly picked up the green. He waved it as the first row of cars passed him. The race was on! Or was it?

Bob Unser, Revson, and Donohue weren't sure whether they had seen a green or not. The electric signal light in turn one was still yellow. Then it turned green. In the brief interval, the lead cars had slowed a bit while the drivers from the back, with a good look at the green flag, began to charge.

A. J. Foyt, whose engine was now started, was pulling back onto the track to join the next pace lap when the flag fell. He was almost hit by the suddenly thundering herd that flashed by.

All this had happened under the direction of the chief steward, Harlan Fengler. Fengler, a stubborn man, the Avery Brundage of Indy, later stated that there was no mixup, no confusion, that he had started the race just as he wanted to.

MAY 27 (LATER)

The race is over.

The fleet car of Bob Unser couldn't stay the course, and in the closing laps it was the *other* car of Dan Gurney's stable, the Mystery Eagle, driven by Jerry Grant, battling it out for the championship with Mark Donohue.

The Mystery Eagle had been so-called because Gurney considered it a mystery why no one would come up with the money to sponsor it. Just in time for qualifying, a sponsor appeared, a large midwestern businessman named Chris Vallo, who didn't like to have his picture taken. More mystery.

Today, the final series of mysteries. How was Grant, a journeyman driver from the Northwest, able to lead the race with ten laps to go against the greatest field in the world? Why did he make an unscheduled pit stop then that cost him the race? Why, now that he had finished second to Donohue, was there talk of disqualifying him?

These mysteries are making it tough for our people in the production truck right now. The race ended at about 1:45 in the afternoon. Our two-hour same day telecast goes on the air at 7:00 tonight. Between now and then, the complete show must be edited.

In the overcrowded mobile unit, editing is moving forward in two small rooms at the same time. Director Chet Forte is supervising one group, A.D. Don Ohlmeyer the other. Producer Chuck Howard and Roone Arledge are ducking back and forth between the two groups, trying to weave it all together.

Listen to some of the bewildering conversation that is typical of a crash editing session:

CHUCK HOWARD: The main thrust of this segment, I think, is the change of lead, from Jerry Grant, to, uh, Donohue.

ROONE ARLEDGE: Why don't we go back about six or seven minutes, and see where we picked it up?

CHUCK: Well, that's really about what we did. I don't know where. . . .

ROONE: What did we. . . . Did you look at that one lap where we were screwed up?

CHUCK: No. That is not in the last three laps. I don't think.

ROONE: Let's get the clock out of there.

OHLMEYER (*at another machine*): We're coming in at lap 183. Instead of lap 184, we'll come in at 183. What do you have at 180? Oh, I'm sorry, go back to. . . .

VOICE (*probably tape operator*): It's no good, we didn't get the. . . .

OTHER VOICE: I'll cue it up. I'll cue it up.

OHLMEYER: Let me see your lap chart a second. Do they have Donohue anywhere a lap down?

TERRY JASTROW (*associate producer*): No, that's the final hundred laps.

OHLMEYER: Why don't you see if you can find out about the pit stops? There's a piece that comes up where everybody pitted.

JASTROW: As a side note, the Gurney people are standing outside. They got this from the USAC people, and it's the same thing that they're questioning, 'cause if. . . .

OHLMEYER: Yeh, but they go back to 107.

FORTE (*working on something else*): Watch this car. Watch the people in the car. Watch the pace car.

MCKAY: We saw Vidan with one finger.

FORTE: Yeah, watch their hands up. Freeze it! See this? They're all saying one finger here.

CHUCK (*back with the other group*): O.K., fine. That doesn't help us, that doesn't really mean a thing to us. Take it back. Take it back. We don't want all this crap.

VOICE: Back up a minute and let it play.

Surprisingly, each of the above people understood what the other was saying. The ABC Sports editing group under pressure is a unique organization in the television business. They speak in a kind of shorthand, possible only because of their knowledge of sport and television, and their experience in working together. This goes for the entire group, from Roone and Chuck, producers and directors and A.D.'s, to the tape editors who spin their bulky reels like a veteran croupier working with a roulette wheel at Monte Carlo.

On this occasion, the normal complications of editing were compounded by the fact that the race result was still in doubt. The Gurney people were, in fact, outside our truck, claiming that the scorers had miscounted a lap and that Grant, not Donohue, had won the race. Meanwhile, Penske was claiming that Grant had illegally been given fuel on his final stop from the tank assigned to Bob Unser's car, not Grant's. This could move Grant way down in the standings, or possibly lead to total disqualification.

I left the truck and started for the press room to see what I could find out about Gurney's supposed protest. On the way, I was met by Moe Campbell, a tall, scholarly looking young man who works with Gurney. He was eager to explain their side of the story to me.

". . . but coming down here," Moe was saying, "Bettenhausen

gets out of the picture basically. Or the big issue is, you go to lap 170 where you've got Bettenhausen and then on the same lap Grant. Then you've got Donohue. Down here, you've got Bettenhausen, Grant, and Donohue. And then it becomes Donohue, having passed both Bettenhausen and Grant."

MCKAY: To get on the same lap? And did he get on the same lap on lap 171?

CAMPBELL: Yeah, he, in fact, had to unlap himself, you know, right there, neither of those guys stopped, I mean there was not a pit stop in there.

MCKAY: Yeah. I have a feeling it could be up in here, that this never happened, therefore the scoring would be right.

CAMPBELL: Well, then, we'll say all right. Yeah. We don't know in the least. We'd like. . . .

It was extremely confusing and stayed that way as the editing team put together its videotape mosaic and the clock moved closer to airtime. The decision was made to play the race present tense, then to have Gurney on live at the end of the show to explain his protest.

Shortly before airtime, Jackie Stewart and I piled into a small car with Gurney, Grant, Campbell, and a couple of other members of the Gurney entourage. Stewart was at the wheel.

VOICE: Hey, move over. Hey, not on my lap, you big mother.

STEWART: Oh I'm not listening to you and I've got a certain standard as to the people I drive.

GRANT (*sitting on someone's lap beside Stewart*): Miserable little Scotsmen, how are you?

STEWART: Well done. Well done.

GRANT: Thank you.

MCKAY: That's the nicest thing you've ever said to him, Jackie.

GRANT (*laughing*): Well, he's a miserable foreigner. I used to know him when he'd stand on it.

STEWART (*also laughing*): Listen, I'll tell you what. Gurney can't afford me drivin'. You never thought I'd drive for you, did you, Gurney?

(General laughter.)

GURNEY: Aw, you long-haired guys. . . .

GRANT: Did you say anything nice about me, Jackie?

STEWART (*still chuckling*): Haven't said a thing nice about you all day, Grant.

GRANT: Goddamn it.

STEWART: We're about to do it, though. Just wait. You'll hear it all tonight . . . if you promise to keep quiet.

All this was in the darkness as the car moved through the tunnel under the silent race course, then maneuvered through the tall steel girders that hold up the grandstand. We all piled out at the foot of the long stairway leading to the television booth. High above the empty Speedway, it was the only light still shining.

From there, we did the show. It went very well, complete with a live interview of Gurney by Chris Schenkel at the end. The result of the race was still in doubt.

Afterward, the weary group of ABC people, including Jackie, returned to the restaurant at the Speedway Motel. There, we were joined by Penske, apparently the winning owner, for dinner. They kept the restaurant open late for us.

Roone says that the surest sign that Wide World of Sports is in town is this scene: a nearly deserted restaurant, with one yawning, lonely waiter glancing at his watch in the corner. The chairs have been turned upside down and placed on top of all the tables, all except one. At that table sits the Wide World group, usually about twelve in number, eating their New York cut steaks, drinking their Beaujolais wine and, says Roone, listening to McKay talk.

He's probably right.

SUNDAY, MAY 28

Usually, we have left the scene of the event by the following morning. In the case of this year's Indy 500, however, I was so tired that I passed up the 7:00 A.M. flight and decided to take the next available plane, at one o'clock in the afternoon. I wandered over to the track.

Our engineering crew was undertaking the depressing job of

breaking down everything they had built up over the course of the last month, packing it away and moving it to the next stop on our endless tour.

Steve Nikafor, one of the top cameramen in the business and one of the most pleasant, was stripped to the waist, hauling dusty pieces of equipment across the infield.

"Hey, Jimmy," he called, "what are you doing here? It's the first time I've ever seen you at a knockdown. Want to give us a hand?"

"No, thanks," I said, "looks like a dirty, thankless job to me. Depressing."

"It ain't so bad," said Steve, "just so you watch for the rats."

"What?"

"Oh, yeah, I'm not kidding. At a big event like this, look at all the food scattered all over the ground and the grandstand. The rats come after it in the night and the next day, they're all over, chewing through cables and everything. A real pain."

Steve Nikafor, holder of a master's degree in education and so skilled with his hands that he built his own house, walked off through the dusty infield laughing.

I walked to the press room, picking my way through the litter, glancing around for rats as I walked.

There was still no decision on the race, but it looked as through Donohue would be confirmed as the winner and Grant would be dropped from second to twelfth for fueling from the wrong tank. Eventually that is what happened, a decision that cost the Gurney crew about $75,000.

There were quite a few people at the track that morning, actually.

Out in the pit area, I heard someone call to me. It was Sam Posey, a race driver from Sharon, Connecticut, who had finished fifth in yesterday's race and was a contender for "Rookie of the Year" honors. (He didn't get it. It went to Mike Hiss.)

Sam is another of the new wave of Indianapolis drivers. He is a graduate of the Gunnery School and the Rhode Island School of Design, descendant of an old Connecticut family. He talks with a flat Ivy League accent, and says he isn't sure whether he is a race driver who paints, or an artist who drives race cars. He is very articulate.

"Say, Jim," he said, "I've been looking for you. I thought that soccer game you had yesterday on Wide World of Sports was just sensational. (He was talking about the tape of the F.A. Cup Final.) That fellow with the broken elbow . . . why, that will become a classic of sport."

"Thank you, Sam," I said, "I'm pleased. You mean that after the race you went back to the motel and watched that?"

"Oh, yes," said Sam. "I thought it was terribly exciting, after that somewhat dull round and round we had here!"

Outside the entrance to the Speedway Motel, I took a final look around as I waited for the taxicab. I probably wouldn't see this spot for another eleven months. Traffic on the wide street bordering the racetrack was sparse now.

A group of men in golf clothes were happily running down the stairway to my left. There is a golf club at the Speedway. The pro shop is in the motel, presided over by white-haired Mike Sullivan. There are nine holes located inside the racetrack, in the infield, and eighteen more outside. It is unlike any other golf course in the world, the only spot I know where a golfer must ignore the scream of racing motors on his left, and the sound of a passing freight train on his right, while standing in the ominous shadow of the Goodyear blimp, cruising overhead.

But then everything about the Indianapolis Motor Speedway is unique. Everything is straightforward, and exactly what it appears to be. There is a flat, straight-faced, old-fashioned midwestern honesty about the whole place, and therein, I think, lies its appeal.

Inside the entrance, I can still hear Jane, the lady at the front desk, laughing as she repeats to a colleague the story she just told me.

"I swear to you," she was saying, "it happened just two minutes ago. This man called while I was handling the switchboard and said, 'Excuse me, please, ma'am, but can you tell me please what time the race starts?' "

"Now wouldn't you think everybody in the whole world would know that our race was yesterday?"

Yes, you would.

5

NCAA Track and
Field Championships

I am having my shoes shined at San Francisco International Airport. When traveling out this way, I always try to allow time for a shine here, because it has one of the finest shoeshine stands left in America. I recommend it to you.

At the head of pier C, where the sign above reads "Gates 20–28, United Air Lines," the Top Hat Shoeshine Stand features regular shines for fifty cents plus tip, wax shines for seventy-five cents, and the "deluxe shine" for a dollar and a quarter. I take the wax, but haven't moved into the heady atmosphere of the deluxe shine as yet.

As I sit here, the Musak is playing, "Ooo, looka there, ain't she pretty?," an old Fats Waller song. I'm on my way back home after our coverage this weekend of the NCAA Track and Field Championships.

This year, they really served as kind of a rehearsal—for competitors, officials, and even for us—for the U.S. Olympic Track and Field Trials to be held in the same place next month.

The place is Stevenson Track at Hayward Field, The University of Oregon in Eugene, Oregon. It's the only place I know where the running track has a different name than the stadium in which it is located.

Eugene is different in other ways, too.

The city bills itself as "The Track Capital of the World." This may be a slight exaggeration, but there is no doubt that track is the warm lifeblood of the community.

Thanks to Bill Bowerman, the track coach at Oregon, developer of middle distance and distance running stars like Jim Grelle, Dyrol Burleson, and Steve Prefontaine, the whole town is track-mad, as spectators and as participants. Any morning, you can see hundreds of citizens out jogging shortly after sunrise. If it isn't the track capital, it most certainly is the jogging capital of the world. Eugene may not be big, but it sure is fit.

Stevenson Track may be the fastest running surface in the world, except for lane one, which tends to be a little lumpy and which also presents a problem because of a white pipe which marks the inside of the track. It is, of course, a synthetic surface, as the Olympic track in Munich will be.

Hayward Field (in which Stevenson Track is located, remember) is anything but ultramodern. Half a century old, it used to be the university's football stadium, but now is used principally for track. The ancient green wooden grandstand looks like something you might see at a rodeo grounds, or at a second division soccer team's grounds in England.

Still, it has a certain charm.

There is an intimacy and a character to old ball parks such as Ebbets Field in Brooklyn or the Polo Grounds in New York (both gone now), or Fenway Park in Boston (still in use). If you ever saw Carl Furillo climb the Ebbets Field wall in search of a fly ball, or Dusty Rhodes loft a pop fly (Chinese homerun) in the Polo Grounds, or any good right-hand hitter drive one into the net at Fenway, you know what I mean.

The many new stadia rising around the country, with their stadium clubs and improved rest room facilities, are more comfortable, more practical, and make more money for the promoters. Like the plastic playing surfaces they contain, they are efficient. But so is a factory, and the sports fan goes to the stadium to escape his factory. Watching on television, it is almost impossible to tell from looking at these stands whether you are in New York, Philadelphia, or Cincinnati.

Character or no character, the Hayward Fields of the world are on their way out, ready to join the leather football helmet, homemade bread, and the corner candy store. In fact, Hayward Field is scheduled to have a brand new grandstand, freshly painted and gleaming in its anonymity.

We found out something we didn't know before at the NCAA meet. There is such a thing as a "fast" water jump or a "slow" water jump in steeplechase running. The shallower the jump, the faster the runner should be able to splash through it.

This came to light when it was discovered that the Stevenson Track water jump is seven inches shallower (therefore, faster) than the internationally approved standard. Local officials of the "Track Capital of the World," embarrassed at such an oversight, promise that it will be remedied by the time of the Olympic Trials.

The fast water jump joins a mental file I've been keeping of other such sports minutiae. Long ago, we found out that there are fast and slow pools in swimming. A pool can be slowed by turbulent wave action bouncing off poorly constructed side gutters, particularly for the swimmers in the outside lanes. The times will be swifter if the end walls of the pool are a touch tacky, rather than slippery smooth. It helps the swimmers get a good push after each lap.

Slalom ski racers are more likely to get bruises on their shoulders when racing in Europe than in America. The Europeans use sturdy wooden poles to mark the course, while we use bamboo sticks. When you hit a European slalom pole you know it.

One of the seething controversies in the world of golf these days concerns six one-hundredths of an inch. The ball used in the United States is 1.68 inches in diameter. The English ball is 1.62 inches. Since the size of the ball is the only inconsistency in the rules of the game today, there is great agitation to standardize the size of the ball. The most frequently heard compromise is for a sphere 1.66 inches across.

Golf ball manufacturers blanch at the thought of retooling for the momentous change.

The NCAA meet also gave us our first look at Steve Prefontaine on his native heath.

Prefontaine is a small, cocky, twenty-one-year-old distance runner from the little seafaring town of Coos Bay, Oregon, who has become a demigod in the state. Male and female students at the university wear T-shirts bearing the red-lettered legend, "Go Pre." The radio station in his home town swears that if he wins a gold medal in the Olympics 5,000-meter run, it will change its call letters to KPRE.

With this sort of adulation, it is understandable that Prefontaine chooses to stay close to home, rather than wander the track world seeking out the likes of Mohammed Gahmoudi, Dave Bedford, and Miruts Yifter. Will that lack of international experience hamper him at Munich, or will he have the advantage of the element of surprise when he faces the toughest field in the games?

This sort of conjecture doesn't seem to interest Pre. He combines a certain Germanic determination (his mother was a German war bride) with a Gallic panache and flair that is summed up in his little mustache and lop-sided smile (his father is of French descent).

Confident? Prefontaine took a victory lap of the stadium, waving to his idolators, *before* his race in the NCAA championships.

WESTPORT, CONNECTICUT—WEDNESDAY, JUNE 7

Back home in Connecticut, I have just heard some good news from Dennis Lewin in the office. I do *not* have to go to LeMans,

France, this week for the 24 Hours of LeMans endurance race. This definitely should strengthen my own endurance. LeMans was going to piggyback with trips to California (U.S. Open), Oregon again (Olympic Trials), Scotland (British Open), Wisconsin (World Lumberjack Championships), and Birmingham, Michigan (PGA), before it was time to go to Munich for the Olympics.

Removing LeMans makes the schedule much easier to live with.

There were several reasons for the change, principally the fact that the race does not look very competitive this year.

SUNDAY, JUNE 11

It's been a beautiful, unexpected weekend at home, and yet motor racing has dominated it, in a sense, even though I didn't have to go to LeMans.

I was sitting in the backyard yesterday, getting some sun and doing research on next week's U.S. Open Golf Championship, a pleasant task, when the mail arrived. In it was a new book written by Jackie Stewart.

I had been thinking about Jackie. Since we worked together at Indy, he had been hospitalized with a bleeding ulcer and had dropped off the racing circuit.

The book was interesting, but not cheerful. Jackie talked a great deal in it about the deaths of his two closest friends on the Grand Prix tour; Jochen Rindt, the Austrian orphan who became world driving champion posthumously, and Piers Courage, heir to the Courage brewing fortune in England. Both had died on the race course.

Jackie is more forthright than most in discussing the ever-present danger of death in his profession, hence his preoccupation with improved safety measures.

I finished the book this morning, and an hour or so later was driving to the Shorehaven Golf Club for a game of tennis with my son, Sean. As I turned on the radio, an announcer was reciting the achievements of a racing driver, declaring at the end that he would be sorely missed.

Someone had died at LeMans. From the announcer's comments, it was easy to figure out who it was, even though I had missed the name at the top of the story.

Joachim Bonnier, Swedish driver turned Swiss businessman, had flown off the course at 190 miles per hour into the woods bordering the Mulsanne straight. In semi-retirement, Bonnier was only in the race to help promote a new business venture.

Jo Bonnier was Jackie Stewart's neighbor in Switzerland, and one of his closest friends among the drivers.

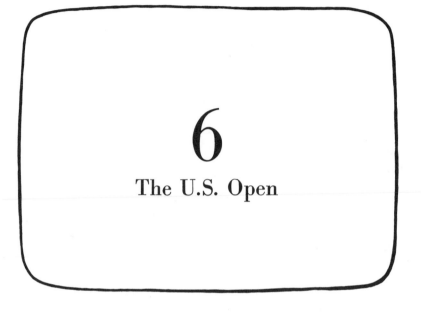

6

The U.S. Open

The view from the window of my room in the Del Monte Lodge, Pebble Beach, California, is fascinating, even in the darkness just after midnight.

I'm looking straight out at the eighteenth green, where the crowd will be gathering in a few hours for the first round of this year's U.S. Open Golf Championship. It is almost certain to be a memorable Open.

For one thing, it is the first time the great tournament has been played here at Pebble, one of the world's most famous courses. For another, Jack Nicklaus, having won the Masters, will try to take the second step on his way to a modern grand slam. The slam, as yet unachieved by anyone, consists of the masters, U.S. and British Opens, and the PGA. Jack likes all of the courses this year (Augusta National, Pebble Beach, Muirfield in Scotland,

47

and Oakland Hills in Birmingham, Michigan), and has consciously prepared himself for a frontal assault.

The trip out from New York was one of those occasions when getting here really *was* half the fun. On the first leg from New York to San Francisco, my traveling companion was Associate Director Jack Gallivan. Jack is an Irishman from Salt Lake City, in his late twenties, freckled and usually smiling through his great red mustache. He appreciates things like good wine, fast cars, deep powder snow, and politics, so he is interesting to travel with.

Jack's father publishes one of Salt Lake's newspapers and owns a television station, but the son has chosen another way. He first wandered into our organization on a temporary basis as car dispatcher during the Winter Olympics in Grenoble, France, 1968. He sat in the lobby of the Hotel Trois Roses all through the games, manipulating cars and drivers by walkie-talkie.

After that, he left us to return to his first love, politics. He became an advance man in the presidential campaign of Senator Robert F. Kennedy. Jack was standing next to the senator in the kitchen of the Ambassador Hotel in Los Angeles. He was one of those who grappled with the assassin, Sirhan Sirhan.

Everything was changed for him that night. He later joined ABC Sports as a production assistant and had since moved up to A.D.

Gallivan was delighted with the acquaintance I made on the plane. It was Isaac Stern, the famous concert violinist, who turned out to be an avid sports fan. Jack sat and smiled through his mustache as Mr. Stern compared his art to sports.

Herewith, some observations by Isaac Stern, aboard United Air Lines' flight 29 to San Francisco:

> *The fascination of sports* is that you can draw a comparison between them and *any* other profession, whether it be composing, playing the violin, or whatever it might be.
>
> *The artist and the athlete* each are first given a talent. This is like money, but it depends whether it is squandered or invested. Henry Aaron has invested and conserved his talent wisely and so he goes on toward age forty in pursuit of Babe Ruth's all-time career home

run record of 714. Denny McLain has squandered his talent, and from a thirty-game winner he descends in a very short time to the minor leagues. The same can happen to a musician.

The first challenge of talent comes when you realize just what it is, a gift—a marvelous, fragile gift that you now have the responsibility to polish and improve. The possibilities for improving the most glorious talent are endless, because the music you are privileged to play is greater than the instrument can produce, therefore you must work and work, forever. You never can completely fulfill the music of the great composers.

Each concert is a competition, not against the music, or the audience, but against yourself, against your own par. Who is to say what par is? To Jack Nicklaus, par may be 69, not 72 as it says on the scorecard. And if par is 69 for Jack today, I am sure that he strives to make it 68 the next day.

Doubt assails the artist each time he plays, and it is the doubt that makes the adrenalin flow, makes him careful and alert to do it right. Too much doubt, though, too much adrenalin, and you can fail, leave your concert in the dressing room, like an overtrained athlete.

There are musicians who have been known to "psych-out" their colleagues in music as in sports. Once in Carnegie Hall, Artur Rubinstein was about to play a concert. Rubinstein is the total artist, the man who can miss a note here and there, yet still communicate the music to the listener better than the rest of us. Backstage was Vladimir Horowitz, total technician of music; sure of every note every time, but without the poetry of Rubinstein.

Noticing that Rubinstein had selected a work with a particularly hard ten-second passage, a brief bit of music known as one of the most difficult in the world to play, Horowitz kidded him.

"Oh, that one ten-second passage," he said, "I know how you must feel."

Whereupon, Rubinstein, suddenly thinking only of the passage, went out and played less than his best, and when he got to the difficult part, messed it up completely.

There is an excitement to the way the ABC Sports clan gathers for the big events like the Open.

We almost missed our connection to Monterey from San Francisco, so Gallivan and I were panting from a long run through the terminal when we boarded the next flight. Laughter and booing greeted us, because there were others of our group already aboard.

Roone Arledge, unknown to us, had been on an American Airlines flight from New York that arrived just ahead of us. Frank Gifford, the former New York Giant pro football star, had come in from Texas to catch this plane, while Chris Schenkel and his wife, Fran, had come on yet another flight, from their Indiana home, by way of Chicago. None of us knew the other people were coming.

After arrival at Pebble, we met others.

In the bar, I found Henry Longhurst, Britain's leading golf writer and broadcaster, who works with us each summer. He was sitting with Bud Palmer (former Princeton and pro basketball star, official greeter for Mayor Lindsay of New York, and veteran sports commentator) and Ken Gordon, a USGA official.

Henry, a rotund, slightly stooped man in his early sixties, had just arrived via an over-the-pole flight, an eleven-hour ordeal that would leave younger men weak for days. But not Henry. Slumped into his chair, he was still good for another few hours conversation before bedtime. In fact, Henry is one of those people who can lead you to think he has fallen asleep in his chair, only to suddenly make an extremely cogent comment that no one else has thought of.

So it was tonight.

Conversation at the table had turned to the great golf ball controversy, the one I mentioned a while ago involving the proposed standardization of the ball at 1.66 inches in diameter, rather than the current American 1.68 or the British 1.62. There seemed agreement that something of the kind would be nice, if it didn't cause total chaos in the ball manufacturing business. Ken Gordon, circumspect in a USGA way, said that the matter had been discussed this week.

Henry Longhurst, chin on his chest, eyes apparently closed, scarcely moved a muscle, but he spoke with authority.

"It wouldn't do at all, you see," Henry said. "The small ball, the original ball, if you will, was well suited to the sort of turf we have in Britain. Now, here come the Americans. Here, you have a broader-bladed, rather coarser grass into which the small ball nestled deeply, causing bad lies. We'll have a different ball, please, said the Americans. Well, fine, then.

"Since that time, the grass has not changed here, basically. Nor has it changed in England. Therefore, I see no reason to make the two countries play with the same ball. Rather, I should imagine that a number of *other* size balls should be used to accommodate other local conditions.

"At very high altitudes, the ball carries unfairly far, because of the light air. All right then, let's bring in a *heavier* ball for those chaps—even things up, you see. In Uganda, there is a devilishly wide-bladed jungle savannah that should require an even *larger* ball. Yes, that's it. More variety of golf balls, not less, I say."

As usual, Henry had left us with nothing to say. So we went to bed.

"One more, I think," he said, "then I'll be right along."

Henry Longhurst is responsible for one very welcome luxury on our commentary towers. A few years ago, he wrote a most polite letter to Chuck Howard, in his post as vice-president of production for ABC Sports and producer of the golf telecasts.

Henry explained that "the ravages of age" had made it increasingly difficult for him to scale the perpendicular ladders that led to our positions on the commentary towers. Sometimes these are very high, a fact which had terrified the rest of us. Mostly out of a wish not to appear cowardly, neither Chris Schenkel, Byron Nelson, Bill Flemming, Bud Palmer, nor I had ever officially complained to Chuck.

He saw the reason of Henry's position, though, investigated the subject, and came up with some marvelous metal stairways, complete with handrails, that wind up through the interior of the towers. We use them all the time now.

And on the survey report turned in by producers when they are ordering the necessary equipment for a golf telecast, you will see as an official designation, along with many technically phrased items, this one: "One (1) Longhurst ladder for each tower."

Like Steve Brodie and Annie Oakley before him, Henry has given his name to the American language.

FRIDAY, JUNE 16

Pebble Beach is living up to its reputation. Double bogies are everywhere and some of the greatest golfers in the world are shaking their heads in disbelief as they look at their scores.

Once upon a time, the land that is now Pebble Beach was all laid out to be a real estate subdivision. That was before a man named Samuel F. B. Morse, descendant of the inventor of the telegraph, quietly burned the plans and ordained that this spectacular piece of scenery would become a golf course.

And so it did, designed by Jack Neville, who is still very much a part of the scene here at age seventy-eight. It is not a course measured by the number of cubic yards of earth moved in its construction. On the contrary, it was subtly placed into the rugged contours that nature had provided. This is not to say that Pebble Beach is ungroomed. It was built with one of the world's first artificial watering systems. Some of the grasses used here are imported, such as alkali grass from Utah, to resist the salt spray that blows in from Carmel Bay.

When the sun shines and the wind is down, you can love Pebble Beach even while it's breaking your heart, but when the weather turns bad—cold and windy as only a seaside course can be—Pebble seems like a work of the devil, all beast, without a single forgiving human trait.

Whether you are trying to hit a delicate little pitch with a trembling hand to the tiny green on the 120-yard seventh hole, or facing the yawning chasm you must cross with your second shot on number eight, you know that you are in a special, truly unique place.

And whether you're hitting into the teeth of a gale on the par three seventeenth with its hourglass-shaped green and frightening rocks below, or finishing up your round along the classic par five eighteenth, where even your third shot, your pitch to the green, may find its way to disaster in the Pacific waters, you feel the combination of legend and stark reality that makes Pebble Beach one of the most famous golfing grounds in all the world.

This afternoon I taped an interview with Bing Crosby for use on the half hour nighttime U.S. Open show this evening (Friday).

Talking with Bing Crosby is a bit like talking with Paul Bunyan. He is a legendary figure who behaves in person just like the legend on the screen. He really does talk in that combination of contemporary slang and polysyllabic words that one remembers from "the old Kraft Music Hall." He really does wear tweed jackets and tweed hats and puff reflectively on a slender-stemmed pipe.

For me, the sensation is amplified, because when I was seventeen years old, I had convinced myself and my classmates at Loyola High School in Baltimore that I could sing exactly like Bing Crosby. An unexpected opportunity to prove this came when our school took over the operation of radio station WBAL for a day as a promotional effort for the station. It was the first time I had ever seen the inside of a broadcasting studio.

Regular announcers stood by our sides as we read commercials and station breaks. The big moment for me, however, was to occur when George Hock and I would sing a duet called "Small Fry." It was a current hit record by Crosby and Johnny Mercer. On this day, I would be Crosby and George would be Mercer.

Stage fright caught up with my partner, however, just as we were about to go into the studio. He couldn't do it, and suddenly I was alone at the microphone, changing my voice from Crosby to Mercer and back again as the song proceeded.

When the day was done, I hurried home to see what my parents and my sister, Mary Louise, had thought of my performance. They were as loyal, as prejudiced, toward me then as they are now, so I assumed the comments would be favorable.

"How did you like the duet, Mom?" I asked.

"Wonderful, Jimmy," said my mother. "You were just wonderful. In all honesty, though, I must say that the boy who was singing like Johnny Mercer really wasn't so good."

That has been a favorite family anecdote ever since, and today, I finally told it to Bing as we waited for a technical problem to be solved before we did the interview. He seemed to enjoy it.

To the average American television viewer, Bing means Pebble. For years now, they have been watching and listening to Bing describing his own tournament here, the annual "Clambake" or Bing Crosby National Pro-Amateur.

In the early 1960s, I awoke on a Sunday morning in the Del Monte Lodge. I could feel that it was cold, but I was not prepared for the sight that waited outside my window.

It was snowing! At a golf tournament.

Roone held an emergency meeting in his suite overlooking the eighteenth and Carmel Bay. Through the swirling flakes, you could see mammoth, foam-crested breakers smashing against the rocks where only yesterday golfers had been retrieving stray shots.

There would be no play that day for sure. But Roone, as usual, had an idea.

At air time, I opened the show standing beside the eighteenth green in the snow and explained the situation. Then some of the golfers, Arnold Palmer included, held a clinic, driving golf balls into the stormy waters of the bay, giving instruction to some of the amateur celebrities on hand.

The next day they finished the tournament. It ended in a tie, and when Doug Ford and Phil Rodgers returned to the first hole for a sudden death playoff, we were unable to show the finish. It was that incident, along with others, that later prompted the PGA to allow playoffs to start at the first available hole of television coverage.

Some golf writers were outraged by this concession, but the golfers didn't seem to mind, and the American golf fan at home finds it much pleasanter to see how it all turns out. So do some golf writers, watching the playoff on television monitors in the press tent, filing copy to beat their deadline, thanks to the hated tube.

Tonight, we had dinner with the most famous caddy in the history of American golf. At the age of seventy, he is a multimillionaire and lives in a magnificent house along the Seventeen Mile Drive here in Pebble Beach with his wife Margaret and their children, John, fourteen, and Cynthia, twelve.

Eddie Lowry didn't make his money caddying. In fact, the peak of his fame in that profession came when he was ten years old, in 1913, at The Country Club in Brookline, Massachusetts.

Photographs show him as a bent-over, round-cheeked lad, with his shirt sleeves rolled up and a cloth cap on his head, struggling to carry a golf bag bigger than he was. Eddie caddied in that U.S. Open for a young American amateur named Francis Ouimet. Together, they brought golf its first popular, romantic, widely followed victory in this country. Ouimet tied the great British professionals Harry Vardon and Ted Ray for the title, then whipped them in an eighteen hole playoff, with a 72 to Vardon's 77 and Ray's 78.

Eddie Lowry never lost his love for golf. In later years, Lowry used some of the money he made as a successful automobile dealer in the San Francisco Bay area to sponsor young amateurs and professionals as they started on the tournament trail.

At dinner with the Lowrys and their kids were Byron Nelson, Chris Schenkel, and Bud Palmer of our group, along with Stewart Hunt and John Murchison, the Texas oil men.

Over dessert, Byron recalled the first Wide World-type overseas operation he did with us. It was at Muirfield, where this year's British Open will be. But this was in 1966, the year Nicklaus won his first British title.

Byron recalled how we scaled our tower at twilight to put some commentary on the edited version of the show as it was fed by satellite back to the States. He remembered how we were caught up in the excitement of what we were watching and talking about on the monitor, and were almost shocked when the show was done to realize that it was now pitch dark. We climbed down the ladder and saw a totally deserted golf course and club house, with only a night watchman and his German shepherd dog standing watch as a mist literally rose over the moors. That inside view of how television works made a strong impression on Byron.

What I personally remember about that trip is Byron Nelson standing in his pajamas in the upstairs hallway of the private home where we stayed, giving me a putting lesson.

SUNDAY, JUNE 18

On this morning of the last round of the U.S. Open, I see a remarkable sight from my window overlooking the eighteenth green. It is seven o'clock in the morning, and yet a crowd has already started to gather, to put down its camp chairs and its hampers of food and drink and to wait for the golfers to come through. Remember, these people are at the *eighteenth* green. In the early morning, they are huddled into parkas and under blankets, because it is cold out there where the wind whips in off Carmel Bay. It will be some *ten hours* before Nicklaus and Trevino, the final pair, come to them.

To be sure, this does look like one of the great closing days in U.S. Open history. Yesterday, the double bogies continued to fly as thick as the birdies. This, to me, is one of the signs of a truly great golf course.

Too often today, a course is called tough, or even great, simply because it is more than 7,000 yards long and somebody has said that par is 70. Birdies, then, are few, except on the par fives. When the pros play the course, there aren't too many bogies either. The classic course, I think, is usually something under 7,000 yards, but so designed that it requires even the greatest golfer to play every club in the bag. It rewards excellence with a birdie, but punishes even slight misjudgments with a bogie or worse.

Pebble Beach is like that. Yesterday, in the third round, the lead switched back and forth as the skills of the players ebbed and flowed. On a chilly, overcast day (more like the British Open than the U.S. Open), many golfers had their chance to take the lead and move in front of the pack.

Yet, when the day was done, who was leading? The greatest golfer in the world, of course—Jack Nicklaus. And who was second? The defending champion, Lee Trevino, naturally. And who was lurking in the wings, figuratively panting and snorting, like an old rodeo bull looking for one more great charge through the arena? Why, Arnold Palmer, logically enough.

All of this made sense, because great courses, in the end, almost always give their rewards to great golfers, and these three are the greatest of their time.

I wonder if Nicklaus is having his recurrent dream this morning as he slumbers while the spectators sit and shiver, awaiting his arrival? I forget how the subject arose, but it was down the coast in San Diego, at the Andy Williams Tournament on the Torrey Pines course last year, that I was talking with Nicklaus about dreams.

I asked him if he dreamed often. As he continued to hit those beautiful, strong, one-iron shots from the practice tee, he smiled and said yes, that there was one dream he had many times. In it, he is walking up the eighteenth fairway in an important tournament when he suddenly and sickeningly realizes that he has twenty-three clubs in his bag! Fourteen is the limit, and the mere presence of twenty-three would cost him the title.

Dream-walking, you know, is always in a kind of slow motion, and as he moves along in the nightmare, Jack surreptitiously throws clubs into the weeds, tries to hand them off to cooperative spectators—and then wakes up.

Dreaming or not, Jack is almost certainly still asleep at seven o'clock this morning. And the spectators definitely are in place, just outside my window in the cold. Traveling as we do to the great sports events, a person can forget what a thrill it might be to see even one memorable sporting occasion in a lifetime.

"It's true," Joe Dey had said last night at dinner, "I have never attended a British Open in my life, but I hope to this year."

It was hard to believe that Joe Dey, long-time head of the United States Golf Association, now the commissioner of Professional Golf, had never seen the British Open in person.

"With the USGA," he said, "I was always busy arranging our own tournaments during the summer months. Since I have joined the PGA Tournament Division, I've been even busier. But this year, I'm going to Muirfield."

Sitting around the table, Bill Flemming, Henry Longhurst, and Frank Hannigan, who had been Joe's assistant at the USGA, all expressed surprise.

To celebrate Mr. Dey's first British Open, I proposed that we all gather for a drink next month at Greywalls, an inn just behind the ancient Muirfield clubhouse. There was agreement, marred only by the muttered comment from Henry that Greywalls would be fine now that it was fixed up after the fire.

"What's that, Henry?" I said. "Greywalls had a fire? A big one?"

"Oh, no," he said, "just the kitchen. Shouldn't have been that big, really. Someone saw the blaze as soon as it began, and put in a call to the Gullane [pronounced "Gillan"] Fire Brigade. There are only two chaps normally on duty there, you see. But one was sloshed and the other was visiting his aunt in Musselburgh, so the fire very nearly got out of hand."

"Henry," I said, "that is a toast if ever I heard one. 'Here's to the Gullane Fire Brigade. One is sloshed and the other is visiting his aunt in Musselburgh.'"

"It's more than that," said the usually conservative Mr. Dey. "It's the chorus of a song. Here's what we'll do. Each of us here agrees to write a verse to go with it and we will recite them at Greywalls next month."

Thanks again go to Henry for a new expression. I still like it as a toast. "Here's to the Gullane Fire Brigade. One is sloshed and the other is visiting his aunt in Musselburgh."

In an unbecoming fit of modesty, Henry Longhurst once said that he thought ABC brought him over here each summer as a sort of quaint, foreign anachronism. As we told him at the time, nothing could be less accurate.

Roone brings him here because he is one of the best golf commentators to be found. We all have grown very fond of him because of his excellent use of the English language and his sense of humor.

Henry has that wonderful way of summing up something in a very few well-chosen words.

Like the time Roone was charcoaling steaks for a large group in the backyard of his home in Westchester County. American outdoor cooking was something new to Henry, so he was more alert to the situation than the rest of us.

Looking back on it, the idea of cooking steer in the midst of a group of people gathered around a swimming pool on a lovely summer night, probably seemed a bit barbaric to Henry, like the scene in Edna Ferber's *Giant*, where the wealthy Texans cook the brains of the steer and serve them from inside the head.

At any rate, Roone, Henry, and I were standing and talking, whiskies in hand, when Roone suddenly interrupted himself in mid-sentence.

"Hold it!" he said, "I forgot about the steaks. I'd better take a look and made sure they aren't burned."

In real or pretended alarm—probably a little of each—Mr. Longhurst arched both eyebrows and turned on me.

"Oh dear," he said. "Has the beast died in vain?!"

SUNDAY, JUNE 18 (1:00 P.M.)

Nicklaus and Trevino are just teeing off.

What an interesting pair they make. Nicklaus—big, blond, Aryan, smartly dressed as he stands holding his driver, brows just slightly knit in concentration, but smiling slightly, too, as he listens to the endless patter of Trevino's monologue. Trevino—chunky, jet-black hair under the tilted-back golf cap, alert eyes constantly peering out from the mahogany tan of his face as he looks around for something else to talk about.

Both men reflect their divergent backgrounds. Nicklaus looks like the son of a well-to-do owner of a chain of drugstores, a country club member from Scioto in Columbus, Ohio. He has the super-confident look of a young man who has had it pretty good all his life. The strength of his body and the precision of his reflexes are controlled by an intelligent mind. He runs his own financial business now, too, having broken from Mark McCormack a couple of years ago.

It's difficult to say where Trevino's confidence comes from, but he exudes it. He was raised in a shack along the edge of a Texas golf course by his mother and his grandfather, a Mexican grave digger, but his real opportunity to play the game didn't come until he joined the marines and went to the Pacific.

Later, at the Tennison Park Public Course in Dallas, he played golf with anybody for any kind of bet. It was there that his now-famous bet that he could beat you while playing with a Dr Pepper bottle began.

They played another game there, too. You played down the first hole, then through a tunnel under a railroad trestle. On the other side, you played across to another tunnel, back through that, and on up to the eighteenth green. The man making it in the fewest shots, of course, was the winner. That usually was Lee Trevino.

Just before the final round of another Open championship, someone asked him if he was feeling the pressure.

"Pressure?" he said. "Hell, this isn't pressure. Pressure is playing a five-dollar Nassau with only a dollar in your pocket!"

Maybe that's where the confidence comes from. Maybe this all just seems so easy and luxurious, after the shack where beans were considered a big dinner, and the tense, hustling rounds at Tennison Park.

Two or three minutes ago, while he and Nicklaus were still on the practice putting green, I asked Lee if he were feeling better today. He has been playing here full of antibiotics, walking around the course half-woozy from the pocketful of pills given him by a doctor in Texas.

He was in the hospital as late as last Monday, suffering from pneumonia. He left against the doctor's recommendation, and has been hacking and coughing his way around Pebble Beach all week. On the practice green, though, he looked better today and wasn't coughing as much.

"Feeling better?" he said. "Hell, Jim, I don't know. I'm like a duck. Every day I get up, I see a brand new world. I can't remember how I felt yesterday, or much of what I did. Half the time, I don't know where I am when I wake up. I just get up and walk outside and see what's going on."

Listening to this new bit of philosophy according to Trevino, Nicklaus continued putting, shaking his head and smiling to himself.

Trevino pointed his putter at Jack.

"If I'd listened to him, I wouldn't have this damn pneumonia," he said. "Really, we were playing together in a tournament a couple of weeks ago, and Jack said my cough sounded terrible, that I should drop off the circuit for a week so I wouldn't get screwed up for the Open. I should have listened to him. I always should. He's the one who talked to me and got me cranked up so that I won those three Opens (U.S., British, and Canadian) last year. I should listen to Jack all the time. Didn't you tell me that, Jack?"

At times you wonder whether Lee is really that friendly or whether all the conversation is an intricate, upside-down psych-out of the opposition. The other golfers don't seem to mind.

Yesterday, Lee played with young Johnny Miller, normally a very quiet man, on the course and off. By the time they got to the hole I was covering, Johnny was gabbing away, telling stories to Lee, who would bend over and laugh as he swaggered along the fairway.

Well, there they go. Big Jack and the "Merry Mexican." I wonder who will win?

JUNE 18 (7:00 P.M.)

Jack won. On the early holes, it looked like it might be a stately march to victory for him. Then came the tenth, a long par four with a cliff on the right side, leading down to the beach. When you least expected it, Nicklaus's tee shot went off to the right and all the way down onto the beach, where non-golf fans were taking a Sunday afternoon stroll. Later, he said that a gust of wind had blown him slightly off balance as he addressed the ball.

For a moment, he considered playing it from the beach, but decided against it and dropped another ball for a one-stroke penalty. His third shot almost went to the beach again! But it hung up in some long grass on a bank to the right of the green. He pitched up and took two putts to get down for a double-bogie six.

Opportunity knocked for the others again on twelve. This is a long par three hole. Jack's tee shot looked just right, but it took a big bounce and went far over the green, ending in a terrible lie under some matted grass. He left his second shot short of the green, moving the ball only a few feet. His third was on but ten feet past the hole. Now, he needed that difficult putt for a bogie four.

This was the moment that meant the Open. Trevino, still in contention, leaned on his putter. On television, Chuck Howard and directors Mac Hemion and Andy Sidaris put up a split screen, showing Nicklaus hunched over the critical bogie putt, and Palmer, further up the course, putting for a birdie. There could be a two-stroke swing here and Palmer would lead.

But Jack, eyes narrowed, lips tight, rolled the ball toward the hole.

Trevino shouted, "Get in, ball!" and it did.

Palmer missed and Jack still led. From there, it was Jack Nicklaus all the way.

I walked in with him and Trevino, wearing a big walkie-talkie arrangement that enables me to talk from the fairway if anything unusual happens.

On the seventeenth, the famous par three on a sandy piece of ground sticking out into Carmel Bay, I walked ahead of the golfers and stood beside the green. A stiff wind was blowing into their faces. The hour-glass green is tough enough to hit any time, but into the wind it is close to impossible. Even if you make the green, it is possible to be in a place where you must use a sand iron to jump over the corner of a bunker.

Nicklaus went to his strength—the one-iron that he so often uses when in a tough situation. Would he play it safe, short of the green, pitch up and settle for a bogie four, rather than take a chance of fading onto the rocks on the right?

It was one of the greatest shots I have ever seen, boring into the wind like an arrow, flying toward me as I stood there. Would it be too long? Long enough? It bounced straight for the pin, hit it, and nearly went into the hole! As it stopped within tap-in range for a birdie two, the U.S. Open for 1972 was over.

Only total disaster on eighteen could stop Jack.

It didn't happen, and now he has two legs on the grand slam. On to Muirfield, to the place where he won his first British Open. But remember who is the defending champion there, too. Trevino.

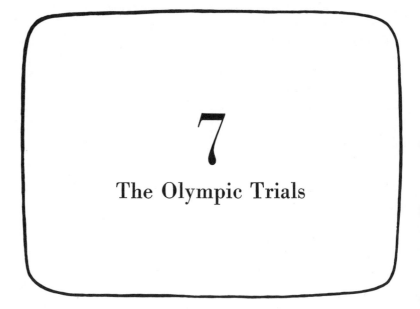

7

The Olympic Trials

If you're going to live a good part of your life on the road, as I do, this is the way to do it—in the Beverly Hills Hotel. The Beverly Hills has a very distinct personality. Long ago, it was the first building of any kind raised in what is now Beverly Hills. In the years since, it has housed the famous and the phony of every era of films and now television. It is said that as many deals are made over breakfast in the Beverly Hills as in the offices of Hollywood all day.

Its architecture, early Hollywood Spanish, gives it a casual, homelike air, which the staff carries through. When you pick up the phone in your room, the operator immediately says, "Yes, Mr. McKay?" (or whatever your name might be), even if you have checked in only five minutes before. I don't know how they do that, but it is one of their special touches that makes the difference.

64

The Beverly Hills has its inconveniences, like the archaic, noisy air conditioners, but they are more than overcome, for me at least, by the rest of it, from the succulent Cranshaw melon for breakfast, to the expert friendliness of Dino, the well-known maître d'hôtel in the Polo Lounge, and Gus the bartender.

There are ghosts in the walls of the Polo Lounge, which got its name more than forty years ago, when there was still a lot of country around the hotel, country through which Will Rogers, Spencer Tracy, and their pals would ride their horses after the polo game. They would tie them up outside the bar, legend says, and hence came the name, the Polo Lounge.

You might guess from the above that there is a bit of the Walter Mitty in me and perhaps even a touch of Snoopy, lying atop his doghouse, dreaming of glory. In my case, the little balloon over Snoopy's head might say, "Here's the well-known sports commentator being greeted by his friend Dino in the Polo Lounge."

A couple of winters ago, Roone Arledge and I rose early in Val d'Isere, France, to get in a little skiing before the day's work began. High above the village where Jean-Claude Killy was born and raised, the day was glorious, the sky blue, the snow white. The fact that neither Roone nor I skied very well didn't bother us at all.

After a few runs, we took off our skis, placed them expertly into a rack, and walked, heavy-footed, into a small bar and restaurant built into the mountainside. The place was almost empty and the sound of our bulky ski boots echoed. Snow flew from them and quickly turned into small puddles on the rough-hewn floor.

At the bar, Roone removed his leather gloves.

"Care for a small cognac to warm up, Jim?" he asked.

"A bit early for me, Roone," I said, "but I guess just a small one."

(Ernest Hemingway would have had a bit of cognac, wouldn't he?)

Casually, I leaned back on the corner of the bar with my right forearm. Then two things happened simultaneously. Roone changed from an international sophisticate into a guffawing maniac, while the bartender put down the rag he was polishing glasses with, stared at me and said, with Gallic disdain, "Oh, non, Monsieur. Non, non, non." He looked like he might cry.

For a moment, I was totally baffled. Then, I raised my arm, feeling a certain sticky resistance as I did so. I looked back and realized that from hand to elbow, I had firmly placed my right forearm into a tray full of peach tarts, just prepared for the lunchtime trade. Walter Mitty had become Stan Laurel. I thought I might cry.

Glancing at me angrily, the bartender, with fine European practicality, gently pushed the tray of tarts back into shape and dusted them off with the bar rag.

I have had my orange parka cleaned several times since, but it is still a bit sticky. Thank heaven the tarts were almost the same color as the parka.

Well, this has been a Walter Mitty day, that is for sure.

I arose at 6:30 A.M. in the Beverly Hills, dressed, went downstairs and asked the early morning doorman to get me a cab.

"Where to, Mr. McKay?" he asked.

"The Disney lot in Burbank," I said. Lord, that sounded glamorous. I thought of all the magazine stories I had read as a kid, which always referred to the movie studio as "the lot," and invariably pointed out that movie stars rose early to do their work. That was it, all right, and this was my first part in a theatrical movie. It would be called *The World's Greatest Athlete.*

My cab driver on the way to the studio was a bearded young man who writes for one of the many underground newspapers in this area. He was a sports fan, though, and said he had the sure remedy for Jim Ryun's hay fever. All the great miler need do, he said, was to follow nature's remedy, one he learned from an old farmer while living in a desert commune.

"Tell Jim to chew on a honeycomb, sucking out the honey as he goes. Do it for a week, and he'll never have hay fever again."

I said I'd tell him.

The Disney lot was just as I had imagined, quiet in the early morning, but with actors and workmen walking about. I went to wardrobe and makeup, and then to one of those huge sound stages that resemble a blimp hangar, or a huge warehouse.

Bob Sheerer, the director, turned out to have been a production assistant on "The Verdict Is Yours," a daytime show I had done at CBS about fifteen years ago. I forget whether Bob said, "Roll 'em," but he definitely did say, "Action."

Now, it is 10:30 A.M. Only three and a half hours after I left, I am back at the Beverly Hills. My first movie role has been completed.

It consisted of the following lines: "I'm Jim McKay, and it's time for sports shorts around the globe. First, we're going to go to Bud Palmer at Maryvale College with a fascinating tale. Over to you, Bud!"

That's it. I hope they don't cut it too much.

JUNE 29 (LATE AT NIGHT)

Today, we took another step on our road to Munich. Roone Arledge, Chris Schenkel, Howard Cosell, Keith Jackson, Murray Rose, Donna de Varona, Erich Segal, and I talked to a group of newspaper people who have been brought here by ABC to preview the fall shows that the network will present in a few months. They have been here all week and today, as a sidelight to the annual presentation, we told them about the upcoming Olympics telecasts. It seemed to go very well.

Howard produced Muhammad Ali as a surprise (the former champion had been having a press conference of his own elsewhere in the hotel). The Howard and Muhammad show was as entertaining as always. They indulged in some badinage and persiflage (as Howard might put it), then Cosell asked Ali a serious question.

"Tell me, Muhammad, can you put into words what it meant to you to be an Olympic gold medalist?" (Ali, then Cassius Clay, was light-heavyweight champion at Rome in 1960).

"Yes, I can," said Muhammad, straightening, pursing his lips, and looking toward the ceiling. "When I was not very old, I loved the gold, and I won much of it. But then the gold led to the green, if you know what I mean, and that was most important."

This was my first meeting with Erich Segal, Yale professor and author of *Love Story*. He will work with me at the games as expert commentator on long distance running events, since his avocation is marathon running. He has participated in the famous Boston Marathon many times.

Segal, I found, is a very small, slight, wiry man, hyperactive, outgoing, and dramatic in speech. He was attired in a light blue, high-fashion motorcycle suit for the luncheon. The jacket had many zippers.

During his remarks he quoted from the poet Pindar, whom he called the world's first sports writer, and stated: " '. . . man,' Pindar wrote, 'is but a dream of a shadow. . . .' "

When it was my turn to speak, I wasn't sure how to react to Erich's performance. After all, we would be working closely together at the games, and it was important that we get along well. I decided to take a chance and kid him a bit.

"Until today," I said, "I didn't realize just how difficult my job will be in Munich. I can see it now. Jim Ryun will be gaining on Kip Keino with half a lap to go. 'He may make it,' I'll say. 'What do you think, Erich?'

"And Erich will reply, 'Jim, man is but a dream of a shadow. . . .' And by the time he finishes that, the race will be over."

Segal leaned back and laughed harder than anybody else in the room. It looked like we were off to a good start.

EUGENE, OREGON—SATURDAY, JULY 1

We're back in Eugene, which really looked like the track capital of the world today. The best track and field athletes in the United States are gathered here now for the quadrennial do-or-die effort to make the U.S. Olympic team. It's quite a contrast to four years ago.

Then, the final trials were held before a comparative handful of people in a sylvan retreat near Lake Tahoe, California, an attempt to simulate the high altitude conditions that the athletes would later face at the games in Mexico City. There was something very nice about those trials—the sweet-smelling, thin air; the cool shadows of the woods through which the track actually ran. There was an air of quiet, almost ascetic preparation about it, more like a seminary than a stadium.

Here, all is different. It's like the weekend of a big college football game. There are flags and bands, and a jam-packed stadium. All of the talk is about the home team, of course, the home "team" being Steve Prefontaine. Here, they are certain he will win a gold medal at Munich.

However, the very first man to qualify for the U.S. team was Larry Young, whose native town appropriately lies in the geographical center of the country—Independence, Missouri.

Larry is a walker, and at 6:53 P.M. today, he came back into the stadium first in his event. The capacity crowd in the old Hayward Field stands gave Larry the kind of ovation he seldom hears in his sport. He loved it.

Since winning a bronze medal for the U.S. in Mexico, Larry has let his hair grow, has grown a full beard, and today was wearing sunglasses under the visor of his cap. He looked like the Larry Young of four years ago wearing a disguise.

He's an interesting man. At age twenty-nine, Larry, the most successful walker in American history, is a college student, an art major at Columbia College in Missouri. He attends Columbia as the recipient of the only race-walking scholarship ever given at an American college. The president, it seems, is a walking fan, one of the very few.

Larry Young, the Missouri metal-sculptor, is on his way to Munich.

So is Dave Wottle, another bit of mid-Americana, who surprised everyone by winning the 800 meters and by doing it in world record-tying time.

Dave isn't even an 800-meter runner. He's a miler whose coach suggested he run the 800 as part of his conditioning and preparation for the 1,500 trial, which is next week.

Wottle is a sight to behold on the track. Thin, almost gaunt, he lopes along in his orange shirt bearing the legend, "Bowling Green" (his university), wearing a weary-looking white golf cap. He first wore it to keep his long hair in place, he tells us, but lately has come to regard it as a symbol of good luck. He'll be sure of that after this evening.

Some people think his victory in the 800 is not a good portent for the United States at Munich, particularly since Jim Ryun had another of his lapses in the closing strides and failed to qualify for this event. The American team, the reasoning goes, will be weaker with Wottle, and without Ryun, in the 800.

Still, a guy can't be all bad when he ties the world record.

As usual, the trials are being conducted against a background of some controversy and grumbling. Four years ago, it was racial. This time, it is financial.

Eugene is about as far from the homes of many of the athletes as it could possibly be, and in keeping with American tradition, they have had to pay their own expenses to get here. A very few were sent by wealthy athletic clubs, but most were not.

A classic case of what the trackmen are talking about is Rodney Milburn, of Opelousa, Louisiana. Rod, in his high-hurdles specialty, is considered one of the hottest favorites for a gold medal in the games. Yet, here is what has happened to him.

Recently, he ran in the AAU championships here on the coast. Just before his semifinal heat, he discovered that somebody had stolen more than $250 out of his locker. Upset, he went out and lost his semifinal heat (although still qualifying for the final). It was a rare loss for him.

Returning to Southern University in Baton Rouge, Louisiana, where he is a student, Rod found that his apartment had burned in his absence, destroying virtually all of his belongings. The school said it wasn't covered by insurance.

In financial trouble, Rod asked the school to pay his expenses to these Olympic Trials, but they refused. Finally, it was his coach who loaned him the money to come.

Make no mistake. American Olympic athletes are amateurs, whether they pay for their track shoes or not. There are even, no doubt, some payments under the table, but if the test of an amateur is whether a guy has trouble paying his rent, they most certainly qualify.

SUNDAY, JULY 2

We're aboard United Air Lines flight 48, the "Red Eye," from Seattle to New York.

Chuck Howard, Dennis Lewin, and I had to charter up from Eugene to make it, but here we are, plodding toward home at 600 miles an hour, contemplating the interesting events of this first weekend of the Olympic Track and Field Trials (we'll be back for more next weekend).

If you are not familiar with the term "Red Eye" as used here, let me explain. The Red Eye is any transcontinental, nonstop, jet flight that leaves the West Coast after 10:00 P.M. Such flights put you into Kennedy Airport somewhere around 6:30 or 7:00 in the morning.

There you stand, waiting for your baggage. The floors are being cleaned with some kind of noisy machine. Under the eerie, fluorescent lighting, the car rental counters stand deserted ("Please use phone to call Hertz," it says on a small sign next to the yellow telephone). Squinting, you can see the sun rising outside the terminal building.

The endless belt that eventually will bring your bag rumbles mindlessly around for long minutes with nothing on it.

Your clothes are rumpled, your mouth tastes of the Scotch whisky you drank on the plane hoping it would help you get a little sleep. Your eyes are red—hence, the Red Eye.

Why do we take it? Well, some members of the ABC Sports staff take it, then go directly to the office. In my case, I'm usually trying to get another day at home before the next trip begins. If you wait until morning on the West Coast, it is the next evening in the East by the time you get home.

Whatever the purpose and no matter how many years you take it, the Red Eye is hard on your body. You have lost an entire night's sleep. More importantly, you have transported your brain and stomach across three time zones.

Perhaps one day, through permutation, man will become accustomed to the time zone phenomenon, but not in my day. We all have an "internal clock," I am told, a psychophysical sort of mechanism that regulates our sleeping and eating, even our bowel movements. But this mechanism knows not of jet travel. You can scream at your brain and stomach if you want, shout that you have now crossed three time zones and it isn't 3:00 A.M., it's 6:00 A.M., but they will not listen to you.

A good many years ago, scientists started researching this very real problem in connection with our space effort. They called it "asynchronosis," a neat coining, I thought. From the Greek, it means, roughly, a lack of timing, or synchronization. Since then, someone has come up with a new phrase, "jet lag," which sounds more like the name of a racehorse to me, and a bad one at that. I'll stick with asynchronosis.

I am also stuck with asynchronosis, it appears. It is even worse when you travel from New York to Europe, and reaches its sickening nadir when you take an over-the-pole flight from Los Angeles to London or Paris.

My worst case of the ailment came this past winter. After describing the U.S. Figure Skating Championships with Dick Button in Long Beach, California, I raced to L.A. International Airport to make an Air France flight to Paris, leaving, as I recall, at 9:00 P.M. At this time, remember, it was already 6:00 the *next morning* in Paris.

The flight was not a good one. Every seat was taken, and the captain must have been suffering from chills or something, because he kept the heat at about ninety degrees all night long.

In Paris, I literally had to run for another Air France flight, the last one that day going to Geneva. It left at 5:30 P.M. Paris time. Upon arrival in Geneva, I was met by a driver (non-English-speaking) who was to drive me four and a half hours into the Alps to a little place called Grindelwald.

Halfway there, we stopped for coffee at a Swiss country bar. As I sat there, half-dazed, listening to yodeling on the jukebox, watching the red-faced countrymen drink their local red wine or beer, it was almost impossible to believe that a few hours ago I was among the oil wells of Long Beach and the used car lots of Los Angeles. It was snowing when we left the bar.

It was almost midnight, local time, when we pulled up at the hotel in Grindelwald. Back in L.A., however, it was only 1:00 in the afternoon.

All that week, I suffered from the classic symptoms of asynchronosis; waking up three and four times a night, exhausted but unable to sleep; wanting to fall asleep at noon on a mountainside, but having to work. It was terrible.

During the long, sleepless night, I tried to use the time as I always do, by reading a book, in this case about the strange things that have happened on the North Face of the Eiger, the local landmark near Grindelwald. The problem there is that your eyes eventually get so tired that you can't read any more, yet you still can't sleep. This is the ultimate Red Eye.

For the record, there seems to be no solution at hand. One scientist suggests that if you drink nothing on the plane and eat very little, your symptoms will be less violent than otherwise, and I think he is right. Still, it is far from a cure, and the Red Eye continues as the chief occupational hazard of my trade.

And here we are, on flight 48, leaning back in the darkness, recalling the other high points of the past twenty-four hours.

Erich Segal's debut as an on-camera sports commentator turned out to be something of a traumatic experience for him. He was standing in the infield prior to the beginning of the 10,000 meter run, admittedly tense, nervous, and somewhat unsure. He had written and memorized his introduction, but the newness of the job was bothering him. In addition, he had a personal rooting interest in the race: the favorite was his former student at Yale (row 17, Classical Civilization), Frank Shorter.

Now, Erich's interest in track is not feigned in any way. He is an authentic track nut, and couldn't possibly have been any more excited at the world premiere of his *Love Story* film than he was before Shorter's race.

Erich launched into his piece. He was really up for it.

When he was about two-thirds of the way through, I saw that there was going to be a problem. About 100 feet in back of

Erich, unseen by him, Bob Seagren was about to start moving down the pole vault runway, attempting a world record height of eighteen feet, five and three-quarter inches.

As Erich talked on, moving toward the climax of his introduction, Seagren began to trot, then accelerate, toward the pole vault standard. It was something like watching two cars at a distance, about to collide.

". . . and then," Erich was saying, "there is Frank Shorter, my former student in row 17 of Classical. . . ."

At that moment, Seagren was airborne, soaring toward the bar, then over, dropping into the pit and leaping out, shaking his fist in triumph. A roar split the Oregon air, suddenly, explosively.

Erich was understandably stunned. Were they cheering his introduction? Of course not. He turned, then suddenly understood.

The piece had to be done over. It was one of my stranger views of a world record—with one eye on Seagren, the other on Erich.

Shorter was very impressive in winning his race. He is a very different kind of runner. With his medium-length hair and neatly trimmed mustache, he looks every inch the Yale man. Even his neat little track suit (he is quite small) could have been tailored at Brooks Brothers. His pace is even all through the race, even on the last lap. He finishes as he starts, hair in place, shirttail tucked in all around, apparently capable of running just as far again.

There was an interesting story in that same race for the home crowd. On the last lap, and most surprisingly, a young man named Jon Anderson sprinted past Shorter's Florida Track Club teammate Jack Bacheler and qualified for the Olympic squad. Jon Anderson is a conscientious objector, currently washing dishes in a California hospital for his alternative service. He is also the son of the mayor of Eugene, Oregon! Anderson was moved to tears by his unexpected showing.

So was the veteran Seagren, gold medalist four years ago in Mexico, now a presumably poised married man of twenty-five and a movie actor by profession, by his new world record. However, Seagren wasn't thinking of the world record when I interviewed him. It was just the matter of making the team.

"Man," he said, "if I hadn't made it, I couldn't have faced my family. I've already made reservations for them in Munich."

One of the little things I'll remember was talking with the mammoth discus thrower Jay Silvester just a matter of seconds before his first attempt in that event. He was talking about the implement he uses, and said, "The kind of disc*i* we use here. . . ." Somehow I was surprised to hear this huge athlete use a Latin plural.

Erich Segal says he thinks that it actually should be "diskoi" since the word originally comes from Greek, not Latin. I really must look it up.

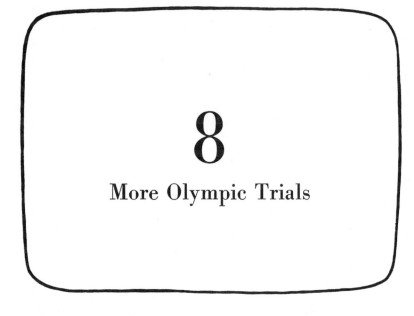

8

More Olympic Trials

Fireworks are breaking over Long Island Sound, the explosions echoing along the Connecticut shoreline, the bright colors reflecting in the water as they drift down from the sky.

My wife and I are standing on the front porch of George and Marjorie Silk's house, at home in Westport, Connecticut. Such occasions have been very few in the past eleven years. Visiting friends, especially on weekends or holidays, is something that simply doesn't fit into the schedule we must keep.

The conversation has turned to expense account stories. These are always a favorite of old reporters. Since our host, George, is perhaps the world's best news photographer (for *Life*), and since my wife, Margaret, was a reporter on the *Baltimore Sun* when we met and still writes a syndicated column on television personalities, it was logical that the subject would arise.

As a reporter on the *Sun*, Margaret had rather a different attitude toward expenses than her male colleagues. It was an approach that dazzled them and she simply confused the company into accepting it.

There was the time, I recalled tonight, that Margaret was sent to Philadelphia to cover a Democratic National Convention and lost sixty-five dollars on the train. She put it on her expense account.

When questioned by the penurious accounting department of the *Sunpapers*, she explained patiently that if she hadn't been on an assignment, she wouldn't have been on the train, therefore she wouldn't have lost the money. The accountants knew there was a hole in that argument somewhere, but they couldn't find it, so they gave Margaret her money back.

Margaret told the story she heard from an editor of the old *Herald Tribune* just after columnist Jimmy Breslin joined the paper. She had asked if the paper was pleased with Breslin, and the editor said that *he* was, but the accounting department *wasn't*, in fact that they were near rebellion on the subject.

An example?

Well, the day before, Breslin had written a very interesting piece on an after-hours bar in Harlem. The piece was fine, but that item on the expense account turned faces blue downstairs. It read: "175 gin and tonics . . . $250.00."

When questioned, Breslin explained. There is no way you are going to get a story like that, he pointed out, unless you buy the house a few rounds.

George Silk told of the time he was a young war correspondent in North Africa during World War II for the New Zealand government. His salary was not large, and the government department which he reported his expenses to was not sympathetic.

There came a time when he was really getting short of funds. Since the people auditing his expenses were civil servants sitting comfortably at home in New Zealand, far from the sounds of Rommel's tank corps, and since those civil servants weren't really too sure exactly what George was doing in the war zone, he decided to play on the guilt complex they might have about the situation and submitted this item: "For repair of parachute . . . $175.00." It was paid without comment.

My contribution was one about Joe Aceti, now an associate director at ABC Sports, but at the time of the story, a production assistant.

Production assistant is the first rung (or to be blunt, the lowest rung) on the ladder of success in television. Production assistants are not paid a high salary, so they must at times become imaginative with their expense accounts in order to make ends meet in the great city of New York. A favorite item among them is a fairly large sum, maybe $150, allegedly paid to someone for trimming branches off trees at golf tournaments so that our cameras will have a clear line of sight. It's a good, solid bit of creative expense account writing.

However, on one occasion, Joe was sent to Scotland to cover a tournament on one of their characteristic seaside links. You've seen the type of course—austere, sandy, treeless.

Aceti returned home and routinely submitted his account with the usual tree-trimming. The next day he received a triumphant phone call from the expense man.

"Ah ha!" he said, "ah ha, Joe, I have finally nailed you. You put in for tree trimming at that British tournament. Right?"

"Right," said Joe.

"Well, I happened to see that program, Joe," the man with the green eyeshade went on, "and there wasn't a single, solitary tree on that entire golf course."

Joe didn't pause for an instant.

"I know," he said. "That guy did one hell of a job, didn't he?!"

THURSDAY, JULY 6

The bags are packed and ready to go again. The list of hotels I'm leaving with Margaret explains pretty well what the next ten days will be like before I return to Westport: the Village Green Motel, Cottage Grove, Oregon; the Beverly Hills Hotel, Sunset Boulevard, Beverly Hills, California; and the Esso Motor Hotel, Queens Ferry Road, Edinburgh, Scotland.

Packing has been complicated for this one. I must take everything I own except my ski clothes. My bathing suit is packed, but so is my long winter underwear. The bathing suit is for possible use in Oregon and Los Angeles, the long underwear for Scotland, at the British Open, where even in July it has been known to get as raw and windy as January at the Crosby.

The trip will be 12,000 miles in ten days.

One of the last preparations for any of my journeys is to check the contents of my toilet kit, known at ABC Sports as my "sock." This phrase originated in the early days of Wide World, when I used to carry some medical aids in my briefcase. So that they would not break on one occasion, I put them inside an athletic sock, which seemed to work so well that I did it on a regular basis for a while. When feeling the least bit ill, I would reach into it for a remedy, an act which Chuck Howard formalized in the phrase, "going to his sock." To this day, you are likely to hear any of the older Wide World hands say something like, "I don't feel so well. I think I'll have to go to my sock."

The actual sock has long since given way to a large toilet kit (traditionally, our daughter, Mary, gives me one every Christmas, because I do wear them out rather quickly). The toilet kit bulges, even though I have tried to reduce its contents to a minimum through the years. In addition to the usual razor, shaving cream, toothbrush, toothpaste, deodorant and aftershave, it holds men's hairspray (I could never work outdoors without it—for twenty years I wore a crew cut because my hair is basically uncontrollable), some antibiotic ointment for any cuts or scratches I may pick up, and two other medicines: a tiny white pill called Lomotil that is just about miraculous in curing that embarrassing international disease known in Mexico as "turista," and another little yellow pill whose name I don't know. (My doctor gave it to me and it wards off nausea.) With these contents safely stowed into the kit, a man can undertake any trip with a reasonable amount of assurance.

There is one other item that need only be packed for foreign trips, since it is readily available here—Alka-Seltzer. In fact, we have devised an international rating system for restaurants based on an Alka-Seltzer scale, something like the famous Guide Michelin in France. Where that guide awards stars for excellence, we award Alka-Seltzers for incompetence. A "two Alka-Seltzer restaurant" can be lived with. An establishment with a "four" rating is to be avoided at all costs. The "six" may require hospitalization.

So much for unsolicited medical advice. Off we go to Cottage Grove, to rejoin the world of track and field.

COTTAGE GROVE, OREGON——FRIDAY, JULY 7

Travel days are storytelling days, both on the plane and after arrival. On the plane from New York to San Francisco today, the stewardess heard us discussing a famous track athlete. "You know," she said, "I had a date with him a couple of years ago."

We asked if she had enjoyed the evening.

"No," she said. "Not at all. It was a double date, my girl friend and I with him and his friend, another big athlete. Believe me, they spent the entire evening comparing their measurements. Not *ours, theirs!*"

She paused to spread a napkin on my tray.

"I specifically remember," she said, "that the guy you're talking about was particularly proud of his thighs."

There are, of course, athletes and athletes.

There was Roger Bannister, first man ever to run the mile in less than four minutes.

The year was 1954, and I was working on a program called "The Morning Show" at CBS at the time. It was trying to compete with NBC's "Today Show" and not doing it very successfully, even though Walter Cronkite was the host. We were an underdog show, and so we were trying very hard to come up with something in the way of scoops on the opposition.

One evening, producer Hugh Beach (a former Colby College English professor who insists that his friends call him "Meathead") was about to leave the office when he took a final look at one of the wire services teletypes.

On it was a "note to editors," a bit of information not meant for publication, but to give clients a lead on something they might want to follow up themselves. This one said that a man closely resembling Roger Bannister had boarded a BOAC flight in London. He denied that he was Bannister, the note cautioned, and his ticket was issued in another name.

If we were to do anything with this, it would be a large gamble at best. But Bannister was the hottest sports story in the world, having broken the four-minute mile the previous week.

There was no videotape at the time, so the only way to get an interview with the English miler would be to take an entire television mobile unit to Idlewild Airport (as Kennedy was then called), hope that the man was Bannister, and further hope that he would agree to an interview. We would also have to hope that his plane was not late. It was due in at 8:00 A.M. New York time and we went off the air each morning at 9:00.

I was first alerted to what was going on by a knock on our apartment door after midnight. Margaret, who wakes up much more quickly than I do, answered.

"Who is it?" she called through the door.

"It is I," said the voice, "Meathead."

Hugh Beach has his own manner of speech—one-third down-Maine, one-third English professor, and one-third Damon Runyon.

He apologized profusely, then begged humbly for the use of a couch to sleep on for a few hours.

"Why?"

"Because your husband and I are on a cloak-and-dagger assignment. We are going to sneak out to Idlewild in the early morning darkness and scoop the hell out of the 'Today Show.'"

By 6:30 in the morning, Hughie and I had arrived at the old "temporary" terminal at Idlewild (so "temporary" that it stayed in use for about twenty years). The hulking CBS mobile unit was already in place and a camera was positioned just outside the customs area.

"Very good," said Hugh to the engineering supervisor on the scene. "You guys do good work. Very good."

At about 7:30, a round, bustling man hurried into the terminal. He looked around at the television equipment and blanched.

"What's this?" he asked Meathead.

Hughie smiled proudly.

"We are meeting Roger Bannister," he said, "the world's first sub-four-minute miler. We are going to interview him on live TV."

The man, a television producer, was astounded and incensed.

"You can't," he shouted, "you just can't. How did you know he was coming, anyway?"

Beach answered the question with a question: "How did you know he was coming?"

"Because he is the mystery guest on our show tonight, and because we are paying his way over here, and you will ruin the whole thing if you get an interview with him!"

The man was the producer of "I've Got a Secret."

Hugh explained patiently that we were in the news business and could not pass up a story to help out an entertainment program. He kidded the producer a bit about his program's parsimoniousness when he found that Bannister was traveling in tourist class.

By eight o'clock I was standing in place as close to the customs area as I could get, microphone in hand, ready to approach Bannister as soon as he appeared.

The plane was late, and time became the enemy. It was 8:15, then 8:30. Half an hour of airtime left. Walter was ready to throw it to us from the studio at any moment. He gambled and built up the fact on the air that we were waiting for the runner.

It was 8:45 when the lean figure of Roger Bannister strolled through customs.

I had never met him, remember. He had been up all night, and had no idea who we were or what we wanted. Cronkite threw it to me as I approached Bannister. On the air, I explained who I was, and asked him if he would tell the American people something about his great achievement.

"I'd be glad to," he said, and launched into an amazingly lucid description of the first four-minute mile. He told of the race

itself, and his pacemakers, Chris Brasher and Chris Chataway. He discussed the medical aspects of the physical problem that had faced him (he was soon to be Doctor *Bannister), and the psychological problems. In all, he talked for almost fifteen minutes, until I finally interrupted him and threw it back to Walter for sign-off.*

It had been as beautiful an interview as we could have hoped for.

Never once did he mention his measurements, or his thighs.

There is a postscript to the interview: Bannister went to Manhattan, for "I've Got A Secret." Before air time, he was glancing at a monitor set when he saw them rolling through their commercials, rehearsing them for air. A Winston commercial appeared.

"Are you sponsored by a cigarette?" he asked.

When told that Winston was in fact the program's sponsor, Bannister apologized, but was firm in stating that he could not possibly appear on any program which featured a cigarette commercial. He left the studio and went back to England.

Ours, then, was the only television interview Roger Bannister did in America in the week after the most famous mile run in history.

Back in the Village Green Motel this evening, I had a late drink with Erich Segal. We talked about critics, among other things.

"Do you know what one book critic said about *Love Story*," Erich said, rhetorically. "He said that he cried when he read it, but he was not moved!"

He told me how the book's title came about. In his workroom, he kept manuscripts for a number of projects he was working on. On the top sheet of each, he scribbled an informal identification, e.g., "history paper," "Greek translation," or whatever it might be. On top of the book manuscript, he scribbled "love story."

Actually, he had a formal title for the book, and he told me what it was, but asked me *never* to tell anyone else—so I won't. It was his editor, I believe, who finally realized the simple power of the identification on top of the novel, and "love story," became *Love Story*. Suppose Erich had just scribbled "novel," or "book"?

Dennis Lewin first noticed that there is something about Erich that reminds you of Woody Allen, the playwright–actor–comedian–clarinetist. It came as an amazing coincidence tonight, then, when Erich mentioned in conversation that he and Woody Allen were classmates at Midwood High School in Brooklyn, New York.

SUNDAY, JULY 9

We're back again in our home-away-from-home, an airplane flying at 35,000 feet, somewhere over San Francisco. The airplane is different this time, though. It is a chartered Falcon fan jet, headed from Eugene, Oregon, to Burbank, California. A swift charter is the only way we can get our job done on this occasion.

The Olympic Trials concluded today, and tomorrow night we must put them on in a videotape special originating from Hollywood. There is a great deal of editing to be done, and tomorrow some bits and pieces of commentary to link the show together, although the basic commentary was done as the events took place.

Our day began at nine o'clock this morning, and for the producer, Lewin, and the associate director, Bernie Hoffman, it won't end until the show goes off the air tomorrow night.

The team selected in Eugene during these two weekends of trials looks quite strong to me, even though it is short of the customary "big names." Among those who failed to make the team were Randy Matson in the shot put and world record holder Pat Matzdorf in the high jump; Jim Ryun missed out in the 800, but made it in the 1,500 in impressive fashion. Lee Evans, the 400-meter gold medalist in Mexico, finished fourth this time and will run only in the relay.

Still, the men who beat out such athletes must have talent of their own, and the times were impressive. Wottle, as mentioned, tied the world record in the 800. So did Eddie Hart and Reynaud Robinson in the 100 meters.

The final events today, for example, saw Rod Milburn, he of the troubled summer, making the team but not winning in the 110-meter high hurdles. Vince Matthews, Wayne Collett, and John Smith may sweep the 400 meters in Munich.

Matthews is an interesting story. He retired after Mexico City and ballooned to more than 200 pounds. His wife encouraged him to jog in an effort to lose weight. As long as he was jogging, he started to run, then to train, with a group of former Olympians who scaled the fence of a locked schoolyard in Brooklyn to train after work in the evenings. They called themselves the "Brooklyn Over-the-Hill Athletic Club" and almost couldn't scratch up the money to come to Eugene. But Vince made it, and now he goes to the Olympics.

The saddest moment of the weekend came when Randy Matson failed to make the team in the shot put. The disappointment must have been deepened for him by the fact that he lost out to Brian Oldfield, who wore flowered bikini bathing trunks and a revealing fishnet shirt while he competed, and ostentatiously smoked cigarettes while waiting on the field for his next attempt.

The coaches have already announced that Oldfield will abandon bikini, fishnet, and cigarettes at Munich or will not compete. Call it regimentation if you like, but I agree with them on this one.

Matson is such a gentleman.

Just after he lost out, we hesitated to approach him for an interview, but of course we did, and he quietly agreed. I could see that Randy, huge man that he is, was on the verge of tears. I hoped that we could get the interview done quickly, but this is seldom the case in television. By the nature of the medium, it is necessary to make sure that the light is such that you can see the interviewee's face clearly. Sometimes the sound isn't exactly right. Almost always, there are people trying to get into the picture, usually in an attempt to wave their hand at somebody back home.

The particular problem on this occasion was that the sun was setting. It was difficult to find a spot on the field where Randy and I would not be silhouetted against the setting sun. When we found a place, it had an ugly scaffold in the background. Four or five moves were needed . . . "two steps to the left, please, Randy," "now, one step back."

All of this while the poor man was suffering through the disappointment of a lifetime. Patiently, he moved around, quietly, uncomplaining. It seemed cruel and yet, if we did not interview him at all, the audience at home, and the press, would ask why. If we interviewed him and his face was an indistinct blob, there would be questions from the office and letters of complaint from viewers.

It had to be done, and when it was, Matson politely answered my questions. When, at the end of the interview, I told him how he would be missed at Munich, Randy muttered his thanks and cast his eyes down. His chin seemed to quiver. Then he shambled off, alone, to return to College Station, Texas, and his job with the Former Students Association. Randy Matson will be watching the Olympics on television.

Frank Shorter, however (row 17, Classical Civilization), will be there, not only in the 10,000 meters, but more importantly, in the marathon. He won that event in Eugene this weekend with ease and should be competitive. He will not be the favorite. That probably will be Ron Hill of England. And there are others, like old Mamo Wolde of Ethiopia and Derek Clayton of Australia.

"Don't you believe it," were Erich's last words to me in Eugene. "Frank is going to win the marathon at Munich."

Those Ivy League guys sure stick together.

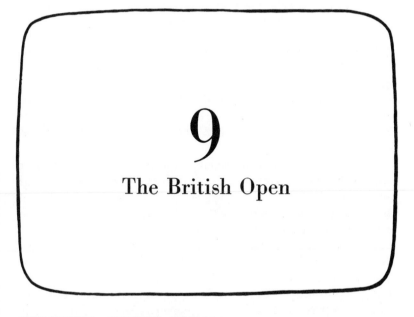

9

The British Open

The trials show was aired, apparently successfully, last night, except that here on the West Coast it was preempted by the extended battle for the California delegation at the Democratic National Convention. When Howard K. Smith read a bulletin that President Nixon had been watching the proceedings but now had gone to bed, Harry Reasoner commented, "Well, the President probably was only waiting up to see the Olympic Trials. Now that they have been preempted on the West Coast, he might as well go to bed."

Dennis and I are flying back to New York right now, where I will change planes, meet Roone, Chuck, Chris Schenkel, Byron Nelson, and director Mac Hemion and fly directly to Scotland for the British Open.

This is my first flight on the new DC-10 airplane, McDonnell-

Douglas's answer to Boeing's big 747. Air travel does get more fantastic all the time. The United stewardess has just brought each of us two carnations in a vase, and now they are announcing on the P.A. system that the champagne punch party is about to begin. The punch is contained in a large metal bowl, with great clouds of steam rising from the dry ice concealed at the bottom. Presumably this is to represent a volcano, since United flies to Hawaii.

A caricaturist is working in the forward tourist lounge. Next week, we are told by the in-flight service director, they will be having a wine-tasting party on Wednesdays and a guitarist entertaining on Thursdays.

We are now beginning a game, with unspecified prizes to be awarded, in which you are supposed to guess the combined age of all the crew members (fourteen in all). The lady behind us just whispered to her husband that she had put down 170. That would make the average crew member twelve years old.

The whole scene is quite a contrast to a decade ago. I suddenly remember vividly a flight out of Bulgaria early one Monday morning. The plane was an old rattletrap, a Russian version of a DC-3. There was no carpeting, bare pipes served as legs for the worn bucket seats. The hostess, yawning as she tried to arrange her unkempt beehive hairdo, was in a rumpled gray suit.

As the ancient crate labored to climb over the Balkans just after dawn, she served breakfast—cold salami, potato salad, and lemon soda.

I hadn't really figured on going to Bulgaria that time.

Chuck and I were at the Grand Prix of Monaco, that anachronistic race through the streets of Monte Carlo, normally one of our pleasanter assignments. It was in the early 1960s, and this particular trip was the first time Roone hadn't come to Monaco with us. His duties as head of the department were keeping him home more all the time now, a tendency not to his liking, but necessary.

On Saturday evening when I came back to the room, Chuck

said that Roone had called and probably wanted me to go directly to Bulgaria for the World Amateur Wrestling Championships rather than return home.

At the time, it was sort of a crowning blow. What with a number of recent last-minute schedule changes, I had had enough.

"Well, I won't go," I snapped.

"O.K., call him up and tell him," Chuck said.

"No."

A few hours later we went to bed. The race was in the morning, and Chuck, a man of methodical habits, went quickly to sleep in preparation for the job ahead. We were staying in separate rooms, but in the same suite and the walls were thin.

Somewhere about four in the morning, the phone rang. Irritated, Chuck answered it. It was Jack Lubell, who had been assigned as producer–director on the Bulgarian show. He wanted to speak to me, to make arrangements for my arrival.

"All right, damn it, Jack," Chuck said, "I'll wake him up."

Chuck called me.

He knocked on my door.

Then he shouted, and pounded on the door. He tried to open it, but it was locked.

"Damn it, McKay!" he shouted, "I know you're in there and I know you're awake. Come out and take this call from Lubell like a man. You're ruining my night's sleep and I have an expensive telecast to produce tomorrow. Goddamn it, answer me!"

There was no reply.

For years now, I have been trying to explain to Chuck that I really didn't hear him, that I was in a deep slumber and wearing ear plugs to screen out the noisy street traffic. Perhaps this is the time to admit that I have been lying.

STILL OVER KANSAS

Dennis wins the age-guessing contest. His prize is an electronic keychain flashlight on which is a full-color picture of the first Studebaker ever made.

EDINBURGH, SCOTLAND——THURSDAY, JULY 13

"Look like the innocent flower, but be like the serpent under it." A Scottish paper used that line from Shakespeare this morning to describe the course at Muirfield, where today they played the second round of this year's British Open. The pressure on Jack Nicklaus here is tremendous. The same newspaper, for example, heads each morning's account of the tournament with a special logo containing a drawing of Jack's face, and the words, "The Grand Slam Open, Muirfield, 1972."

Well, it may be, because Nicklaus is only one shot behind after thirty-six holes, but frankly, he hasn't looked that good in putting together rounds of 70 and 72. He said as much himself today.

Tony Jacklin, the golfing idol of his home island, and defending champion Lee Trevino are the co-leaders. Tied with Nicklaus a stroke off the pace are Peter Tupling, a young Briton who led the first day; Johnny Miller, the young American with startling rounds of 76 and 66; and the veteran swinger of the tour, Doug Sanders.

Sanders would be the leader tonight, except for a horrendous seven on the eighteenth hole, a par four. "This course is lying there waiting for you," he said afterward, "and if you snooze, you lose."

Tupling, a youngster who surprised everyone in the first round with 68, made a refreshing comment after that opening round. In this day of the cool, often arrogant athlete, it was good to hear a man say, "Let's be reasonable. There is no way I can win the Open, I'm not that good a player. One day I hope to be, but I'm not now."

It's eleven o'clock at night as I sit in my room at the Esso Motor Hotel, and the sun is setting, slowly. Scotland in July is almost perpetual daylight, being a much more northern country than one realizes until you look at an accurate map of the world.

My feet hurt. I walked eighteen holes with Nicklaus this morning, and eighteen more with Trevino this afternoon, and it was worth a couple of blisters. The day was unbelievably warm for

Scotland, as beautiful as yesterday's opening round had been depressing, rainy, and windy.

The change in the weather fooled Nicklaus this morning. He started out wearing a cashmere turtleneck with an old golf shirt underneath it. Then the sun came out. All through the first nine, he was uncomfortable, and his game looked it, lacking the fire and certainty he had displayed at Pebble Beach.

He thought of simply taking off the turtleneck, then realized that he had cut the collar off the old shirt underneath. "That would have looked kind of silly in the British Open," he said later, so he asked his wife Barbara, walking in the gallery, if she would run ahead, to Greywalls, where they are staying (remember, it's just behind the clubhouse), and get him a lighter shirt.

At the end of nine, Jack ran to the hotel, took the shirt from Barbara, went into the men's room on the lobby floor and changed it. "I called myself a few names while I was in there, too," he told me afterward.

The episode seemed to help him somehow. He went out and pulled his game together on the back nine for the 72 that keeps him in contention tonight.

Trevino was as talkative as ever as he put together a very nice round of 70. There is a bit of tension in his pairing for the first two rounds. Neil Coles, a phlegmatic British golfer, has complained at being paired with the defending champion on the first two rounds for the second year in a row. Last year, he was put with Tony Jacklin, who had won in 1970, and he told the committee that it hurts his concentration when the gallery stampedes to the next tee for a better view of the champion while he, Coles, still may be putting out.

They asked Trevino about the situation in the press tent. He leaned forward on his elbows, paused, then said, pleasantly, "Well, they're his people."

So they are. Not a chicano to be seen anywhere, except Lee.

Coles was silent throughout today's round, sometimes leaning on his driver and staring out to sea when they had to wait to tee off. Not so Lee. Since he had no partner to talk to, he often aimed his comments at me, as I stood back against the gallery ropes. They were meant, however, for everybody, and the large gallery loved them, perhaps even more than the crowd at Pebble Beach.

On the sixth tee: "I thought I'd never get here. The guy who was supposed to pick me up at Prestwick didn't show, so we had to take some kind of a bus. Do you know the driver didn't know the way? We got lost and the same tractor—so help me, a tractor—passed us four times. Oh, well. . . .

"I'm staying at this old castle and they had a special oldtime kind of dinner. We had to eat everything with our fingers, except a piece of fish. They gave me a toothpick to eat that. Hell, I've got a cat back home in Texas who eats with a fork!"

On the tenth tee, they had to wait again, and once more, Lee strolled over to the gallery rope and started talking to me. His Scottish caddy finally tired of the colloquy, and in the imperious, protective manner that Scottish caddies have with their golfers, he addressed the defending champion sternly.

"Here, here, now," he said, "That'll be enough with the press."

"He's not press," said Lee, "He's television. Is that all right?"

Despite his strict discipline, Lee's caddy seems pleased with his assignment. Not so Neil Coles' caddy.

The man carrying Coles' bag is a classic Scottish caddy of the old school. He is in his sixties, saggy of shoulder from long years with heavy bags, red of nose from the cold, windy weather and the whiskey that cures it. On the back nine today, he plodded along, looking angry, in his heavy tweed jacket and cap, despite the unexpected heat. As I walked along the rope, he approached me.

"I tried to tell him," he said bitterly, "There was no way for him to get there with a three iron on that last hole. You saw where it went. I'll tell you what else I told him. I told him I didn't come here to waste my week.

"Why, I caddied for Alf Padgham when he won the Open in 1936 at Hoylake. I'm no Johnny-come-lately, you know!"

Caddies like Coles' man are beginning to disappear and it's a shame. They have been a colorful part of Scottish golf for a long time.

For a quiet man, Neil Coles certainly has stirred things up this year.

Max Faulkner, the first British golfer to adopt loud colors in his golfing clothes, had a caddy years ago even more colorful than he was. They called him "Mad Mac." For reasons never revealed to the public, Mac wore five neckties at all times on the course, along with an old, moth-eaten overcoat that reached to his shoe-tops. When lining up putts for Faulkner, he used a pair of beat-up binoculars. They had no glass in them. Still, the strange pair—madcap Maxie in his lavender knickers and Mad Mac in his five ties—won the British Open in 1951 at Portrush.

Coming off the eighteenth late this afternoon, I met Joe Dey. Remember that the commissioner of the American pro golf tour is attending his first British Open. Remember, too, that he assigned a group of us back in Pebble Beach to compose verses to go with the toast to the Gullane Fire Brigade.

Well, Joe is having a marvelous time. He was happy and smiling when I met him today, and immediately asked if my verse was ready. When I confessed that it wasn't, he said, "Well, mine is," and produced it from an inside pocket.

He admitted that a Scottish friend with whom he is staying had composed the bulk of it, then read it aloud, standing tall beside the eighteenth green under the gentle sun of Scotland:

> "We've got helmets bright and polished.
> Our axes, too, are sharp.
> But if you get a conflagration,
> Just start to play your harp.
> For we're in the bar at Bissett's
> Drinking beer. We've got it made.
> The mustachioed commandoes of the Gullane Fire Brigade.
> > Here's to the Gullane Fire Brigade. One is sloshed
> > and the other is visiting his aunt in Musselburgh."

We passed through the little seaside town of Musselburgh, on the Firth of Forth, as we returned from the course tonight. Roone, Chris, Byron, and I were riding in the ABC Sports limousine, chartered through a young Scot named Bob, who also drives it. Bob keeps his Daimler meticulously clean, and even has a special ABC Sports pennant mounted on the left front fender, whipping in the wind like the flag of an ambassador on his way to the United Nations. This year, Bob has added the Olympic rings as a special touch.

The car rented for the drive from St. Andrew's, Scotland, to Manchester, England, in early July of 1961, was a car of a different order—an ancient Humber sedan, underpowered and over-used.

We had filmed a head-to-head affair between Arnold Palmer and Gary Player over the Old Course at St. Andrews. Margaret and I had flown off to Paris for our first trip to that great city. Roone wanted to stay and play a couple of rounds at St. Andrew's, then fly down to the British Open in England.

Roone Arledge has a real love for the great sporting venues of the world, as he does for fine food, good wine, good music, and expertly tied fishing flies. These passionate interests are one of the secrets of his success at ABC Sports.

Roone has a special attachment to the Old Course (he is today, in fact, a member of the Royal and Ancient Golf Club of St. Andrew's).

Others on the trip, though, had a different idea. Chuck Howard, director Bill Bennington, and A.D. Marvin Schlenker thought it would be more fun to drive through the Scottish countryside, down past the lake country and into Manchester.

Roone disagreed, but finally gave in—on one condition, that as they drove, they would stop somewhere at a typical old English country inn, where they would have roast beef and Yorkshire pudding, and a pint or two of good beer, followed by Stilton cheese soaked in port wine. It was so agreed.

Only after leaving St. Andrew's and getting well out into the country below Edinburgh did they find out that their driver, a rather grouchy old fellow, had never been outside his home county in his life. He had no idea where an old English inn might be. In fact, he was lost. The Humber was hot and terribly uncomfortable.

The search for the inn went on far into the evening, too far, in fact. Then they began settling for lesser restaurants, but they were closed for the night.

Finally, tired and rumpled, they threw themselves on the mercy of the unfriendly proprietor of a combination bowling alley and pub. Please, could he give them something to eat, anything?

Grudgingly, he did.

It was cold spaghetti on white bread, not exactly what Roone had planned for dinner on the night of his birthday in 1961.

GULLANE, SCOTLAND—FRIDAY, JULY 14 (5:27 P.M.)

By Scottish standards, we are having a heat wave.

With the temperature at a torrid seventy degrees, the spectators have literally started peeling off their shirts as they walk the course, to stay cool and to catch a little rare sun tan. It makes an incongruous sight, here on the dignified fairways of Muirfield.

On the way out here this morning, we passed a beach and it was paved with sun-bathing bodies, all of them a pasty white, untouched by sun for many a month. There will be some bad sunburns around here tonight.

Aside from the white skins, the sight at this moment is just beautiful. I'm following Jack Nicklaus and Gary Player, and color is everywhere. The fairways are a soft green, not vivid as at home. The sky is blue, accented with floating white clouds. Beyond the course, ships are slowly moving along the huge Firth of Forth.

A scoreboard, in the foreground of my view right now, has yellow signs, along with red indicating under par, green for even, and black for over par.

In the midst of the scene, separated from the pale-faced gallery by a hundred feet on each side, are the suntanned figures of two of the game's great competitors. Jack Nicklaus is wearing a white golf shirt, light-blue pants, and white shoes. He is very blond, his face a study in concentration as he strides forward.

Playing with him is another tight-lipped man, little Gary Player of South Africa, not in his traditional black today. He has on a white cap, blue and white striped shirt, white pants, and white shoes. Even the caddies, in their drab tweeds, contribute to the color. They are wearing yellow bibs, bearing the names of the golfers.

There is only one flaw in the lovely scene before me. It looks like Jack Nicklaus is playing himself out of the British Open right now, losing his bid for the modern grand slam. He hit a poor tee shot here on twelve, left his second in the rough. He has just hit to the green, but is forty-five feet from the hole. Two putts will leave him five shots behind the new leader, Sanders, four behind Jacklin, and two behind Trevino. And soon there will be only eighteen holes left to play.

7:10 P.M.

I still find it difficult to believe what Lee Trevino has just done.

Listen to his own description of it:

"The fourteenth is where it all started. I hit a four-iron to twenty feet and holed the putt for a birdie. The fifteenth, another twenty-footer for a birdie three. The short sixteenth—the grip of my six-iron came off so I wound it back up and hurried a six-iron into the right bunker. I had a bad lie against the back lip and downhill. I haven't been playing those bunkers too well and I came out strong.

"The ball hit the pin on the first bounce and went in. If it hadn't, it would have gone into a bunker on the other side.

"I made two. I could have made five.

"I go to the seventeenth feeling pretty good and I really mellow the drive. I was swinging at the world. Five-iron, two putts, another birdie.

"On eighteen, I hit the ball as hard as I could and cut a five-iron through the green. I chipped thirty feet and when it started rolling, I knew it was in.

"Another birdie. I can't remember ever having five birdies in a row."

Lee went on to explain that his magic weapon this week is a forty-year-old ladies' sand wedge, Helen Hicks model, that he fished out of one of those barrels full of old clubs you sometimes see around pro shops.

With his inborn sense of showmanship, he calls the club "Miss Helen."

Trevino, with his round of 66, still only leads Tony Jacklin by one, since Tony had a fine, fighting 67. Sanders finished weakly again and is four strokes back. Jack Nicklaus is six strokes behind Lee Trevino. It looks like the grand slam will not happen this year.

Tomorrow's story, it appears, will be Lee Trevino going for his second British Open in a row, a feat that was last accomplished by Arnold Palmer in 1961–62.

Just before Trevino started his historic string of birdies today, the tension between Neil Coles and his caddy exploded. Coles fired him, right on the course, at the thirteenth hole! A Scottish pro carried the bag the rest of the way.

What makes this whole story the more remarkable—aside from Coles' normal quiet temperament—is that the caddy, Arthur (Chinji) Maidment by name, is on an annual retainer from Coles and has been caddying for him for fourteen years.

In the press tent, a Scottish golf writer thought it would blow over.

"As your gossip columnists say," he told me, "a reconciliation is shortly expected."

11:30 P.M.

At dinner tonight, Georges Croses showed me an invitation he recently received to the wedding of Mlle. Marie Chasteignez, of Rouillon, France. She will wed a count.

George, who is the European representative for ABC Sports, smiled his soft French smile as he showed it to me.

"*La petite Marie*," he said. "How do you say, Jim—time flies?"

It was June, 1962.
The first time we went to LeMans, France, the year before, we

had stayed at the Hotel de Paris, an old, noisy hotel in the middle of the city, but about the best one there. This time, through Monsieur Mordray of the Automobile Club de l'Ouest, we were to stay in an honest-to-God 900-year-old château with a French marquis and his family.

It seemed that the local bishop had a drive on to build a new church. He had prevailed on some of the well-to-do local ladies to rent out some of their rooms at the time of the twenty-four-hour race, with the proceeds to help build the new church. It sounded great.

Roone, Chuck, and I headed down from Paris in a little Simca with great expectations. The ride was not without incident. At one point, about twenty miles after passing through Chartres, I got a ticket, payable on the spot, for passing across a solid line. I was terrified at the time, because I didn't have my driver's license with me. As the gendarme, attired in full motorcycle leathers, approached the car, I hissed at Roone to pass me his license. He did, but slowly, chuckling softly.

Although my French has never been better than adequate, I have always prided myself on at least trying to speak the language. On this occasion, though, I became the complete tourist, muttered, "Je ne parle pas Français," while Arledge and Howard hooted at me. He glanced at Roone's license (we couldn't look less alike), nodded, and told me that would be twenty-five francs. I thought I had best understand that, paid it, and drove on.

Not five miles later, we got behind a sand and gravel truck, spewing tiny pebbles behind him. One of them hit the windshield, which exploded into a tiny mosaic pattern on my side, making it impossible to see, unless you stuck your head out the window.

Further down the line toward LeMans, we found a Simca dealer, who, fortunately, had a spare windshield ready to install. In fact, he had about twenty of them sitting there, leading us to believe that exploding windshields must have been a common failing with Simcas in that area. It also explained to us why the car rental lady in Paris had said that the insurance covered everything, except (so help me) the windshield.

It was late, then, when we arrived in LeMans, but no matter. We would simply ask someone to direct us to Rouillon, which, we had been told, was only about five miles from the city. There was still about a half hour of daylight.

Oddly, the gendarme we asked said he didn't know where Rouillon was. We were also greeted with a shrug of the shoulders at the Total gas station. After two more blank looks, we began to get a bit edgy. Finally, a passerby who spoke no English, understanding the single word, Rouillon, nodded assent and pointed the way for us.

Out in the country, the light was failing. We came to a crossroad, where Roone had to get out and read a rusted metal sign, the right half broken off long ago. It did say, under the rust, "Rouillon, 5 km." We came to a tiny town with the usual large church in the center, and a small shop with the red, diamond-shaped sign over it that indicates a tobacconist. The shop was closed.

The town was Rouillon, all right, but there was no sign of a château, and no one to ask. It was dark now. We drove further, into the black countryside, and could have been on an uninhabited planet.

We saw lights off the road. This must be it, we thought. In the weak headlights of the car (incidentally, we couldn't figure out how to keep them on without holding the switch continually), we made out a sign at the entrance to the estate. It read, "Centre Insemination Artificiel." An artificial insemination center? Since we were all city boys, we didn't know whether that meant for animals or humans, so we half expected to see Peter Lorre answer our knock at the farmhouse door. The man was red-faced, gruff, and dirty, and smelled terribly. But he growled at the word "Rouillon" and pointed back in the direction from which we had come.

Back and forth we drove, for another half hour, until finally Chuck spotted a pair of large, rusted gates back from the road. It was unlikely, but certainly worth a try. Roone and Chuck opened *the gates and they creaked, just like in the movies. We drove down a long dirt road, into a dip through some woods. The trees were dense and tall. Then we started uphill, and as we did, the bright, metallic moon came out from behind a cloud.*

Silhouetted in front of it, suddenly, unexpectedly, was a building that seemed to rise to the sky. It must be the château, but what a dark, foreboding place. We drove around to the front of the building and it was totally dark, except for one light in an upstairs window.

It was silent—and then there were screams, female screams, and from around the corner of the building came a girl about twenty, and two younger girls—one about ten or eleven, the other perhaps six or seven. They were laughing, thank God.

The older girl ran up to the car.

"Hello, there, can I help you?" she said, in an accent that sounded like Piccadilly, not LeMans.

"Well, not unless this is the Château Rouillon."

"It is," she said. "I'm the baby-sitter and you must be the chaps from the ABC of America."

We said that we were. She invited us to come in, then turned to the two little girls.

"The marquis and marquise will be home shortly, but here are their daughters. They've been waiting up to see you."

The two little girls stood on the sides of their shoes, giggling and looking at the ground. The older one had a finger in her mouth, around which she murmured, "Bon soir, messieurs."

That was Marie, age eleven. And now she's going to be married.

GULLANE, SCOTLAND—SATURDAY, JULY 15 (1:05 P.M.)

Well, they've all teed off now for the final round.

Trevino was talking as he walked down the first fairway, of course, still "swinging at the world," as he says, still "mellowing" his drives.

Jacklin was modest, but determined, very tough somewhere

underneath, and always more confident when he is at home on his island.

Nicklaus looked more relaxed, oddly, than any day so far. He was looser, less mechanical.

Near the clubhouse I saw the Hon. William Whitelaw, former majority leader of the House of Commons, now carrying the weight of the world on his shoulders as the man assigned to straighten out the affairs of Northern Ireland.

Roone was host to a very pleasant lunch for "Willie" Whitelaw, as the distinguished statesman likes to be called, a couple of years ago in a private room at the "21" Club in New York.

Mr. Whitelaw was captain of the Royal and Ancient Golf Club of St. Andrew's at the time, a great honor in Britain. At lunch he told of a letter he had received from one of his constituents just after his election to the post.

"I remember it very vividly," he said. "Here's what the chap wrote:

My dear Mr. Whitelaw,

For twenty years now, I have been casting my vote for you to represent my interests in the House of Commons. This you have consistently refused to do.

Now, I read that you are to play golf at my expense.

I hope you lose your balls.

"Delightful letter," Willie Whitelaw said, laughing, "Absolutely delightful."

2:55 P.M.

This may turn into one of the great golf tournaments of all time. On another glorious day, even warmer than yesterday, Jack Nicklaus has finally caught fire, birdieing three of the first five holes. Trevino has a bogie and no birds so far, so the standings look like this:

Trevino	−5
Nicklaus	−3
Jacklin	−3
Sanders	−3

I'm on my tower now, ready to put commentary on our video-tape of the action, which will be relayed by satellite to the States later, so that it can be seen at home at a reasonable hour. Chris and Byron are on the anchor tower behind the seventeenth. My location is behind the fourteenth green, but from here I can see quite well the twelfth green, the entire short thirteenth, the fourteenth, the fifteenth, sixteenth, and most of the seventeenth. One of the advantages of the flat, barren Scottish courses is that you can see a lot of the action from one spot.

You can also hear the roar of the crowd distinctly from any part of the links. It rolls across the rippling ground and must be audible aboard the ships moving up and down the Firth of Forth. There is a great roar right now, because Nicklaus has just birdied the ninth, Trevino has taken another bogie, and they are tied for the lead! Jack has made up six shots in nine holes, with nine still left to play.

From here on the golf course will be a great arena, more so than any golf course I've ever seen. In addition to the fine visibility afforded by the geography here, they have put large grandstands at various points. The largest of all is at the eighteenth green, where 6,000 people are already jammed into a horseshoe-shaped wooden bleacher that gives the finishing green the appearance of a bullring.

3:15 P.M.

The grand slam bid of Jack Nicklaus is still alive. Another great shout is spreading out across Muirfield like the concentric ripples when you drop a stone into a pond. It emanates from the tenth green, where the man from Ohio has just made another birdie. He has the lead, with eight holes left.

What a time for my monitor to go out. That is exactly what has happened, so Roone and Chuck will have to "talk me through it," telling me through my little earpiece what pictures they are displaying on the tube at any moment.

We've done it before. At the opening ceremonies of the Winter Olympics in Innsbruck, Austria, 1964, we found out just before airtime that my monitor had a picture on it, but the wrong one, the picture intended for Europe, not America. They talked me through it then, and they will now.

Roone and Chuck are my good friends when we are not working, but when lashed into that working rig of microphones and tiny loudspeakers, I hope it does not sound maudlin to say that we are more like brothers. It is as if we have been doing this all our lives. We understand what the other person is trying to do most of the time without any words being spoken. When they are, they are brief and to the point.

4:48 P.M.

Since the last entry, I have been busy describing, along with Chris and Byron, an incredibly exciting series of holes.

Nicklaus began to stumble a bit after the birdie on ten.

On the sixteenth, a hole he probably will long remember, he made four for a bogie on the short hole, where Trevino blasted into the hole from the bunker yesterday. Meanwhile, both Trevino and Jacklin, playing together, have steadied.

Nicklaus has finished now, Trevino and Jacklin are walking up to the seventeenth green. These two are tied for the lead, and a disappointed Nicklaus trails by one. Both of them will have to bogie the seventeenth or eighteenth for Jack to get a tie and a playoff tomorrow.

As I stand by the eighteenth green now, watching on a BBC monitor and listening to Chris and Byron describe the action, it looks like Jacklin will win his second British Open. He is well on the green on the par-five seventeenth with his third shot. Trevino, on the other hand, has suddenly come apart. He lies four and still is off the back of the green. Even if he gets down in two

from there, a tough job, he will drop into a tie with Nicklaus.
Jacklin, with a routine two-putt green, will lead.

4:50 P.M.

This is the most exciting golf tournament I have ever seen.

Lee Trevino has chipped into the hole for a par five, keeping
him one stroke ahead of Nicklaus! Now, Jacklin three-putts for a
six. Where he figured seconds ago to gain at least one stroke,
more likely two, he now has lost a shot to the amazing Trevino.

5:10 P.M.

It's over, and Trevino has won his second straight British
Open. He is standing just in back of the eighteenth green, talking
of course, this time to the crowd.

"There's a lady down in Dallas," he said, "I call her my second
mother. She says that God is a Mexican, and I believe her!"

He was referring to the miraculous quality of his golf here,
birdieing the last five yesterday, using a golf club like a magician's wand on seventeen today, pitching or chipping into the
hole *four* times during the tournament.

Everyone likes Trevino, admires his feat, and is congratulating
him.

Still, there is an undercurrent of disappointment here, because
Nicklaus has lost his courageous bid for the modern grand slam.
He lost to Lee by a single stroke, with Jacklin third (he also
bogied the eighteenth).

Jack must remember with pain not only Lee's chip-in on seventeen, but his own bogie on sixteen.

Doug Sanders couldn't quite keep up with the powerful front-
runners on the final nine, but he gave it a noble try. Six years ago
here, he lost to Nicklaus by a stroke. Since then, he lost to him at
St. Andrew's by missing a short putt on the final hole, then being
beaten in the eighteen-hole playoff.

Usually, Sanders' manner reflects his colorful clothing. He is
cocky, wisecracking.

Today, though, as he walked off eighteen, his world-weary, creased face was a portrait of exhaustion. And he sounded more like a twelve-year-old after losing a Little League championship than the famed swinger of the golf tour when I congratulated him on a great effort. There was no brashness, no glib reply as he looked straight at me.

"Jim," he said, "I tried as hard as I could."

As for Nicklaus, his small smile is more resigned than sad as he shakes Trevino's hand. "Lee," he says, "Why don't you go back to Mexico?"

Trevino hugs him and they laugh.

MIDNIGHT

We are getting into Bob's limousine, ready at last to leave Muirfield.

We went off the air a few minutes ago after transmitting to-day's excitement back to the United States by satellite. Chris, Byron, and I, sitting together in the commentary booth, just had to do a few short passages to link things together, the bulk of the description having been done as the events unfolded.

Sitting up there, fifty feet above the ground in the only lighted space for a mile around, we must have looked like some strange trio of lighthousekeepers, there on the shores of the Firth of Forth in the cool night.

When we came down, I saw Dick Ebersol, the Yale man who serves as Roone's assistant and occasionally produces shows. I had last seen Dick in Eugene, Oregon, at the Olympic Trials, less than six days ago. Since then, he had been to Greece, where he produced a special Olympics show written and narrated by Erich Segal, in which Bill Toomey and Rafer Johnson, both Olympic decathlon champions, went back to the ancient Olympic stadium and recreated the pentathlon competition of those days.

And now here was Ebersol, just arrived in Gullane, Scotland. We do, indeed, get around.

"I must tell you how I left Erich," he said. "You know how excited he gets, how wrapped up and interested in what he is doing? Well, there he was, telling me to say hello to you and Roone. There he was, standing in the lobby of the Athens Hilton, holding an ancient spear and shield and wearing an old Greek helmet."

Yes, sir. It really looks like the Olympics will be an interesting assignment.

Now Bob's limousine is passing the old clubhouse at Muirfield. In the dark, it sits, silent, stolid, and I think of Tony Lema.

They called him "Champagne Tony." He was the Trevino of his time, a poor kid from San Leandro, California, who strode a golf course with the dignity of a prince.

When he came to St. Andrew's in 1964, he had made it to the top, seemed to be on the verge of greatness. It was the first trip he had ever made outside the United States and he wasn't really sure what it would be like.

He played in Philadelphia, at Whitemarsh, caught a plane afterward, on Sunday night, and flew the Red Eye to Prestwick. After the drive across Scotland, still without sleep, he played nine holes on the Old Course to see what it was like.

At about eight that night, I interviewed him on film in the backyard of the private home where he and Sanders were staying for the tournament. It was cold and windy. In the interview, he said how fascinating it was to finally be in Scotland, the home of golf. He complimented the Scottish people on their friendliness, and said that, all in all, it was a wonderful experience.

Then he asked me if we were finished. When I said we were and assured him that the camera was turned off, he shook his head in disbelief, then leaned toward me.

"Jim," he said, "Isn't this the most miserable goddamn place you've ever seen?"

He was to change his mind, and the British would change their mind about him. The nickname, "Champagne Tony," had misled them. They expected the ultimate in what they consider American gaucbery and arrogance, a loud-talking, blustering braggart. He was not that kind of man, and he soon disarmed them, first by answering a Scottish newsman's question about where he stood on the money list in the States by saying, "Let's see. I think right now, I'm third in money-winning and first in money-spending." They liked that.

Then he went out and won the British Open on his first attempt, beating high winds and Jack Nicklaus in the process, and they liked him even more. And he grew to like, then love Scotland.

In 1966 at Muirfield, he didn't play well. Back in the pack, he teed off early on the last day. As I started out toward the commentary tower, I saw Tony, leaning against the side of the doorway of the old clubhouse. He was smelling a rose.

"Where did you get the rose, Tony?" I asked.

"Jim, I just don't believe these wonderful people. You know how badly I've been playing. Well, when I came on the first tee this morning, the gallery was small, but a pretty girl stepped forward and handed me this. 'Good luck, Tony,' she said. I responded in typical Lema fashion by putting my tee shot in the left fairway bunker. But that isn't all.

"By the time I was coming up to eighteen—I played badly again today—there was almost no gallery left. But as I was about to address my second shot to the green, an old man called from the side of the fairway. 'Lema,' he called, 'Lema!'

"'Yes, sir?' I said.

"'Lema,' he said. 'You're the greatest. Please come back to Scotland.'

"I just can't believe these people, Jim."

He smelled the rose again.

"I'll come back here as long as I can walk."

Those, I assure you, were his exact words.

A few weeks later, he was dead, victim of a freak private plane crash, on a golf course, in Illinois.

And now, the limousine is out of the Muirfield grounds, on the main road. Off to the left, rising from the fog that has begun to creep over the moor, is a strange tower. It is the structure where the Gullane Fire Brigade dries its hoses.

Behind the tower is the firehouse. There is a light in one window, behind which, presumably, sits one fireman, getting sloshed on good Scots' whisky, while his colleague visits his aunt, in Musselburgh.

10

World Lumberjack

Championships

"Sweet Corn and Other Things Ahead." That is the crudely hand-painted legend on a sign at the side of route 12 just outside Woodstock, Vermont.

It refers to a roadside vegetable stand, but to Margaret, our daughter Mary, our son Sean, and me, it seems to sum up the wonderfully warm tastes, smells, and experiences that we have found in the country's most beautiful state. And it seems to promise more in the unknown future.

We built a house in Vermont two years ago, "for the kids and their friends," in a very special place called Sonnenberg ("Sunny Mountain"). There we ski in the winter, swim and play tennis and golf in the summer, look at the flaming leaves in the autumn, and stay away in the springtime (April and May), when the land turns to mud for just a little while. At Christmas, we go into the

109

woods and cut down our own Christmas tree and ski it down the mountain. (I didn't even ski when we started to build the house, although I had been reporting on ski races for about fifteen years.)

We sat down one evening to sketch out our plans for the house, Margaret and I. On a piece of yellow paper, I drew a small box.

"That is a sauna," I said. "Now, let's design the rest of the house."

We did, and it is beautiful, and the only trick (a difficult one), is getting up there frequently enough.

Well, we're in the house above Woodstock this weekend, and right now I am treading the fairways of the Montague Golf Club in Randolph, Vermont, with my friends Sheldon Dimmick and Hans Kurash.

The Montague Golf Club couldn't offer greater contrast to last week's British Open at Muirfield. To be sure, Montague has been here longer than you'd think—all nine holes of it. Originally, some rich man from New York built it and used to graze his cows on the same grass where he played golf. For that reason, they had wire fences around the greens, so the cows wouldn't mess them up. It costs fifty dollars a year to belong to Montague, I believe.

The clubhouse is a small, weathered, wooden building. The front steps are worn concave in the middle from the passage of many thousands of golf spikes through the years. Inside, the young pro, Jim McAtee, will sell you clubs and golf balls. He will also sell you a ham sandwich, which he slips into a little warming oven to make it taste better.

Beside the steps is a drinking fountain, with a small plaque indicating that it is dedicated to an older lady who has been playing the course for about half a century.

As for my playing partners, Sheldon Dimmick is my banker in Randolph. He started as the bank's janitor when he was a very young man, and now is the president. He still keeps janitor's hours, rather than the so-called "banker's hours," however. If you call the bank very early in the morning, it probably will be

Sheldon who answers the phone himself, invariably with a single word that sums up the directness and economy of the true Vermonter.

"Bank," he says. That's all.

Someone told me that Sheldon handles more small business loans than any banker this side of Boston.

He is chewing tobacco as we walk down the fairway, telling me, as always, that I should stop running around the world.

"Just give speeches here in Vermont," he says. "I'll fix them up for you."

My other partner, Hans Kurash, is the man who built Sonnenberg. He was a successful builder outside Philadelphia who had a dream of building the kind of houses he wanted to at the pace he wanted to build them, in Vermont. In the dream, he and his son, Ralph, would build the houses (with their own hands) in the summertime, and run the ski area in the winter.

That was six years ago. Now there are twelve houses and a ski area. There is a nine-acre lake, where there was nothing, and a couple of tennis courts. To ski at Sonnenberg, you must make a reservation a day ahead, and when Hans decides he has enough, he takes no more reservations. So there is never a lift-line.

In frankness, I must say that Hans's golf game, from tee to green, needs work. Once on the putting surface, though, he is incredible. He only took up the game a year ago, yet he regularly makes putts of anywhere from ten to forty feet.

Why?

"Simple," he says. "I've been doing carpentry now for thirty years. I have a carpenter's level in my head. Can't you see the way that green breaks off?"

And he knocks in another one. It's kind of annoying.

The crowd at the Montague Golf Club is a cross-section of Randolph. Everyone knows each other—bankers, lawyers, shopkeepers, housewives, and a retired eighty-one-year-old postman called "Babe." Babe plays just about every day. We passed him a while ago, and I asked what he had on his first nine.

"Forty-three," he said, apologetically. He was walking fast, though a trifle stiff of leg, carrying his own bag. "Could do better, but the damn poker game didn't break up until four o'clock this morning. Serves me right."

That's Vermont.

FRIDAY, JULY 28

I'm in a ski resort called Telemark, near Hayward, in northern Wisconsin. A minute ago, I killed a mosquito as big as a fly in the bathroom, but aside from that, everything is fine.

Imagine all the people of the world placed in a sort of police lineup—people of every country, every color, every size and shape, every walk of life. Suppose you had the opportunity to pause, at least briefly, and talk to all of them. Well, that's something of what it is like to work and travel for ABC Sports. The kaleidoscope of people has continued as I made my way here for the World Lumberjack Championship.

There was a stop in Chicago to play in the annual golf tournament for the clients of ABC Sports. That means the sponsors—company presidents and ad managers, advertising executives and our own people. We play golf, then eat and drink and tell stories. It's a pleasant day and has been a very successful occasion for a number of years now.

Next day, I flew to Hayward on Air Wisconsin's Champagne Flight, the only such flight I know of on a feeder airline. Shortly after takeoff on the 6:00 P.M. flight, the fifteen passengers in the little Beechcraft 99 hear a message on the P.A. from their pilot.

"Folks," he says, "There are two hampers sitting in the aisle of the airplane. In one is some snacks and little hors d'oeuvres. In the other is chilled champagne. Feel free to help yourself."

The two hampers are prepared each evening by a Mrs. Roy Shwery. She is the wife of the president and founder of the airline.

At our flight's one stop, Wisconsin Rapids, I was interviewed by the public relations staff of Air Wisconsin—the president's daughter, Catherine, and her husband, a young Englishman who started his adult life as a London bobby, came to North America

Indy 500

Hoosier hoopla, hot dogs, beer, magnificent racing machines, thousands of balloons rising against a Memorial Day sky, brave drivers, and sudden death.

Why do we watch men driving at Indy? Is it to be part of a mammoth spectacle? Is it the piercing, high-pitched whine of 30,000 horsepower flat out? Is it the ghoulish anticipation of death? It is all of these, I think, except the last. We watch, not hoping for death, but wishing to see men *defy* death, approach it, and conquer it. We identify with them, slumped in a horizontal position, all but invisible under their heavy helmets.

To sit in an Indy car in the quiet of its garage is to learn a new appreciation of the driver's courage. He is wedged into place; strapped tightly at shoulders, chest, waist, and thighs; surrounded by highly volatile racing fuel. Behind him is the mighty power plant; in front, only a fiberglass shell. Alone, in his machine, on the race course, the driver is a frail and vulnerable human being.

1 2 3

What sort of person becomes a race driver? All sorts, it seems. [1] Mario Andretti spent much of his childhood in an Italian displaced persons camp. [2] Lloyd Ruby keeps coming to Indy even though he feels that "Lady Luck just never has been with me in this place." [3] A. J. Foyt, a tough Texan, three-time Indy winner, financially secure, will race on anything from asphalt to dirt. [4] Al Unser has won the big race once, as has his brother Bobby. Another brother, Jerry, died on the track. [5] Phil Hill, a three-time winner at Le Mans, a former World Grand Prix champion, races no more; he restores antique cars and music boxes, and collects rare piano rolls of classical music. [6] Peter Revson, a could-be jet-setter, prefers the dangerous business of racing to cosmetics; his brother Doug died at the wheel.

4 5 6

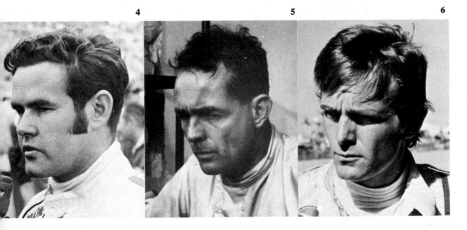

Golf

Jack Nicklaus and Lee Trevino: together they form a golfing legend that is being written right before our eyes. Nicklaus: big, blonde, Aryan, super-confident; the strength of his body and the precision of his reflexes controlled by an intelligent mind. Trevino: raised in a shack on the edge of a Texas golf course by his mother and his grandfather, a Mexican gravedigger. They are the same age, thirty-three. Although they were born worlds apart, they share the inherent qualities of gentlemen and sportsmen. When before have we heard one great athlete say of another, as Lee did of Jack, "He is the greatest golfer in the world— it's an honor to beat him just once in a while"?

Nicklaus and Trevino are the emerging commanders of the "army" that once was Arnold Palmer's alone. At forty-three, Arnie plays on, still thrilling the loyalist members of his legion with an occasional charge, fighting on, figuratively panting and snorting, like an old rodeo bull looking for one more great charge through the arena.

Olympic Trials

As the 1972 Olympic trials approached in Eugene, Oregon, many observers openly disagreed with America's system of selecting its track and field team. Each athlete, no matter what his reputation or record, got one and only one chance to make the team.

[1] Rod Milburn, the best hurdler in the world, was beset with personal problems: money was stolen from his locker; a fire gutted his apartment; he was nearly penniless after paying his fare all the way from Louisiana.

[2] Jim Ryun, on the comeback trail after his disappointing showing in Mexico City, had become lost in the middle of the pack.

[3] Reynaldo Brown, high jumper, looked like a sure thing to make the team, along with Pat Matzdorf, the new world record holder.

In the end, Milburn made his event with a second-place finish; Ryun made it in the 1,500 but failed in the 800; Brown didn't make the team; neither did Matzdorf.

Most foreign athletes—the Soviets and Germans excepted—don't have the problem Americans do of making their own team. Kjell Isaksson of Sweden, for example, was an automatic choice for his country, where world-class pole vaulters are not frequently found. His problem in Munich was an Olympic imponderable: injury.

XX Olympiad

ABC at the ready in Munich.

[1] The set where Chris Schenkel would act as host for the network and where, later, we would spend the long hours of sport's most terrible day.

[2] The control room. Right to left: Jim Jeannette, associate director; Chuck Howard, v.p. of production; Roone Arledge, executive producer; Larry Kamm, director (he shared that seat with Don Ohlmeyer); and Vern Hendrickson, technical director.

All was silent and anticipatory, like a Christmas garden waiting for the kids to descend with shouts in the morning.

1

2

This is the ABC crew of some 250—or at least as many of them as could get together at picture-taking time. In the front row, from left to right: Geoff Mason, production coordinator; Marvin Bader, production manager; Jim Spence, v.p.; Dennis Lewin, producer (behind Spence's left shoulder); Julie Barnathan, v.p. of engineering; Howard Cosell; Chuck Howard; Erich Segal (behind Howard's left shoulder); the author; Roone Arledge; Chris Schenkel. Fifth from the right is expert Gordon Maddux; on his left are Peter Jennings and Frank Gifford; at the extreme right is Doug Wilson, producer.

The Games of the Twentieth Olympiad began with the voices of children, the youngsters of Munich bearing flowered arches they had made themselves, singing an old English canon rota. The day was perfect, the setting much more Hansel and Gretel than Hitler and Göring.

1   2

Each day at Munich brought a new surprise, and one never knew whether it would be comedy, confusion, or chaos. In the marathon, the surprise was fraud. A young West German student [1] entered the stadium first; he was not an entrant; he had in fact sneaked onto the course just before the finish. It wasn't funny, detracting as it did from the victory moment of America's Frank Shorter [2] first United States athlete to win the event since 1908.

In the 800 meters, Dave Wottle provided the surprise. He ran at the back of the pack until the last 200 meters [3]; then he burst forward with an unbelievable closing sprint that beat out Arzhanov, the Soviet favorite, for the gold medal. Dave received a surprise later himself. Only under questioning by the press did he realize that he had stood during the national anthem wearing his good luck golf hat [4]. Later, on television, he apologized to the American people: "I'm just sick about it."

3   4

2

1

It was an Olympics of total unpredictability. Steve Prefontaine [1] was so confident of his abilities at the NCAA championships that he ran a victory lap around the stadium before the race. At Munich he ran himself to exhaustion, staying with the leaders until the final steps when he stumbled and fell across the finish line, fourth in the 5,000 meters.

Olga Korbut [2] was an 83-pound second-stringer on the Soviet gymnastics team, but a teammate's injury gave her the chance to compete at Munich. At the end of the competition, she stood on the victory stand, a triple gold medalist, smiling and waving, living in a world where everyone was her friend.

For the McManuses (AKA McKay, as it says on the passport), Munich was a family experience never to be forgotten. [1] Margaret took the sun in front of ABC equipment trucks with Frank Gifford and Chris Schenkel. [2] Mary met younger members of the ABC team, like production assistant Dorrance Smith, just behind her, and the entire Canadian swim team (male). It was all fun for her until she stood beside the camera and saw the helicopters rise with the hostages inside. "They were so close," she said, "but nobody in the whole world could help." [3] Sean, wearing his "only vestige of legality," the ABC windbreaker that got him into the opening ceremonies when there weren't enough tickets to go around. Later, he sat in a corner of the control room, watching his friends, the men of ABC Sports, cover a story of life and death rather than of victory or defeat.

Suddenly, on the fifth day of September, the television screens of the world showed an ordinary concrete apartment building rather than a stadium. Inside the building were Arab terrorists and the captive Israelis. On a rooftop, at left of the photograph, lay police snipers waiting for an order to fire that never came in the Olympic Village.

There were spectators that day, too; thousands of them, a hundred yards from the terrible room where the hostages stood helpless. The spectators, and the world watching, had no idea how to help.

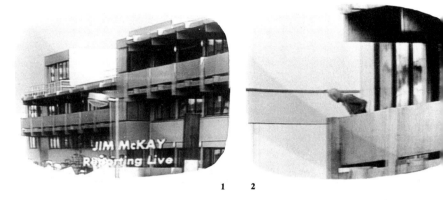

1   2

It would be tedious to detail everything we did and said after Roone cued me to talk on our first live transmission that day, but certain sights and thoughts do float to the surface of my mind. The heads of the terrorists, popping out of windows and doors regularly like some sort of dreadful puppet show, turning from side to side, alertly spotting their adversaries [1]; the man in the mask [2]; the man in the white hat [3]. The man in the white hat conferred with a negotiator for the Germans [4]. . . . The terrorist grew apprehensive during one of the meetings. "You are going to do one of two things," he said. "Either you are going to kill me or try to take me as a counter-hostage. In either event, I think you should know that you are going with me." From behind his back, he produced a hand grenade, its pin already pulled halfway out.

3   4

1   2

[1] An Israeli producer-reporter told me the early details of what had happened. [2] Hans (Jonny) Klein, Olympics press chief, issued bulletins to the press of the world all through the day, the night, and the early hopeless hours of the next morning. [3] Manfred Schreiber, police chief of Munich, was the man on the spot, his actions a matter of international discussion between the German and Israeli governments. [4] Konrad Ahlers, official West German government spokesman, was hopeful in an interview with us just after the false report that the hostages were safe. Like us, however, he was waiting for the definitive word. "A bad outcome might reopen old wounds," he said.

In the end, the outcome was the worst possible, and the watching world had a new wound, one that would not heal for a long time.

3   4

MANFRED SCHREIBER
Munich Police Chief

The Games of the Twentieth Olympiad shredded the emotions of the world with their joys and sorrows, their excitement and tragedy. The gold, silver, and bronze of the medals gave way to the blue steel of rifle barrels.

A security man in an athlete's warm-up suit, gun in hand, his face a study in sad determination, seemed to sum it all up. As he walked, he mirrored the events of Munich as indeed the Games themselves mirrored the state of the world in 1972. Confused. Violent. Still, moving forward.

to work in aerial exploration of the Arctic, then met Catherine.

In Hayward, we were greeted by the promoter of the World Lumberjack Championships, Tony Wise. Tony is a low-key wilderness millionaire who talks so low and so fast that it is sometimes difficult to understand him.

"He's the Jack E. Leonard of the north woods," someone said.

Tony owns the ski resort where we are staying, among a great many other things.

He loves his country and his background. In fact, to this day he sleeps in the bed in which he was born.

He also has another peccadillo in the area of tradition. Wherever he moves, no matter how big or how modern the house, Tony insists on taking with him, and using, his mother's old G.E. refrigerator, the kind with the big coil sitting on top. A couple of years ago, his house burned down, and his wife reportedly was somewhat depressed to find that one of the few surviving items was the old coil-top refrigerator.

As I said, the world is one long, dizzying, and fascinating array of different human beings.

SATURDAY, JULY 29

We have just heard three national anthems, played on somewhat scratchy records, here in the Lumberjack Bowl in Hayward, annual scene of the World Lumberjack Championships.

They were "Oh, Canada," "God Save the Queen" (for the contestants here from Australia and New Zealand), and our own anthem. It occurred to me that the next time I see flags raised and anthems played will be far from here, at the Munich Olympics.

The view from my commentary position gives a graphic illustration of the world as God made it, and the world as Man is remaking it to his *own* image.

While the anthems were being played, I looked first to my right. All I saw was the blue water of an inlet from the Namakagon River, surrounded by an endless forest of evergreens, growing right down to the water's edge. Overhead, a sky was blue as the one we saw in Scotland last week.

Then I looked to my left. First, I saw the ugly wood and cloth fence erected to keep out nonpaying spectators ($3.50 for adults, $2.50 for teen-agers, $1.50 for children). Beyond it was a highway under repair, dusty and grimy, with trucks and bulky campers moving along it slowly and noisily.The power and telephone lines that thread a skein of ugliness across America are there, of course, and advertising signs: "Logger's Cove Travel Trailer Park." And another big one, courtesy of the U.S. Government, apparently trying to explain why the road is all torn up reads: "New jobs for your community in partnership with your U.S. Department of Commerce Economic Development Administration."

But inside the Lumberjack Bowl, the scene is pleasant.

This is a legitimate event, not a put-on. The contestants, except for the girl log-rollers, are real lumberjacks, and they care a great deal about winning these titles.

There is log-rolling, properly called "birling," for men and women. There's been a world championship in birling since before the turn of the century. And there is tree-topping, in which men climb identical eighty-foot poles, then saw off the top of the pole. Whoever's wood chip hits the ground first is the winner. Speed-climbing contestants use the same poles, but they have a simpler object. Just climb up the eighty feet, ring a bell, and climb down. They do it in something under thirty seconds. Then there is wood-chopping, both American style (standing on a horizontal log and swinging between your feet), and Australian style (standing up, whacking at a vertical log). And axe-throwing, at a target.

Families compete here, like the Fishers, from Stillwater, Minnesota, and the Scotts, from Nova Scotia. P.A. announcer Joe McKenna has just introduced one of the Fisher girls competing in the birling.

"This girl's been raised on a log," he said. "Her father's been rolling for more than twenty years."

SUNDAY, JULY 30

We're sitting on an old park bench—producer Doug Wilson, director Larry Kamm, unit manager Ted Payne and I—in front of the terminal building at the Hayward airport. The bench is the waiting room.

I paced off the terminal building itself, and it is twelve feet by twenty-five, including the men's and ladies' rooms and the ticket counter. Behind the ticket counter, the only decoration is an old airplane propeller with an American flag sticking out the hole in its middle. To the side of the counter is a small card table, where they sell Baby Ruths and Hershey Bars. Outside, in addition to the park bench, there is a Coke machine and two gas pumps.

This rustic air depot is on its way out, though. The lady at the counter told me that by this time next year, they will have a brand new terminal building—"all rough-cut and stone," she said.

The Lumberjack Championships are over, and they were a rousing success before a full house on another gorgeous day. They were climaxed with a major upset in the men's birling contest. This pitted Phil Scott (of the Nova Scotia Scotts) against Jim Fisher (of the Minnesota Fishers). Scott was the defending champion and favorite. As they started out on the big log, it was man against man, family against family, and nation against nation.

Phil Scott came out of nowhere a few years ago to dethrone the Wickheim brothers, of Sooke, British Columbia, whose personal fiefdom the world of log-rolling had been for some years. Phil had participated in a canoe race across Canada that ended at the scene of the great Expo then being held in Montreal. As he and his brother wandered through the various exhibits, they came upon the Wickheim brothers, putting on a birling exhibition.

The Scotts were fascinated, asked the Wickheims how a fellow could get started in the sport. Jubiel Wickheim gave Phil a few tips on technique, then suggested he go home to Nova Scotia, practice, and save his money all winter, then next summer go to Hayward and enter the novice class at the world championships. Phil Scott did as he was told, except that he was a bit short on the money. He flew to Duluth, Minnesota, then had to hitchhike the rest of the way to Hayward.

Having gone to all that trouble, and after watching some of the competitors practice, he decided to enter the big event itself rather than the novice class. He won the world title on his first try, beating Jubiel Wickheim.

Well, the next year, a chastened Jubiel came back and beat Phil, then prudently retired as the world champion. Phil has dominated the scene since.

Whenever I talk about the Wickheims, I think of a story an advertising friend told me. His client wanted to use log rollers in a commercial, so he called ABC Sports and found that the best were the Wickheims, out in western Canada. He called them, made a deal, and sent them their airplane tickets to New York.

A few days later, he received a call from Northwest Air Lines in Seattle.

Had he purchased tickets for two gentlemen named Wickheim?

Yes.

Is he willing to authorize the overweight charge they will have on their transcontinental flight?

Sure, how much is it?

Seven hundred and fifty pounds.

My friend suddenly was more attentive.

"Seven hundred and fifty pounds?" he said, "What the hell is it?"

"Well, sir," said the air line spokesman, "It looks like a great big log."

One of the Wickheims was put on the phone, and patiently explained that it was necessary to bring their own log with them for the commercial.

My friend protested that there were plenty of logs in New York State.

Again, the Wickheims were patient.

As any birler knows, the only acceptable logs are made of western cedar. Anything else sinks too low in the water and is impossible to work on.

The agency paid for the overweight.

The match between Phil Scott and Jim Fisher was best two of three falls, with the men moving to progressively smaller logs during the competition. First comes the big red log, fifteen inches in diameter. The contestants roll on that for five minutes and then move to the white log, an inch smaller. After five minutes on that log, they move to the blue, then to the gold, or "final," log, which is used until the conclusion of the match. But once they have moved to the gold log, the contest usually ends quite quickly. The slenderer the log, the more difficult it is to stay on, and the gold log is very slender, indeed.

The match went the full three falls. We covered it with one camera dangling from a 150-foot crane, another in a rowboat. It looked like rub-a-dub-dub, three of our men—cameraman, assistant, and rower—in a tub. Other cameras were in more normal locations.

Most surprisingly, it was young Jim Fisher, recently returned from service in Vietnam, who won that final fall.

The measure of a sport's legitimacy, to me, is the degree of genuine interest and enthusiasm it engenders in the people who participate in it. By that measure, the lumberjack sport qualifies easily.

As Jim Fisher leaped back onto the dock, he was met by a swarm of friends and relatives, hugging him, pounding his back and lifting him in the air. He had returned the world log-rolling championship to the United States for the first time since 1954.

I moved in quickly to get a reaction from Jimmy. He was incredulous, disbelieving of his own accomplishment. Then, just like someone who has won the U.S. Open or been elected to the U.S. Senate, he turned serious.

"Jim," he said, "it's been a long way to the top."

We leave Hayward, then, home of "the world's largest mounted muskie." That's a fish that hangs on the wall of a local bar. Hayward, a beautiful vacation land where one of the things to do on Saturday afternoon is to go downtown and watch them make fudge in the window of the candy store. Hayward, where people come from the big cities to see how mid-America was in days gone by.

I guess that's why Tony Wise keeps his mother's old coil-top refrigerator.

11

ABC's Olympic Preparation

Charley Franke, of the ABC Press Department, is with me as we ride back from Philadelphia in a rented limousine.

The PGA golf championship last weekend, which figured to be the climax of the golfing year such a short time ago (until Trevino chipped in on seventeen at Muirfield), became instead anticlimactic. It was a good tournament on a good course (Oakland Hills in Birmingham, Michigan), with record crowds and sunny skies. Still, we had all been looking forward so much to the possibility of Nicklaus's grand slam, that it was more a weekend of fun, than of building tension.

Its highlight for us, in fact, was an outdoor cookout at Bill Flemming's house. Bill, who has been a commentator on Wide World since its inception, lives close to the course in Bloomfield Hills. He and his wife, Barbie, invited the entire ABC crew over for some of Bill's specially done barbecued chicken.

The countdown to Munich and the Olympic Games can be

119

heard loud and clear now. Yesterday was a 7:00 A.M. to midnight work day and today will be another.

The Olympics project that many people in our department have been working on for several years really started to surround me immediately after my return from Hayward. First came the beginning of a pre-Olympics show, to be aired the night before the games start. Doug Wilson is producing, Don Ohlmeyer is directing. I will be writing and doing commentary on much of the program. It will be a continuing project, something we will work on, no doubt, until shortly before it goes on the air.

Yesterday, I started to work with another of our young ABC Sports producers, Brice Weisman, on a special feature of this year's Olympics coverage. Since at last we will have enough time to document a great sporting occasion the way we have always wanted to, Roone and Chuck have come up with some really good ideas for in-depth coverage, not only of the events, but, more particularly, of the people.

For several months now, Brice has been working on a series of filmed features exploring the personalities, home surroundings, and training methods of many of the world's great athletes. Yesterday, I wrote scripts and recorded twenty-three of them. We also attended another pre-Olympics press luncheon, this time for the New York disciples of the printed page.

The idea of the personality pieces (they'll probably be called "up-close and personal") can be shown by the contrasting thoughts of two American swimmers.

One piece is on Mark Spitz, the brash young Californian by way of Indiana University who announced that he would conquer the world four years ago in Mexico and ended up an embarrassed Olympian. Mark is back, older, perhaps even brasher, but certainly more mature as a swimmer, thanks in great part to his coach at Indiana, Jim (Doc) Counsilman.

Spitz was asked what he thought about to avert boredom during the endless miles of training laps: "I picture a different beautiful girl I know at the end of the pool," he said. "A different one on each lap."

The other American swimmer is Mark Chatfield, another Californian. Mark is a serious student of the cello, and when he was asked the same question, he said that he mentally selects a favorite piece of music and imagines it being played perfectly, on a cello, from beginning to end.

We did twenty-three of those yesterday. By the time we finish them, again probably in Munich, there will be between fifty and seventy-five.

This morning, the rented limousine and Charley Franke picked me up in Connecticut shortly after seven so that we could drive to Philadelphia and I could appear on the Mike Douglas show—to talk about the Olympics.

That has been done.

The other guests were Ralph Nader and his sister, and Rich Little, possibly the country's best mimic, whom I had last seen when we rode together on a plane from Calgary to Toronto about a year ago. At that time, he must have done about a hundred different voices for Doug Wilson and me during a three-hour trip.

This was the first time I have appeared on Mike's show. He does an excellent interviewing job—smooth, easy, listening to the answers, yet keeping things moving. I think, to use the phrase of our trade, that Mike does his homework.

When we get back to New York, I will go to the ABC tape room to work with yet another producer, Ned Steckel. Tonight, we'll record a review of the 1968 Olympics for this week's Wide World of Sports. My on-camera position will be in the tape room, where the idea is that I am looking through the old tapes with tape editor, John Croke. Johnny, an old Wide World hand on the engineering side, will have a line to speak. It is reported that he got a haircut this morning and has been clearing his throat for a week.

Yes, the countdown for Munich has indeed begun.

JOHN F. KENNEDY INTERNATIONAL AIRPORT,
NEW YORK—FRIDAY, AUGUST 18

Suddenly, it is time to leave for Munich. I say suddenly because that is the way it always seems to come upon me.

We finish one Olympics, have a party, and kid each other about the fact that the next one is only four years away.

We talk while we work on other shows, worry that another network may get the rights. One day, Roone wraps up the rights and we start thinking of ideas.

We hear stories about what went on when Roone went to meet with the people in the new city, and develop a new interest in books about that part of the world. It still seems very far away.

Every few months, one of us says to the other, "You watch. Suddenly, one day, it will be here."

And suddenly, one day, like Christmas, or April 15, or the day your child leaves for college for the first time, it is, in fact, time to leave for the Olympics again. That is today.

This time, we are all going together—Margaret, Mary, Sean, and I—which makes it a very special Olympics for me. None of them have ever been to a Summer Games, although Margaret did go with me to Grenoble for the Winter Olympics in 1968.

Margaret was going to join me in Mexico for the Summer Games four years ago, but the very day I left (she was coming down two days later), Mary was taken to the hospital for an emergency operation. Instead of strolling through Chapultepec Park, she sat up in the hospital room for forty-eight hours, then nursed Mary back to health for the rest of the games.

Neither of the kids, as I said, have been to any Olympics. They are excited about it, but neither they, nor anyone really, can know what the Olympic Games actually are until they see them. It is not a big track meet or sporting festival, alone. It is the largest regularly scheduled gathering of mankind.

When you have seen one, you remember it all your life. Whether pleasantly or unpleasantly, or something in between, depends on the games of that year, which events you see and what you bring to the scene yourself. Certainly, beauty, to an extent, *is* in the eye of the beholder.

And sport, to paraphrase something William Saroyan once wrote, is caring. If the athletes don't care, and the spectators don't care, then there is no sport, just a meaningless dumb show.

The fact of the Olympics is that everyone does care, for whatever their personal reasons. Some of the reasons are crass, to be sure—money, status, ego-trips, nationalism—but others are not. To be the only person on earth to win the gold medal in any event in any given Olympiad is an honor worth striving for. Having won it, you are given the responsibility of taking care of it. If you should lose it, or if it is stolen, it will not be replaced.

To say that because they are worthwhile the Olympics have no problems would be like saying the same thing about life. The Olympics are perpetually involved in problems and controversy.

Right now, as we prepare to board Lufthansa's flight 401 for Munich, major trouble has already erupted at the games.

Ethiopia first, and now other black African nations, is threatening to withdraw from the games if Rhodesia is allowed to compete. This is a very complicated, totally political affair, not without hypocrisy on both sides.

Last year, the black nations *did* agree that Rhodesia could compete if it marched behind the Union Jack of Great Britain and used "God Save the Queen," as its anthem. Since Rhodesia has completely broken from the former mother country, this was technically as unrealistic as the United States marching behind the British flag. Still, it was agreed upon.

Now, the black nations have changed their mind at the last minute. It seems an obvious power play. Get rid of Rhodesia, they are saying, or lose many of the top competitors in track and field—Kip Keino of Kenya, for example.

It would be a strange turn of events if they all went home. When the Olympics were last held in Germany, Hitler made it clear that black athletes were not really welcome. It was doubly embarrassing for him when Jesse Owens, a black American, was the hero of the games.

Now, we face a situation where the black athletes of the world are welcome in Germany, but may not compete at all. There are even rumblings that the black Americans may boycott the games, but this is hearsay at the moment.

It looks like ABC, at any rate, is ready to go. We had our big production meeting late Monday. Roone presided and introduced Chuck, who then conducted the meeting. Geoff Mason, associate producer who has been paving the way in Munich, had returned for the occasion. Others had flown in from all over the country—producers, directors, commentators, everybody who would be involved on the production side.

Everything is waiting for us—hotels, commentary booths, studios, tape rooms, offices, our own cafeteria, sauna, swimming pool, massage facilities. It is now up to us to get ourselves there and be prepared. Even on that front, we have considerable help.

Normally, on Wide World and the other shows I work on, I do all of my own research. For the Olympics, though, Terry O'Neil was hired a year ago, just after graduation from Notre Dame, and given Olympic research as his total assignment. Since then, he has been all over the world, talking to athletes and coaches of many nations.

Today, he produced the first volume (there will be three all together). There are 539 pages in it, covering the opening ceremonies, track and field, and miscellany. Miscellany delves into such matters as the history of the ancient and modern games, historical anecdotes, eligibility codes, city of Munich, drug tests, sex tests, maps, and a conversion table.

The only mixed signal I have heard of in the ABC operation so far concerned a pamphlet put out by a group called Peter Glenn Associates bearing the ABC Olympic shield on its cover. The booklet is accurate and very complete, giving daily schedules for all events in the Olympics, lists and suggestions on hotels, restaurants, night clubs, shopping, and so forth.

In fact, the compilers seem to have become overly zealous in their dedication to completeness. There is a category, which nobody seems to have noticed until the booklet came out, entitled "Ladies of the Evening." It is exactly what the title implies, a list of houses of prostitution in the Munich area. *Variety*, the show business newspaper, made note of the category last week.

As we were about to leave Westport today, one more anecdote filtered back from the Segal–Toomey–Johnson expedition to the ancient Olympics stadium in Greece.

The two former decathlon winners, Bill Toomey and Rafer Johnson, if you recall, were re-creating the ancient pentathlon, a five-event competition involving wrestling, jumping, throwing, and a foot race. When they came to the foot race—one stade, about 200 meters—Toomey made a false start. Professor Segal, a stickler for historical accuracy and a stern disciplinarian, quickly pointed out that in the ancient games the penalty for a false start was that the offending athlete would be *whipped*.

A whip had been provided for this possibility.

The starter, wincing a bit, laid a soft blow on the bare back of Toomey. The whip generated more speed than he thought and opened several bleeding little stripes on Bill's body.

O.K., so much for historical accuracy, but the vagaries of modern technology had intruded. Something had gone wrong with the camera and the "take" was no good.

"Sorry, Bill," said director Lou Volpicelli, normally a most sympathetic Neapolitan. "We'll have to whip you again."

They did. This time, the starter tried to be so gentle that he came up short and hit Toomey in the face.

The picture was fine this time, but the sound was bad. Toomey finally rebelled, refusing to be whipped yet again.

Someone muttered a suggestion that they whip a stand-in, gently, just for the sound.

The young Greek boy who had been hired by Volpicelli as a general assistant for a few drachmas a day will never know how close he came to corporal punishment on that afternoon. All that saved him, frankly, was the flat refusal of production assistant Andy Crawford to supervise the whipping.

"Lou," Andy said to his director, "I know I'm supposed to do whatever you tell me, but I don't get paid enough to tell that kid we are going to whip him. Whip me if you want."

Volpicelli, thinking, no doubt, of the reaction in the office when word filtered back that he was whipping his production assistants, shook his head sadly and decided to stay with what he had.

MUNICH, GERMANY—SATURDAY, AUGUST 19

We are in Munich, one week before the opening ceremonies for the games of the Twentieth Olympiad.

It is time to meet the ABC cast of characters as they assemble. The hotel room assignment list here at the Munich-Sheraton reads like a family tree of our organization:

Twenty-first floor

Roone P. Arledge (rm. 2108)—As president of ABC sports, Roone is the architect of ABC's Olympics coverage. It was he who got the rights, fought for the amount of air time needed to do the job, and supervised the planning. He will be in the control room actively producing each night's telecast here in Munich.

Roone is in his early forties, red-haired, with the strong build of an offensive guard. He has the inner fire that is traditional with red-headed people, but normally it is kept under tight control. Those of us who work with him closely know when the fire is burning brightly, however. A pinkness of cheek and a faraway look in his eyes are the first symptoms. When he begins to pick at the front of his shirt, as if it is fitting too tightly, real trouble may be brewing.

Arledge is the man who has built the ABC Sports Department. He was still in his twenties when he came to ABC from NBC to produce NCAA football. Soon, he was originating Wide World of Sports, then expanding the department's operations to the mammoth scope they have today.

He has been an innovator, in terms of the kinds of sports presented on television and in the techniques used to cover them. Underwater cameras and cameras dangling from 200-foot cranes, as well as cameras attached to racing cars, racing boats, and racing skis, have been the most visible evidence of the Arledge touch.

More important, I believe, has been the subtle, underlying philosophy of concentration on the individual, the human being who strives for excellence. It is summed up well in the weekly opening of Wide World of Sports: "Spanning the globe to bring you the constant variety of sport—the thrill of victory and the agony of defeat, the human drama of athletic competition. This is ABC's Wide World of Sports."

Roone is notoriously difficult to reach on the telephone, but when you *do* get to him, you have his total attention, and he is ready with answers to your questions. He has thought it out. He will not be rushed or panicked into a decision.

Total billings when he came to ABC Sports were about $2,000,000. This year, they will be more in the area of $130,000,-000.

Nineteenth floor

Charles W. (Chuck) Howard (rm. 1923)—As vice-president in charge of production of ABC Sports and approaching the witching age of forty, Chuck Howard is still as youthful-looking as he was when he came to ABC Sports from the Chase Manhattan Bank more than a decade ago. He will be Roone's top aide here, as he has been since his days as a production assistant. In addition, he will produce, on location, the opening and closing ceremonies, some swimming, and all of the track and field events.

Chuck is tall, short-haired, volatile. Next to Roone, he is the best producer of sports events in the business, I think. In addition to his executive duties, he produces NCAA football and our major golf telecasts.

His loyalty to Duke University is exceeded only by his encyclopedic knowledge of sports. At the slightest provocation, he can come up with the names of third-string college football cornerbacks, golfers who did *not* qualify for the tour in last year's rookie tournament, or drivers of Formula Three race cars.

Eighteenth floor

Jim McKay (rm. 1810)—Host of ABC's Wide World of Sports, commentator on major golf telecasts. I will handle Opening and Closing ceremonies, gymnastics, track and field, and the pre-Olympics program.

Bill Flemming (rm. 1811)—Commentator on Wide World of Sports since its inception. He also works on NCAA football and golf.

Once upon a time, back at the University of Michigan, Bill wanted to be a doctor. He still has a most impressive vocabulary of medical terms (did you know that funny growling you get in your stomach sometimes is properly called, "Borburigny"? So Flemming tells me).

Bill is a top professional at his trade, and runs a tight commentary booth. He loves to research his event. He and I, through the years, must have walked a few hundred miles on golf courses together, looking for first-hand information on what is happening.

Chris Schenkel (rm. 1812)—Chris will be the host of the games of the Twentieth Olympiad for ABC television. He is play-by-play commentator for ABC on NCAA college football, NBA basketball, the Professional Bowler's Tour and golf.

Chris and I have worked together, on and off, for more than twenty years. Together, we did the first program ever produced by a group called Sports Programs, Inc., headed by Ed Scherick. Sports Programs, which operated out of a hole in the wall on West 43d Street, later became ABC Sports through a complicated series of events. (Ed Scherick became a successful movie producer.)

Chris Schenkel is one of the most truly friendly people I have met. When he thanks somebody on the air for their help—be he promoter, greenskeeper, or statistician—Chris really *means* it.

He and his family now live by a lake in Indiana, his beloved native state.

His job here, acting as host in the studio, will be a subtly difficult, marathon job. His basic office hours will be 1:00 to 4:00 A.M.

Keith Jackson (rm. 1813)—Keith's route to network sports commentary led from his native Georgia to the state of Washington to Los Angeles, where he lives now. Keith is big and strong, and a skilled professional play-by-play man.

Once, when we were golfing together, I saw him hit a drive at least 280 yards.

"Good Lord, Keith," I said. "What a drive!"

"I'm not happy with it, Jim," said Keith, looking down at his driver. "I think I'll have to change to a D-5 shaft."

Kind of a perfectionist, Keith is.

Frank Gifford (rm. 1814)—He was once one of the great stars of the National Football League, but Frank is not an athlete cashing in on his former fame. Rather, he has used that previous career as the entrée to a new one. He has worked long and hard to become a professional at a very different business, sports commentary, and he has succeeded.

Frank is a quiet, low-key person who wears well.

When Roone originally wanted him for Monday Night Football, he was still tied to CBS.

"I'll tell you who would do a hell of a job for you, though," Frank said. "Don Meredith. He'd be terrific."

Thus the seed was planted for the eventual team of Frank, "Dandy Don"—and "Humble Howard."

Howard Cosell (rm. 1815)—Howard Cosell is—Howard Cosell. Persistent interviewer, opinionated editorialist, Howard is a former lawyer with the photographic memory and forensic talents often associated with that calling. (You see? As soon as I start writing about Howard, I use words like "forensic.")

Howard ad-libs all his material and, yes, he is exactly the same off-camera as he is when on the air. He doesn't enter a group, he envelops it.

In personal conversation, he speaks in "Cosellisms."

A month or so ago, I came into the office (one of my rare visits there), at a time when everyone was out to lunch. Howard happened along, smoking his ever-present cigar. With no one to hear except the two of us, Howard put an arm around my shoulder, looked me in the eye, and said, "Jim McKay, you are an extremely talented, albeit diminutive, man."

That's Howard.

Bill Russell (rm. 1816)—Former star and coach of the Boston Celtics professional basketball team, now expert commentator on NBA basketball. A former Olympian, he will cover basketball with Frank Gifford.

Extremely intelligent, strong, and articulate in his opinions, he is a talk-show regular. He gives the appearance of a loose, relaxed giant. When he laughs, almost seven feet of coordinated human body goes into motion at once. Yet, as a player and coach, he was often said to be tough, hard, bitter. I think it would take a long time to know Bill Russell completely.

Bill Toomey (rm. 1817)—Bill Toomey was almost thirty years old when he won the decathlon four years ago in Mexico City which, in itself, should tell you he is a very determined man.

Bill is here with his wife, formerly Mary Rand, who was an Olympic track and field gold medalist herself for England.

Toomey, son of an advertising executive, is making a smooth transition from athlete to businessman, working with sponsors as spokesman and also as idea man. He plays bit parts in movies and does track commentary regularly for CBS. Here, he will be one of the experts working with me on track and field, handling the sprints, hurdles, and field events.

In Bill's manner, there is more of Madison Avenue than the locker room. In conversation, he speaks softly, but is given to puns and one-line gags. Shortly after winning the decathlon, for example, complaining of the strict amateur standards imposed on American athletes, he said, "Hell, I'm the only thirty-year-old in Laguna Beach still living with my folks."

He was also the only decathlon man who used to drive to the meets in a Mercedes-Benz 230SL, with his vaulting pole, in two pieces, lashed to the roof of the little sports car.

Bill is a leader in the athletes movement for reform of the U.S. Olympic Committee and the AAU.

Erich Segal (rm. 1818)—Author of *Love Story*, professor at Yale University, next year will instruct at the University of Munich, as it happens, teaching Latin and Greek—in German.

He is a marathon runner by avocation, frequent competitor in the Boston Marathon, who will function here as expert on long-distance running and Olympic history.

Some find the diversity of his interests unpleasant. "What makes Erich run?" they ask, speaking figuratively.

Others find a sort of modern Renaissance man in someone who operates in the fields of scholarship, literature, films, television, and sport.

Here, he is working for French radio—in French—as well as for us.

He is an interesting person, animated and graphic in conversation, except for certain occasions when he seems not to be with you at all. Then his eyes glaze a bit, and he glances around as if looking for an escape route.

Marty Liquori (rm. 1827)—Middle-distance runner from Villanova University who would be competing in the 1,500-meter run here except for a foot injury that has put him out of action. Marty will do commentary on the 800 and 1,500 with me.

He seems shy on first meeting, almost unconfident. This is a false impression.

In his running career, he has epitomized what I think of as the Eastern-type runner, bred on the cold and windy early spring training fields of New York and New Jersey, hardened in the winter indoor meets, where elbows in the ribs and splinters in the rear end are a normal part of the event.

Eastern track men live hard and run tough in a sport that is not widely followed in their part of the country, except for a few meets at Madison Square Garden.

Marty is very much that kind of a runner, and that kind of a young man.

Bob Beattie (rm. 1828)—A Colorado transplant from Manchester, New Hampshire, and former assistant football coach at Colorado University, where he was also ski coach. This led to the job as first national ski coach of the American Alpine team. There he built a group headed by Bud Werner, Bill Kidd, and Jim Heuga, dubbed them "The Tough Americans," and invaded Europe, looking for improved starting positions in the international seeding and then victory.

His endless discussions (with F.I.S. officials abroad for the better seedings, with groups of every sort at home to get more money for the team) paid off in the Winter Games at Innsbruck in 1964, when Kidd and Heuga won silver and bronze medals in the slalom. They were the first American men ever to win a medal in any sort of skiing event in the Olympics.

Since then, Beattie has branched out into half a dozen other enterprises, the most public of which is a pro ski tour, which he invented and organized. He also works with me as expert commentator on international Alpine events.

Here, oddly, he will be doing play-by-play on volleyball and weight-lifting.

Bob is a great salesman, and he has convinced Roone and Chuck that he can do those sports effectively. Don't bet against him.

Peter Jennings (rm. 1829)—Former anchor man on the ABC Evening News, he is now ABC News correspondent in the Middle East. He is here to cover the sidebar stories, the nonsports aspects of the games. This could range all the way from a story on a beer hall to another on Dachau. Again, it is part of the effort by the Sports Department to cover these games in a way that has never been done before.

I have met Peter only briefly before this week. It will be interesting to see how he fits in with our group.

He did one other story for sports, by the way. When the American volleyball team played in Havana last year, trying to qualify for the Olympics, Peter was sent in at a time when it looked like his Canadian citizenship might be needed for us to gain entry to Cuba. As it turned out, he did a fine sports commentary job. Hence, his presence here.

Others on the eighteenth floor, whom you either have met earlier in this book or will in the pages to come are Fred Schuhmann, George Milne, Charley Baldour, Jacques Lesgards, Marvin Bader, Phil Levens, and Georges Croses.

Seventeenth floor

If the eighteenth floor basically is the commentators' floor, the seventeenth is dedicated to producers and directors, plus a few experts, three publicists—and Julie Barnathan.

Julius Barnathan (rm. 1723)—Julie Barnathan is a small, dynamic executive, currently vice-president in charge of engineering for ABC. Julie, especially now that he has lost some thirty pounds preparing for the Olympics, looks more like a former college middleweight wrestler than the doctor of statistics he is.

The mind that earned him his Ph.D. has been used in many areas by ABC.

As head of engineering, however, he has been particularly important, revamping the department and coming up with innovations that are of great benefit to the Sports Department especially. He has worked hand-in-glove with Roone on the Olympics project. The dizzying technical facilities needed here all have been worked out under Julie's direction.

Lou Volpicelli (rm. 1712)—The previously mentioned Luigi is really not given to production assistant-whipping. Rather, he is a warm, sentimental man, a talented sports director who will prepare Italian meals for us at the drop of a pepperoni. He has found Italian restaurants around the globe, in Munich, Zurich, or Tokyo, as easily, it seems, as in Rome.

Doug Wilson (rm. 1713)—A prime example of the wildly assorted staff that Arledge has put together. Doug was once a professional singer, later an NBC page, today is an ABC Sports producer, also capable of directing.

He is our music specialist, often spends long hours in the record library searching for the few notes of music that will most appropriately fit behind one shot in one of our "scene-sets." For our tenth anniversary program of Wide World, Doug composed a special song and sang it on the show.

One story may explain him best. Margaret and I were sitting in Vermont at dinner one night when the phone rang.

"Hi," said the wistful voice of Doug Wilson, "I'm in a phone booth in Pocatello, Idaho."

"O.K. What's up?"

"I would tell you two things," he said. "First, I have just produced a regional University of Idaho football game here. At the opening, instead of college football marching music, I used Judy Garland singing, 'I was born in a trunk in the Princess Theatre in Pocatello, Idaho.' We piped it into the P.A. so the whole crowd could hear it."

"My second bit of news is that I have finished the song."

Doug was referring to a song he had been working on for about six months.

"That's great," I said, "I can hardly wait to hear it."

"You don't have to wait," said the small voice on the other end of the transcontinental telephone connection, "I have my guitar with me in the phone booth."

He sang the song for me, a soft, sad ballad called, "It's Already Yesterday."

Margaret put her ear to the phone and listened with me while Doug sang his song. It was beautiful.

So is Wilson.

Chet Forte (rm. 1716)—Although only five feet, nine inches tall, Chet was the highest scorer in the school's history when he played basketball for Columbia University. He was an All-America the same year as Wilt Chamberlain. Now in his mid-thirties, Chet can still match baskets with the top pro players in informal shooting contests. These days, though, he is chiefly known as producer-director of "Monday Night Football."

Chet is highly intelligent, given to hypochondria, and still a bachelor. In the travels of the Monday Night gang, he is well-equipped to trade comments and stories with the likes of Cosell and Meredith, but might just as easily be seen in a quiet, earnest conversation with Gifford or Roone.

Chet is a strong member of the ABC Sports production group.

Andy Sidaris (rm. 1717)—Andy is a Greek from Shreveport, who worked on off-shore drilling rigs as a kid, graduated from Southern Methodist, and today is as hip a Hollywood cat as you will find.

The Sunset Strip manner is in great part a masquerade for Andy, however. At the core, he is a very smart and talented director, possessed of a lightning-quick sense of humor. One-liners flow from him.

"Man," he will say, "I took a plane ride last month that was the world's worst. Don't ask why. The food alone was enough. Man, in first class they gave you a live turkey and a knife. Back in tourist, they threw a box of Crackerjack on the floor and let them scramble for it."

Some of the others on the seventeenth floor are: *Dennis Lewin*—Another former NBC page, now, at the age of twenty-six, the coordinating producer of Wide World of Sports; *Geoff Mason*, a young former yachtsman from Marblehead, Massachusetts, now associate producer of the Olympics coverage (he and Marv Bader have been the principal advance men here); *Don Ohlmeyer*, a mammoth, twenty-five-year-old Notre Dame graduate, now a director; *Larry Kamm*, from New York and Northwestern, who will share the studio directing chores with Don.

The publicists on the floor (Irv Brodsky, Otto Penzler, and Tom Mackin) have requested that for the duration of the Olympics they not be called by *Variety*'s term, "flack," meaning a publicity man. Over here, they pointed out, "flak" still means antiaircraft fire.

Sixteenth floor

The sixteenth floor contingent is led by *Jim Spence*, vice-president in charge of program planning for ABC Sports. Jim and Chuck Howard started out as the two P.A.'s in the department more than a decade ago, and have risen in rank together. While Chuck deals in production, Jim deals in the acquisition of rights to events and a myriad of other aspects of the sports television business. Jim is quiet, but direct in manner and as honest as anyone I have ever met in our business.

Roone's assistant, *Dick Ebersol*, is also on the sixteenth floor, along with most of the associate directors, production assistants, and the researcher.

Among them, these people comprise the reasons for the success of ABC Sports. Diverse in personality and talents, they share a dedication to getting the job done, whether it takes an hour or a week of uninterrupted hours; whether it means a glamorous function of some sort, or the most menial of tasks.

Titles in our department mean something, all right, in terms of prestige and money, but none of our people let a "job description" stop them from doing whatever is necessary to solve the problem at hand.

That is the end of my testimonial to the ABC Sports Department, but this book would be incomplete and unfair without it.

The theater, in the form of the Olympic grounds, is complete. The audience is assembling from all over the world. The players —the athletes of 120 nations—stand in the wings. More than 100 television cameras are in place, waiting to record the proceedings and flash them around the planet.

The curtain rises, and the drama will unfold, but first there will be the overture, the opening ceremonies, one week from today.

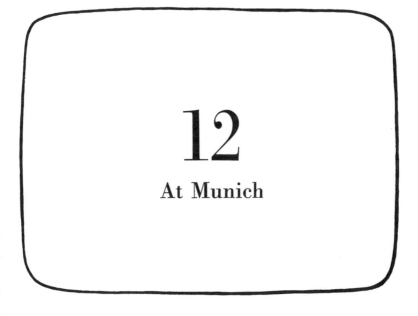

12

At Munich

This may be the last quiet moment any of us will see for a while.

In the basement of the Munich-Sheraton, I have just stepped out of the sauna with Bill Toomey, who is a bit of a sauna freak like me. I am looking across the beautiful indoor swimming pool toward the outdoor terrace. It is not crowded.

Outside, a few people are sun-bathing, my wife among them.

Inside, Erich Segal is standing by the bar in track clothes. He has just returned from running the second half of the course to be used for the marathon ("The runners are bitching like hell," he says. "There is a long stretch where they have to run on gravel. It's terrible on the feet.").

On a yellow plastic chaise longue, the inert body of Doug Wilson lies. He has been up for something like forty hours com-

137

pleting the pre-Olympics show that will air tonight, the last evening before the opening ceremonies. As he lies there, Wilson's right eye is half open, but unseeing. He is out cold.

The scene is peaceful, conducive to looking back over the week since we arrived, remembering little things.

There was the athlete from New Zealand who approached one of the pretty, uniformed German girl Olympic guides. Persuasively, he told her of his loneliness and her charms, suggested dinner for that evening. He was a young bachelor athlete halfway around the world from home. She was a single German girl. What could be nicer . . .

"Excuse me, please, for one moment," the girl said.

She went directly to the remarkable computer they have installed here for the games, filled with millions of facts about the Olympic Games, history and records, the city of Munich—and the athletes. With practiced fingers, the girl fed her new friend's name into the computer. In a matter of seconds, the information she had requested came out. There was his name, birthplace, residence, date of birth, athletic records, and the notation: "Married, three children." She returned to the New Zealander, said she had enjoyed talking to him, declined dinner, and left.

The car-dispatching office at Barnathan's Bungalow, in fact our entire motor pool, is under the direction of our old friend Kurt Fuchs, the stolid, graying "Silber Fuchs" (Silver Fox) of Munich. Fuchs, for more than a decade now, has been our driver, interpreter, arranger, and comrade.

Originally, Kurt learned his English from listening to the American Armed Forces radio station here in Munich, but by now his grammar is more ABC than AFN. If things aren't going well, it is a "bad scene" to Fuchs. Early this week, I asked him if he was enjoying some particular aspect of his job.

"Of course," he said in his gruff, Bavarian accent. "You know I like all those jazz."

"At first," he said, "When you came over, only Roone was a vice-president. Now he is a president, and Chuck and Jim Spence are vice-presidents. Well, then, now I am a vice-president, too . . . vice-president of transportation."

Just to keep his drivers aware of who is who, however, Fuchs has taped two pictures to the wall, like "Wanted" posters in the post office. One picture is of Roone, the other of Chuck. Under Roone's is the legend, *"Chef Ein"* ("Boss number one"). Under Chuck's it says, *"Chef Zwei"* ("Boss number two").

There was Fred Schuhmann solving the problem of the empty ice-machine. On our eighteenth floor at the hotel, the ice machine seemed to be perpetually empty, unless you got there very early in the evening. This was a considerable inconvenience for several days until I mentioned it to Fred.

"Very simple," said the vice-president of production services, who solves problems of studios, engineering facilities, cafeteria supplies, or new Olympics uniforms as a matter of daily routine. "Just get it from the nineteenth floor."

I asked him why there was an ample supply on the floor above, if there wasn't here.

"Just look at your room assignment list," he said. "On this floor, almost every living soul is an American and therefore a conspicuous consumer of ice with his drinks. Chuck Howard is the *only* American on the nineteenth floor. The rest are Europeans, who, as you should know, almost never put ice into anything. Ergo, one goes to the nineteenth floor for your ice."

Mostly, this week, for me, has been taken up with the aforementioned pre-Olympics show.

We shot many on-camera pieces at various locations around town, like the busy intersection at the Odeonplatz, past which the marathoners will run; the various Olympic stadia, indoors and out; the little pond in front of the former swimming pool house of the king of Bavaria, another point on the marathon route.

If you are confused by the designation "swimming pool house" for something that belonged to a king of the mid-nineteenth century, let me explain that this little house contains what may very well have been the world's first indoor swimming pool. As you walk through the several rooms, it looks like a sumptuous small residence, with expensive furniture and wall hangings. Then you walk through a door and suddenly find yourself on a small balcony, looking down into a big, empty swimming pool, about twenty yards long by twelve yards wide. On the wall is a huge, ornate faucet, which was used for filling the pool with water from the lake.

At any rate, most of the week was taken up with these things, and finally, yesterday, we went into the tape rooms and studios to put the whole thing together. While Wilson and Ohlmeyer and the associate editors worked with the tape men, I wrote my commentary and narrated it, bit by bit, as each part was ready. Doug was also pulling little pieces of music from his own secret sources, adding them as we went along.

Roone was overseeing all, all twenty hours of the session, which ended for me at 6:30 this morning, and for the others about an hour ago.

The first thing I wrote was what we call the "tease," a hopefully attention-arresting bit of pictures and words that comes on before the announcement of the name of the program or anything else.

In this case, we began with short scenes from Mexico, 1968, and Berlin, 1936, then showed the television tower that symbolizes the games about to begin. We finished the tease with a series of faces:

… but the games in the end will depend on the human beings involved, as they always have, on individuals, like:

Dorando Pietri, staggering into the stadium in 1908 in the marathon, unable to finish, being helped toward the finish line by officials, and then disqualified …

Jim Thorpe, the world's greatest athlete, forced to return his gold medals for playing semi-pro baseball …

Paavo Nurmi, the "Flying Finn," won ten medals, seven of them gold, in the 1920s …

Babe Didrickson was a tomboy out of Texas when she won at Los Angeles in 1932.

This was Jesse Owens in 1936, shaming Adolf Hitler with his talent and quiet dignity …

Bob Mathias, a seventeen-year-old boy, amazed the world by winning the decathlon in 1948 . . .

Cassius Marcellus Clay winning the light-heavyweight gold medal in 1960 at Rome. Even then, he was moving—and talking—like a potential world champion . . .

Al Oerter—four times in a row, he won the gold in the discus . . .

Don Schollander—He did it quicker, winning four golds in *one* Olympics . . .

The feat of Bob Beamon could last a hundred years, breaking the world long jump record by almost two *feet* . . .

And Kip Keino, the cop from Kenya, scoring a historic upset in the 1,500 meters in 1968, beating . . .

Jim Ryun—Ryun, who now returns for one last try, another shot at Keino, a final breathless dash down the stretch, reaching for the rainbow, an Olympic gold medal.

Certain small things come into my mind as I think back over the long session, like my first thoughtful look at the master control room, where so many people—among them Roone, Ohlmeyer, Kamm, Mason, along with the technical directors and the video and audio men—will spend most of the Olympics.

As they sit at the controls, they see a bank of twenty television screens, or monitors, labeled, "Line," "Preview One," "Preview Two," "Matte," "Effects," "Cam One," "Cam Two," "Machine One," "Machine Two," etc.

There are endless audio circuits, and an array of colored control buttons in front of the T.D. that would make a science-fiction movie seem out of date.

Roone has the facility to talk to everybody—producers, directors, and commentators—wherever they may be, at whatever Olympic venue in Munich.

God knows how many hours they will put in, here in this dark, cheerless room, already embalmed with that special canned smell which newly installed air conditioning systems impart to a place.

Sometime in the course of the twenty-hour session, in the middle of the night, it seemed, I looked up and my daughter was standing there with her new friend, Vicki Gifford, Frank's daughter. They had been to the discotheque in the Olympic Village and now had four Canadian swimmers (male) in tow. They were having a marvelous time.

Frank Gifford was there with us all night, by the way. He came with Roone to do his own piece, but stayed to keep us company and marvel at the wonders being performed by the producer, director, and tape editors.

About 3:00 A.M., I went over to the other ABC building, to our own cafeteria. It is not one of our triumphs. The men manning the cafeteria are German sailors in uniform, giving you the feeling that you are eating in a badly run submarine. The sailors' uniforms are smudged wih memories of yesterday's pig's knuckles. The only items left on the menu at this hour are cookies in little cellophane bags (good) and chicken soup (atrocious, unless you like lumps of grease the size of marbles in your chicken soup).

On the walls of the cafeteria are signs hardly worthy of a creative organization: "Happy is the next man's face, when you are sure to clean your place." And, so help me: "This is *your* cafeteria. Please keep it clean." To this moment, at least, the signs are not being heeded—especially by the sailors.

I will remember Doug Wilson, standing in the littered control room of studio B at about 3:30 A.M., all alone except for the audio man and T.D., rumpled and weary, with legs apart, an eye on the monitor and an ear to the commentary I was speaking, pointing at the audio man and saying (I could hear him in my small earpiece), "Ready the flute section and have the woodwinds stand by!" There wasn't an awake musician within many miles, but Doug was referring to some tiny musical sections he had edited together for the past hour or more that he felt would add something to the program.

He was right, but at the time, I neither thought the music worth the trouble it had taken, nor did I see anything amusing or ironic or romantic about the scene. We had been winging along toward completion of the long session at about one o'clock when Doug started searching for the elusive flute part. I had been writing, then recording, writing, recording, in a kind of rhythm. As long as you keep moving in such a pattern, you can go for a long time. I had to stop while Doug tested flute sections.

"Not there. Not quite," he would say to the audio man. "Gee, I hate to bug you with this, but if you could just go back a couple more bars. . . ." And the flute would play from the record, over and over, and over—to the point where I sat in the commentary booth, my head sagging on the table, the flute obligatos piercing my brain like tiny needles, less than painful, but more than ticklish. Finally, I jumped from the chair, flung my notes on the floor and rushed past Doug into Roone's office.

"All right," I said, "Now I'm really sore!"

Roone and Gifford, drowsing in their chairs, had last seen me as a hardworking, rational person about an hour before. Now they saw a haggard, harassed figure—sore, about something.

"What are you sore about?" Roone asked.

"Wilson," I said "Him and his goddamn flutes! What are we doing here, a television program or a flute concert? I am really sore! There comes a time when you do the show or fall asleep. Which do you want?!"

Roone chuckled, which made me angrier. Then I laughed, too. Doug came in and said he was sorry, but the flutes were ready now, if I wasn't too tired.

We did the piece, which was much better with the flutes added.

This sort of thing happens fairly frequently in our group.

Of all the pieces we put together, I think my favorite was the one on the history of the marathon. Obviously, I can't show you the pictures—the strangely moving old newsreel segments Don Ohlmeyer had come up with, the wonderful footage from the Rome Olympics film. I can't re-create here the musical accompaniment—something by Isaac Hayes—which gave the entire piece its dreamlike quality.

I can, at least, recall the words:

You must run the marathon by yourself, every step of the way, or not at all.

In the first modern Olympics at Athens in 1896, Spiridon Loues won Greece's only track gold medal to this day. The king shared his victory . . . but he won it alone.

You must run the marathon by yourself, or not at all.

Fred Lorz won a permanent spotlight of notoriety by accepting a lift in an automobile for part of the course in St. Louis, 1904, and temporarily being acclaimed the winner.

The automobile, remember, was still new at that time, and used primarily as a rescue vehicle in the marathon, as you see it here. But Lorz used it unfairly.

You must run the marathon by yourself, or not at all.

Have you ever had a dream where you are running toward a place you want to reach very much, but the harder you run, the slower your legs move, the heavier they become?

This happened to Dorando Pietri in London in 1908, but it *actually* happened, as this exhausted, confused little man from Italy was turned in the *wrong* direction by officials as he entered the stadium at the end of the marathon.

What could have gone through Pietri's mind as he lay on the track in a state of collapse?

Was he thinking at all when the fluttering, gesturing badge-wearers literally dragged him across the finish line, almost as if *they* were winning the race?

All they brought him was disqualification and near-death in the hour after the race.

You must run the marathon by yourself—and you must run every step of the way.

Forty years after Dorando Pietri, the marathon returned to London in 1948. History repeated itself.

Ettienne Gailly of Belgium entered the stadium in the lead. Four hundred more steps and he was the winner. But his legs were weights of iron. This time, no officials steered him wrong, but none helped him, either, as he was passed by Delfo Carbrera of Argentina . . . and then by Tom Richards of Great Britain.

For Gailly, the gold had faded to bronze . . .

You must run the marathon by yourself—and you must run it in your own way.

Like Abebe Bikila, the Ethiopian palace guard, at Rome in 1960.

Bikila's way was to discard his shoes after the start, to run in his bare feet, as he had done in the mountains of his homeland.

Bikila was alone, but he carried a symbolic message when he finished first at the Arch of Constantine, winning the day at the victory symbol of his nation's conquerors.

You must win the marathon by yourself, on your own two feet and legs.

And at Tokyo, four years later, it was Bikila again, this time with shoes, who made athletic history by repeating his victory, an unprecedented achievement.

Bikila, alone and on his own two feet, winning in Tokyo . . .

Four years later, he failed to finish in Mexico, and since then was the victim of a tragic automobile crash. He is paraplegic and will not run on his own two legs again.

The marathon is more than a race.

It is a nightmare come to life, and you must run it by yourself—or not at all.

In time, I shuffled into the darkness outside our technical center. It was almost dawn, but the moon was still out, a translucent cloud, outlined in black, filtering its bright, reflective rays. The plastic roof over the Olympic grounds was visible, a few lights beneath it making it just possible to discern the great stadium. Poles on the spreading parking lot bore clusters of amber lights, one over the other. In the early morning haze, they looked like great, immobile fireflies standing at attention. It was all silent and anticipatory, like a Christmas garden waiting for the kids to descend, with shouts, in the morning.

That was just hours ago. Now, it is afternoon. Wilson sleeps, Erich talks, Toomey plunges into the pool, and Margaret lies in the sun.

And tomorrow, the games of the Twentieth Olympiad begin with the opening ceremonies.

13

The Olympic Flame—
and the Games Begin

As he had many times before, Chuck Howard said the words in my ear through the small, almost invisible earphone.

"Go Jim," he said.

I started our coverage of the games of the Twentieth Olympiad with these words:

> Was it almost four years ago that the Olympics ended in Mexico? Has it really been that long since the sombreros rustled in the night, since the soft strains of "Las Golondrinas" filled the light air of Mexico City?
>
> Richard Nixon and Hubert Humphrey were engaged in an elec-

tion campaign then. The world was still stunned by the Soviet invasion of Czechoslovakia. All of us were four years younger as the spectators waved their soft farewell to the athletes of all the nations.

The athletes, if you remember, had broken through the barriers restraining them and danced with each other, needing neither common race nor common language to communicate with each other, to say that they had experienced a wonderful time and wished it could go on forever.

But the time had come to say, "*Hasta la vista*" to the Mexicans, to go home, some to retire, to tenderly put the irreplaceable gold medals in a hallowed personal place, others to train and train until the next time, on another continent; then to speak in another language, to hear the cries of "*Willkommen*" in Bavarian dialect . . . in Munich.

The Olympic flame was extinguished, and in the black night, the athletes went home.

These were the words. The pictures were videotape of the closing ceremonies in Mexico. Then, down below in the control room, director Andy Sidaris punched up a camera with a live picture from the stadium in Munich. After all the preparation, our telecast of the Munich Olympics was underway.

As Erich Segal and I sit in the commentary position, a large, temporary wooden platform perhaps twenty feet square constructed especially for ABC, a memorable panorama spreads out before us.

We are high on the rim of the stadium, nestled just underneath the enclosed booths where the other nations will do their commentary. The reason for our outdoor position is so that we can be seen on camera occasionally (the platform is also one of our camera positions). A bonus of the arrangement, though, is the fact that it *is* outside. This always makes me feel less detached from the event. An indoor, glass-enclosed booth gives you the feeling that you are an outside observer, separated from the event and even from the other spectators.

I have always felt that a television reporter should convey the feeling as well as the fact of the event he is covering.

The Olympic Stadium is, of course, filled. Forty-seven thousand are seated (at a legal price of $33, up to $750 per ticket on the black market, we are told). Thirty-three thousand more are standing, packed in as tightly as safety will allow on the "terraces" at either end of the field. Standing room tickets are five dollars.

The great stadium nestles into the expertly landscaped Olympic grounds here on the Oberwiesenfeld. Although we are high above the ground on our side, the opposite side of the stadium is approachable at its very top from ground level. Sitting in full view, then, from our position, are the Sporthalle, on the left, where the gymnastics will take place, and the Schwimmhalle, on the right. Further to the right, there is a softly rising green hill, on which many more thousands of spectators stand, looking at the scene from afar.

And in back of it all looms the television tower, with its revolving restaurant. On the observation platform atop the restaurant, hundreds more are jammed together, looking toward the stadium.

It is a grandiose scene, and yet there is a friendliness and intimacy about it, a pleasantness accentuated by the gorgeous summer weather—blue skies above, the temperature about seventy.

There is no question that the Germans have achieved their first objective—an Olympic grounds that speaks more of Hansel and Gretel than Hitler and Göring.

Beneath the man-made beauty of the scene—the work of 550 architects and engineers, 400 construction companies, and 6,000 workers—lies a typically European historical background.

The land we look at was a farmer's field long ago. More recently, by which I mean 100 years ago, it was a training ground for the troops of the king of Bavaria. By the early 1930s, it was an airplane landing field, principally for light aircraft. It was here that Chamberlain landed on his way to see Hitler. From here he left, having won "peace in our time," he thought.

After those days, the area went swiftly downhill, becoming literally a trash heap. Here, the rubble of Munich was brought after the Allied bombings of World War II. In time the rubble, thought to contain the bodies of many undiscovered bombing victims, formed a great, ugly hill. That hill has now been re-shaped, seeded, and criss-crossed with quiet walks to form the fairyland hillock we see to our right at this moment.

Scattered through the grounds are some 3,000 newly planted trees, mostly lindens, brought from downtown Munich, where they stood in danger of destruction by the bulldozers making new highways and a subway. Many of the linden trees are half a century old, but ninety-nine percent, they tell us, have survived.

Europe is old and it is small compared to America, so it knows that it must hold onto what it has, that it must preserve and conserve, not squander.

The moment has arrived now for the lighting of the Olympic flame; Gunter Zahn, a young German runner selected for his fine build and classic running style rather than his achievements or fame, is circling the running track with the torch, escorted by four other runners—one from Europe, one from America, one from Africa, and one from Oceania.

It is the climactic moment of ceremonies that have been just beautiful to this point, from the moment when the Greeks entered first, as is their traditional right, followed by the other nations in German alphabetical order. Under this system, Egypt ("*Ägypten,*" in German) came just after the Greeks.

For the first time, music characteristic of each nation, 120 in all, has been played as the countries entered the stadium. The music has sounded marvelous as it fills the bowl, emanating from the best public address system I have ever heard.

Comments from the P.A. announcer, a local actor named Joachim (Blacky) Fuchsberger, have been softly spoken and helpful.

It has given me a wonderfully warm feeling to watch the athletes from every corner of the world enter the stadium, smiling, in their native dress—dashikis from Africa, blazers from Britain, Bermuda shorts from Bermuda, ancient tribal garb from Mongolia. (I remember the Mongolians arriving, unannounced, in Innsbruck for the 1964 Winter Olympics, apparently unaware at that time, that you had to enter the games much earlier. They were allowed to compete, and the name of one of their girl cross-country skiers still sticks in my mind. It was Jigjigy Jazvan-dulem.)

Some of the German signs being carried to identify the nations have looked strange to us, such as *"Elfenbeinküste,"* for the Ivory Coast; *"Jungferninseln,"* for the Virgin Islands.

Little Liechtenstein is here, that tiny principality of sixty-two square miles, nestled in the Rhine river valley between Austria and Switzerland. I smiled as their flag-bearer—a very straight, but not young, man—entered the stadium.

During the rehearsal of the parade yesterday, I walked down the line of flag-bearers looking for bits of information. When I came upon the man from Liechtenstein, I asked him who he was.

"Oh," he said, "I am not an athlete. I am Baron Falz-Fein of the Liechtenstein Olympic Committee. The fact is," he lowered his voice, "they are letting me carry the flag as a birthday present. I will be sixty years old during the games."

And there was the baron, proudly bearing the flag of his minuscule homeland. What did de Coubertin say about the Olympics? That the object is not to win, but to take part? Liechtenstein, at least, believes this.

I will confess to a totally unexpected twinge of patriotism—or nationalism, or chauvinism, or sentimentality, or whatever you deem it to be—when the American team walked in.

Olga Connolly carried the flag. Olga, the controversial, outspoken liberal mother of four, wife of hammer-thrower Hal Connolly. Olga, the former Czech athlete who met her husband when both competed in the Olympics.

When the flag came in, I suddenly found that I couldn't talk. I can't explain it in any rational way. I didn't expect it. This hadn't happened to me at any previous Olympics. But this time, I just couldn't say anything, for perhaps twenty or thirty seconds.

The emerging nation of Lesotho entered, with one athlete carrying the flag, followed by three officials. The one-man Olympic team is Matsopi Mourosi, a world-class sprinter. Mourosi was a South African, black in color. Because of his color, and the fact that South Africa has been banned from the Olympic movement for its racial policies, Mourosi quietly moved to Lesotho, an enclave completely surrounded by South Africa. He volunteered as an Olympic team, an Olympic Committee was formed by the country and here he is today, proudly bearing the Lesotho flag, preparing for his upcoming competition with the likes of Valeri Borzov, Eddie Hart, and Lennox Miller.

Yes, I have been aware as the parade progressed of the underlying political maneuvering that preceded it. Rhodesia, is in fact, conspicuous by its absence. The I.O.C. threw them out earlier this week in a total capitulation to the black African nations, all of whom now have stayed for the games.

But politics is not visible in the faces of the athletes, and the opening parade cannot reflect a perfect world when one does not exist. What we are watching does not show us how things are, but how they might be one day. The Olympics are more hope than history.

Now, as the torch-bearer mounts the steps on the far side leading to the receptacle for the flame, I see, from the corner of my eye, my seventeen-year-old son, Sean, sitting on the edge of our platform, his feet dangling over the side. I know now why I thought it was so important to bring my family here. A while ago, I rather remarkably was able to find Margaret and Mary (she's nineteen) in their seats in the stands through my binoculars. Sean is in the booth not through special privilege, but desperation.

The most difficult thing to accomplish this week has been the acquisition of tickets to the opening ceremonies for our families. ABC had a limited number of tickets, which were reserved for a large group of visiting VIP's the network has brought here.

Eventually, I was able to get two seats. These I gave to Margaret and Mary. Sean became a subject for secret operations. Early this morning, he was able to sneak in as far as our graphics room, located under the stands. There he stayed, until what he thought was an appropriately busy moment to make his way to my position. His only vestige of legality was an ABC windbreaker.

Twenty minutes before we were to go on the air, live to the

States, I was crushed when our unit manager, Marshall Lopez, slipped into the booth and said, "Jim, I'm sorry, but Sean got caught. I saw him being hustled out by a guard downstairs."

I felt terrible. Sean had come all this way, taken his chances, and now had lost. A bad lesson for him, not a good one.

At ten minutes until air, I was going over my notes and talking with Chuck about how we would do the opening, when suddenly, I heard a voice behind me.

"Hi, Dad," said Sean.

I have seldom been so glad to see anyone.

"How did you do it?" I asked him.

"Oh, I don't know," he said, in the indefinite way prep school seniors have of explaining things. "I just kept trying different gates and getting thrown out until finally one guy let me get by. Then I climbed over that plastic fence back there. Can I help you guys?"

I told him no, just sit down, stay out of the way, and enjoy.

So all of the family is here.

After the entry of the teams, we saw a welcome to the athletes from 3,200 Munich school children. They had made horseshoes of flowers themselves. They danced with them while singing an old English canon rota, then gave them to the athletes.

It began, then, with the voices of children, greeting the nations to what have already semi-officially been called "the serene Olympics."

The air and the mood and the colors and the music and the costumes all were light and pleasant. Perhaps this would be the Olympics to heal old wounds, to change old images, to suggest that men and nations can change, for the better.

There were short speeches, by Willi Daume, president of the Organizing Committee and old Avery Brundage, serving out his last term as president of the I.O.C. There was the official welcome by the head of the West German State, President Gustav W. Heinemann. Every modern Olympics has been opened by a head of state except at Los Angeles in 1932, when Herbert Hoover found his campaign schedule too heavy to allow a visit to the games.

The Olympic flag has been raised, to a disappointing new arrangement of Spiro Samara's Olympic hymn, composed originally for the first modern games in Athens.

There was a lovely ceremony for the handing over of the official Olympic flag from the Mexicans to the Germans. The Mexicans brought it in to the music of the mariachis and dancing, in brilliant, varicolored costumes, by the Ballet Folklorico Mexicano. They were met at the midpoint of the homestretch on the running track by a little German oom-pah band and Bavarians in *Lederhosen* and those pointed hats with the feather sticking out. Officially, the Germans were called the Vereinigte Bayerische Trachtenkapelle of Bernau and Ruhpolding, the Goasslschnalzer and the Oberbayerische Preisplattler from Berchtesgaden and Chiemgau.

Sometimes I think the Germans make up those words to test commentators.

Everything, as you would expect, is magnificently organized, a wry contrast to the games of 1968 in Mexico. Mexico, a small country not known for efficiency, ad-libbed its way through the Olympics in a way that all of us remember fondly.

It was great to watch them prove that they really could put on the big show.

But there were, unquestionably, ad-lib aspects to it.

Michael Samuelson, an English friend and film maker, was in the stadium at Mexico checking out his camera positions on the day they rehearsed the opening ceremonies. Remember that here, in 1972, they have been arranging the music for a year and a half.

On the day before the games opened in Mexico City, several hundred musicians sat in the empty grandstand. There were so many of them that their conductor had to address them through a loud-hailer. He had not seen them before, these men who had been recruited from all the orchestras of the nation.

Michael Samuelson speaks Spanish, so he was able to understand the leader when he said to his men, slowly and distinctly,

his words echoing off the vacant seats: "Please raise your hands,
all of you who know Beethoven's Ninth!"

The Olympic oath was led by the pretty German girl track
star, Heidi Schuller. She was the first female to administer the
oath to the other athletes:

> In the name of all competitors I promise that we will take part in
> these Olympic Games, respecting and abiding by the rules which
> govern them, in the true spirit of sportsmanship, for the glory of
> sport and the honor of our teams.

The flame has been touched off now, by the young German
athlete dressed in immaculate white. Frankly, the flame and its
receptacle are something less than we had expected, somewhat
on the small side, not particularly artistic in appearance.

The gas jets that feed the flame are visible, sticking up in the
middle in an unattractive way.

The total emotional impact of the ceremonies, though, is just
what you would hope for. Only one more item remains on the
program now, an oracle of the god Apollo, set to music by
Krzysztof Penderecki.

Its words seem appropriate, not as a statement of the world as
it is today, but as an aspiration for Olympiads to come:

> Keep to the old customs: protect your country, avoid war and
> give the world a sign of brotherly friendship whenever the joyful
> time of the four-year games approaches.

All is anticipation. In sixteen days, we will know everything
that has transpired in the games of the Twentieth Olympiad, the
good and the bad, the surprises and the heartbreak.

Now, we know nothing.

SATURDAY, AUGUST 26 (11:00 P.M.)

There are two addenda to today's opening ceremonies.

One is a frustration: for three days, I have been trying to find out from every source I could think of, the names of the four runners who would escort Gunter Zahn when he carried the torch into the stadium. No one knew, but all seemed to assume that they would be purely symbolic men of their continents, as Zahn himself was symbolic.

Sitting high above the track, neither Erich Segal nor I looked at them closely when they entered the stadium. Only tonight did I find out, when Margaret happened to mention it, that two of the four were Kip Keino and Jim Ryun. It is a small thing, but very frustrating, just the same.

The other addendum is something I am glad I didn't know until tonight. Our daughter Mary very nearly didn't get into the ceremonies.

She had a ticket, you will recall. This she tucked into the pocket of her jeans while she and Margaret made their way through the crowd thronging the gates. When they arrived at the first row of gates (there were *four*, at each of which you had to show your ticket), Mary reached for the ticket and it was gone, stolen!

Incredible coincidence intervened. Just as they were about to leave, to go back to ABC and watch on television the ceremony Mary had been looking forward to for a year, Doug Wilson appeared, like a genie from a bottle.

As soon as he found out the situation, he took off his ABC jacket and somewhat in the manner of Sir Walter Raleigh, spread it around Mary's shoulders. Then he presented her with his credential and left, saying that he didn't need anything to get in.

This was a lie and Wilson knew it as he disappeared, swallowed by the 80,000 pushing toward the entrances.

The jacket and credential worked.

About a half hour later, Margaret and Mary were interested to see a prosperous looking man enter their row, clutching a ticket. Quickly, Mary leaned across and looked at it. It was hers, all right.

"That's my seat!" she announced.

The man, who either didn't speak English or didn't want to admit it, made himself very small as he sat down.

There was room for everybody, but whether the well-dressed chap was a thief, or whether he bought the ticket from a pick-pocket for a princely sum, we will never know.

But Mary saw the ceremonies.

14

Double Duty–Gymnastics,
and Track and Field

Certain expressions become almost thematic at long sieges like the Olympic Games.

Here in Munich, it appears that the phrase of the week is "Do you have your yellow ticket?" Whenever you call room service in the Munich-Sheraton Hotel, for whatever meal it might be, they ask you this question. The yellow tickets were issued to us shortly after arrival, and are specifically printed with the date and the meal. In other words, you cannot use an August 29 ticket on August 30, nor a lunch ticket for dinner.

Room service just asked me the question when I called down and ordered a filet mignon and a bottle of beer.

Tonight's gymnastics competition ended a little more than an hour ago. I came right back, and when I arrived, Margaret asked me if I realized I hadn't eaten dinner since last Saturday night.

I hadn't thought about it, remarkable for a man who makes a point of eating three formal meals every day of his life.

The reason has been simple—the busiest schedule I've ever had, and in many ways, the most rewarding. We came to do the Olympics. We've been preparing, as you know, for a long time, and nothing else is really important until we finish. This is one of those rare occasions when food and sleep can come later.

Tonight, however, we pause for a filet and a beer. As we do, I realize that it seems a long time since the last previous dinner on Saturday night. At that time, Margaret, the kids, and I had eaten in the Stube downstairs in the hotel with Doug Wilson, Bill Flemming, and Bob Beattie. It occurred to me then that, in this age of specialization, ABC Sports still expects scope in its people.

Beattie, for example, the ski coach and entrepreneur, must become a kind of instant expert on volleyball and weight-lifting. Flemming has been cramming on a new event here called white-water canoeing. Bill, of course, has been doing things like that for more than eleven years on Wide World.

Twenty-four years and eight months ago, I entered the television business with station WMAR-TV, channel two in Baltimore. It was the first station in the city.

All of us in the production end were newspapermen quickly recruited for TV duty by our employer, The Baltimore Sun-papers, except for one man. His name was Paul Knight. He had previously been with a TV station in Philadelphia, wore a thin mustache, and talked in show business language that we sometimes didn't understand. In the year 1947, these things added together made him a television expert.

During our first month on the air, since we had no studio as yet, we did many different things around town, using our mobile unit. We did sports events, amateur shows, city council meetings, sermons, everything and anything.

For three hours every afternoon, we just pointed a camera out the window of the newspaper building and let the people at home watch the traffic. We got a bit of publicity with that idea when a thief entered a store in full view of the camera, and exited fast, with the police in hot pursuit. It was sort of a news scoop, television's first in Baltimore.

It was a hectic month, and Paul Knight was everywhere. He wasn't pleased with my work. He was friendly and pleasant, but not pleased.

"Jim," he would say, "somewhere in this video game, there is a spot for your announcing talent, but we haven't found it yet."

Paul was a big believer in specialization, the specific man for the specific job.

Then one night, we did professional wrestling from an old barn of an arena call the Coliseum. It was the usual nonsense ("The Super Swedish Angel," a 300-pound, bald, kindly grandfather was cast as the villain in the main event, I remember), and I felt demeaned as I reported on it. I didn't lie, though, doggedly calling it "red" on the man's face, not "blood," since I knew it was liquid dye from a concealed vial, and trying to keep my tongue firmly planted in cheek during the matches.

The next night, we televised a sermon by then-Monsignor Fulton J. Sheen. I served as announcer, quietly commenting from the organ-loft of a Catholic Church. Afterward, our group retired to a bar on Cold Spring Lane to relax and discuss our latest problems.

Paul Knight, however, was truly pleased for the first time all month. Raising his glass of Scotch, he proposed a toast to me.

"Why?" someone asked.

"Because," Knight said, completely serious as he spoke, "we have now found out what Jim can do in this business. You have been just great the last two nights, Jim. We have found your specialties—wrestling and religion!"

Fortunately, ABC Sports takes a broader view, feeling that a reporter, given a reasonable amount of time to prepare, should be able to cover any story.

The first problem as we began our gymnastics coverage was trying to explain to the audience, with some degree of clarity, just how the sport is scored.

The first three days are team competition. Each member of each team competes on all apparatus, first in compulsory exercises, then in optionals where they can devise their own program at will. The lowest mark for each team on each piece of equipment does not count.

While the team competition is going on, the athletes are also *qualifying* for the individual finals later on. In the women's competition, for example, the top thirty-six girls in total marks go on to the individual *all-around final*, in which they all compete again, in one evening, on all pieces of equipment. In addition, the top six finishers on *each* piece of equipment in the team competition go into an individual final on that piece of apparatus. Having tried to explain the situation on Sunday, we then tried to keep score.

Scoring in all sports here in Munich is computerized, and it is well done. However, the scores are computed periodically in gymnastics, not constantly and instantaneously. This means that we must attempt our own speedy calculations.

As we do on Wide World of Sports, we try to tell a running story, to keep you informed on what each performance may mean in the overall picture *as it occurs*. To accomplish this brain-wearying task, I had Tom Maloney, a former U.S. National team coach and one of the sport's true experts, computing figures at my side, along with Bob Kelly, our production assistant.

Tom and Bob fed me the necessary figures constantly, on little pieces of paper that littered the booth after a while. As I did the commentary with our on-the-air expert, Gordon Maddux, I tried to translate the numbers into a reasonably coherent running story.

"If Tourischeva gets a 9.6 here," I would say, for example, "the Soviet girls will take the lead."

The running story is my job, along with trying to point out the human aspects of the competition. I leave all the technical commentary to Maddux. Gordon, who is the gym coach at Los Angeles State College, has been doing an outstanding job at his first Olympics.

Sunday (compulsory exercises for men and women), Monday

(optionals for women), and Tuesday (optionals for men) were complicated days, then. Only when the optionals were finished, did we finally determine the team championships.

In advance, it sounded like a dull aspect of the games, but it didn't turn out that way. The human stories started popping to the surface immediately.

Bright and early on Sunday morning, America's Cathy Rigby appeared for her set of compulsory exercises.

Cathy looked like the big story in this sport for the United States, and possibly one of the great stories of the Olympics. Two years previously, when Wide World covered the World Gymnastics Championships in Ljubjana, Yugoslavia, Cathy had stunned the crowd by taking a silver medal in the individual competition on the balance beam. In fact, it was the first medal of any kind ever won by an American, male or female, in a world gymnastics meet. Since she appeared on Wide World that day almost two years ago, tiny and blonde, in a lime-green costume, Cathy has been written about and photographed more like a pro football star than a gymnast.

Last spring, I went to her home in Los Alamitos, California, and to the tiny gymnasium in the rear of a Protestant church where she trains with her teammates on the SCATS gymnastics team. The room is startlingly small when you first enter it, a great contrast to the beautiful arena here, and its 11,000 spectators.

In the little gym back home, Cathy was relaxed and loose, although she was obviously very tired, with dark circles under her eyes, when she finished her normal seven- to nine-hour day of practice. She was full of confidence, and so was her coach, Bud Marquette.

"Yes, sir," Bud had told me, "She'll win a gold medal in Munich in the balance beam, I really believe it. And four years from now, she'll be the all-around champion."

"If I win a gold medal, will you let me go skiing next winter?" Cathy had asked.

Here in Munich, Cathy's mood has been different. She has looked nervous. At times, her lip has seemed to quiver a bit when she talks. It is understandable, since she carries the hopes of her country totally on the small shoulders of her tiny body. Cathy is four feet, eleven inches tall, and weighs ninety-three pounds.

Some say she has also been shaken by the controversy going the rounds here about a nude action-picture of her in last week's issue of *Sports Illustrated* magazine. Both Cathy and Coach Marquette deny that this has bothered her. The picture was taken about two years ago, in the presence of the coach and Cathy's mother, with their permission. It is one of a series *Sports Illustrated* took, portraying modern athletes nude, the way they competed in the ancient Olympics.

Of course, there were no women in the ancient Olympics. In fact, if a woman was caught trying even to look at the nude men as they competed, she was executed. Still, this was the idea of the magazine story.

Cathy and Bud are satisfied with it, but many people here think that, rightly or wrongly, it has tarnished the image of "America's Pixie," that Bud has previously encouraged.

It was a strange sensation to see 11,000 people gathered in a gymnasium with sunlight streaming through the big window early on a Sunday morning. It made it difficult to realize that every small movement on the various pieces of equipment was just as important to the girls as it would be in the individual finals later in the week. Yet, if you don't perform well in the team competition, remember, you won't even qualify to participate in the finals.

Cathy Rigby made the first big news. It was a bad slip on her favorite event, the balance beam, that slender chunk of wood (four inches wide, resting on metal legs four feet above the floor) on which the girl gymnasts perform their most dangerous exercises. Considering the slip, Cathy got away with a pretty good mark. Still, it meant that more pressure would be on her in the optional phase Monday night.

As a team, the American girls did better than expected. An excellent group performance in the optionals could give them a bronze medal by Monday night. Their competition comes from the Hungarian girls, a very capable team.

MONDAY, AUGUST 28

The Olympics have a new emotional favorite. Out of nowhere, in a matter of a few seconds on the uneven parallel bars, the name, face, and figure of Olga Korbut have become the focus of the story in the Sporthalle. She is the tiniest of all the girls here. Even Cathy Rigby outweighs her by ten pounds.

Since she was a last-minute replacement (one of the Soviet gymnasts had broken her wrist), the Soviet team brochure doesn't include her biography with her famous teammates, Ljudmila Tourischeva and Tamara Lazakovitch. We had to do a rush research job to find out that Olga is seventeen years old, from Grodno, Byelorussia, that she took up the sport at age ten, and went to her first national championship just three years ago.

Her best finish was in the Soviet National Championships last year, when she took second place on the balance beam. Tonight, she looked like a potential Olympic gold medalist. Olga was good on all the equipment, but the arena exploded in sound when she emptied her unexpected bag of tricks on the uneven bars.

She did an upward back-somersault off the higher of the two bars that led to a series of amazing maneuvers, some of which had never been seen before. Gordon Maddux, who brings a marvelous enthusiasm to his expert comments, could only whoop and clap his hand to his head in astonishment.

"Oh, my—wow!" were his exact expert comments.

"What do you think she'll get for a mark?" I asked him.

"I don't know, but I'd give her an eleven!" he said. (Ten is a perfect mark in gymnastics.)

Little Olga smiled, a great broad smile that takes up the entire bottom half of her face, and waved to the crowd like a veteran. She had stolen the show from her teammates, although collectively, they took the team title with ease.

In contrast, Cathy Rigby met disaster. The event in which she hoped to reach the individual finals and have a chance at the gold medal was the balance beam. When she came to that specialty tonight, the Americans were locked in a tight battle with the Hungarians for the team bronze medal. Rather than take a chance on blowing the chances for the U.S. squad, Cathy, after conferring with Bud, left out her most difficult maneuver, an aerial (this is a complete aerial somersault, beginning and ending on the beam). The rest of her routine was fine, but the mark, without the aerial, was not good enough to qualify her for the balance beam final, nor to give the United States third place.

Things happen that suddenly in sport. In the course of one short performance on the balance beam, the Cathy Rigby story ended for these Olympics.

With an even shorter routine on the uneven bars, Olga Korbut, unheard of in America before tonight, is a new household word.

TUESDAY, AUGUST 29

All of the competition was dedicated to the men this time, with the powerful Japanese team easily defeating the Soviet men. The American male team was a tremendous disappointment, performing at less than their potential all through the team competition.

Bud Marquette came to the booth for an interview. He obviously was steaming, said that he had some things to say, all right. I guessed that he might be angry with the American team coach, Muriel Grossfeld. Bad feeling between them has been long and bitter.

But that wasn't it.

Bud was incensed at the judging by officials from Eastern Europe, from the Communist bloc of nations in the women's competition.

On camera, Bud said, "I have no hesitation in saying that this has been the worst rape in the history of amateur sport!"

In the interest of objectivity, Roone immediately asked us to get an interview with someone from the other side.

We found Larissa Latynina, a former great Soviet gymnast, now an official.

Through an interpreter, I told her what Bud had said, and asked for her comment. When the interpreter translated the part about "the worst rape . . ." her face seemed to flush, but she maintained a pleasant smile.

Her answer, whether true or not, was a diplomatic masterpiece: "The American girls," she said, "they are so pretty, so lovely, that I suspect we judge them a little too liberally, if anything. But then, they are so graceful and have such potential that we wish to encourage them, because we feel that one day, very soon, they will be truly competitive with our Soviet champions."

Comrade Latynina could be a capable member of the Soviet diplomatic corps. Perhaps she already is.

WEDNESDAY, AUGUST 30

Now the filet has come, and been eaten, and the beer glass sits empty on the room service table, bits of foam drying on its interior.

It is Wednesday night and, as someone once said, what a difference a day makes.

Olga Korbut, Monday night's Cinderella, carried the metaphor too far tonight.

In the individual all-around championship, she was leading when she moved to the uneven parallel bars. The crowd leaned forward in anticipation. This was where she had brought them to their feet two nights ago, with that sudden display of teen-age virtuosity. Here, already leading, she certainly would wrap up the all-around gold medal for one of the great Olympic stories.

But she didn't. As she swung onto the lower bar to begin her routine, her feet hit the floor, and it was as if the clock began to strike midnight. She swung onto the upper bar, continuing her routine, then missed badly.

You could almost see the carriage turning back into a pumpkin.

But she kept going, and at the end ran, tears running down her face, to her coach, Paolina Ashtakova. It was over. As I watched, I remembered Ashtakova herself, "The Russian Birch Tree" they called her then, crying in Rome in 1960; but her tears were for victory, not defeat.

Doug Wilson, producing and directing, punched up a memorable shot as Olga walked to the next part of the competition. It was a closeup of the small face, chin wrinkled, tears still drying, the eyes seeing only darkness in the future. In youthful despair, there is no tomorrow.

They reached the balance beam, where Olga would perform next, and, as she slumped into a chair, a woman left her place in the stands, waved off a guard, and walked toward Olga.

Where she had gotten the flowers I don't know, but she had them in her hand. She gave them to the little girl, with a sympathetic word and a gesture of compassion, then went back to her place.

I don't know who the woman was, but here, in the most public of places, it was very much like a mother kissing a child's bruise, to make it better.

THURSDAY, AUGUST 31 (11:45 P.M.)

The filet again sits on the room service table as I try to think how to organize my thoughts. This has been a day of fantasy become reality.

It began with routine at ten this morning in the Olympic outdoor stadium, turned to nightmare in the late afternoon, then reverted to fairy-tale in the evening. On each occasion, there were many witnesses; 80,000 in the stadium this morning for qualifying heats in track and field; 80,000 again this afternoon; and the usual 11,000 plus in the Sporthalle for the gymnastics tonight.

I suppose the only way to tell the story is chronologically.

The lobby of the Munich-Sheraton was jammed this morning. For the first day of track and field competition, an additional wave of people had washed into the hotel from everywhere, it seemed. There were men in fezzes, and others in straw skimmers with bands made to resemble the Union Jack of Great Britain. There were Africans in tribal headdresses and Mexicans in sombreros. It was almost as if the opening day's parade was going to reassemble there in the hotel.

"Jim, hey, Jim!" someone called through the crush around the concierge's desk.

I turned, and there, almost invisible among the milling people, was little Jackie Stewart. I had left him in Indianapolis less than three months ago, but it seemed a long time. Since then, the Scotsman had been hospitalized with that bleeding ulcer, had fought his way back, and had resumed motor racing after a midsummer layoff.

And here he was at the Olympics.

"I'm only here for the day," he said, "but I had to see something of the Olympics."

Jackie is a sports fan as well as a participant. We had just missed him at the British Open in July. He had come out of the hospital near his home in Switzerland to see the tournament for one day, before going down to London to receive the O.B.E. from Queen Elizabeth. The world of sport spins more quickly every year, it seems, and Jackie spins right along with it.

Then he was gone into the crowd, and I went to the car where Henry Meyer was waiting to drive me to the Olympic Stadium. Henry is a young South African student assigned as my driver here. He comes from a German-speaking part of South Africa, so his English is acquired. His accent is unusual, not Germanic, more like old-British-Army-officer seasoned with a touch of Carnaby Street. His favorite word is "fantastic."

"Fantastic!" Henry said, as we reached the Olympic grounds and saw the crowd pushing toward the entrance gates.

On this crisp, pretty morning, I was not prepared for the sight of the stadium. At 9:45 in the morning, for a program that included only qualifying in women's long jump and javelin throw, and heats in men's 100 meters and 400-meter hurdles, the bowl was filled to the brim. I had heard that the Olympics were a virtual sellout in advance, but somehow I had assumed that did not include these morning sessions with no finals. I suppose I was prepared for a crowd of 15,000 or 20,000 people. Instead, here was a throng filling the stadium, 80,000 strong, just as at the opening ceremonies. Each seated person was paying the equivalent of sixteen dollars to watch qualifying action.

On the platform, our little band of commentators was assembled for the first time. I was seated on a stool, from which I could watch the monitors in front of me and consult my notes, while at the same time have a good general view of the stadium. The experts took turns using another stool to my left—Bill Toomey for the sprints, hurdles, and field events; Marty Liquori for middle-distance races; Erich Segal for long-distance running and erudition; Fred Thompson for the women's events.

Two athletes, a professor, and a lawyer. To my right sat Jim Dunaway. Jim is the Eastern editor of *Track and Field News*, the sports' authoritative publication in the United States. He is also an ad man and frequently published magazine writer (*Esquire, Sports Illustrated*, etc.). Jim has worked with me on statistics, information, and timings for five or six years now, including the Mexico City Olympics. To his right, working in something of the same areas for producer Chuck Howard was Fred Baer, a West Coast Dunaway, a real expert on the sport.

With Chuck and Andy Sidaris in the control room, and Roone back at the studio master control point, we were ready to go.

Chief attraction for the Germans this morning was the appearance of Heidi Rosendahl in the long jump. The West German girl didn't let her fans down. Before the day was done, she had won the gold medal, by *one* centimeter (that is just about the width of your little fingernail).

The American focus was on the men's events—making sure that our three entries made it safely through the first round in the hurdles and the 100 meters. They all did, but in the 100, young Reynaud Robinson, in his first Olympics at age twenty, pulled up after qualifying, and there was an unconfirmed report that he might be slightly injured. One person said they thought he had pulled a hamstring.

Still, the morning was without major incident. The afternoon figured to be the same, with finals scheduled only in the ladies long jump and the 20-kilometer walk. Mentally, I was already looking forward to the evening, when I would be working on the women's individual finals in gymnastics.

Basically, we were recording today's track and field events just to be on the safe side, to make sure that we were showing the pictures and saying the words in case some totally unexpected occurrence should pop up.

In fact, the major subject for conjecture among us was whether the Olympic officials would allow Dave Wottle to compete in the 800-meter heats while wearing his golf cap. Marty Liquori thought they might not, that it would be a potential danger to following runners if it should fly off.

Dave appeared on the track with the cap, ran, and qualified easily for the next round. There were no questions asked about the now-familiar cap.

Some drama developed, though, in another heat of the 800. Rich Wohlhuter, a 1971 Notre Dame graduate, had surprised everyone by qualifying for the games. He looked very good in doing so at the trials, coming off turn four with a fine closing kick to make the team, helping to squeeze out Jim Ryun in the process.

Today, Wohlhuter brought the crowd to life when he suddenly fell down on the backstretch of the first lap. He lost many yards before getting to his feet, and seemed to be out of it. But he kept plugging, cheered on by the 80,000 now. By turn four of the second and final lap, he was in position to move into the top three (three in each heat qualified for the next round).

He kicked, although you could see that he was panting, laboring. He moved into the top three and the crowd cheered louder, until he finally ran out of gas with a couple of meters to go, and missed qualifying by a step.

Then came the second round of heats for the 100 meters, the quarterfinals. The semis and the final would be tomorrow.

The first heat was called at 4:15 in the afternoon. Rey Robinson would be in this one for the United States . . . or would he? As the athletes took off their sweat clothes, Robinson was not there. An official went out and removed the marker with the lane number from behind his position.

"Well," I said, "It looks like the reports about Robinson are true. He did pull up this morning, and now, apparently, can't make it for this round. A tough break for Rey and the United States' hopes of holding onto that 100-meter gold medal against the likes of Borzov."

The next heat was called. Eddie Hart would be in this one for the United States.

But Eddie wasn't there, either.

The block was removed from his lane, while Dunaway and Baer shrugged their shoulders at me, and Toomey and I admitted that we had no idea why Eddie wasn't there. Another injury seemed to be the only logical explanation.

The heat went off without Hart, and the United States was now down to one athlete in the classic event the country has dominated since the origin of the modern Olympic Games.

Heat three was called. We leaned forward on our stools, straining to see the runners as they emerged from the tunnel onto the track.

Robert Taylor was there. At least he had made it. The swift, strong-running flanker back for Texas Southern University had only qualified third in the Olympic Trials, but Hart and Robinson had to tie the world record to beat him out, and Robert had other credentials. He beat Borzov on a relay anchor leg back in 1970, and in recent weeks, on his way to Munich, he had defeated Robinson, Jean-Louis Ravelomanantsoa of the Malagasy Republic and Don Quarrie of Jamaica in a 100-meter race in Oslo.

Taylor is good, then, some think potentially the best of the three Americans, but as he jogged near the starting line this afternoon, concern was evident in his facial expression. He shook his head as he warmed up, sucked in deep breaths and blew them out, like a man who is tense, nervous.

It was just at that time that Chuck Howard spoke into my earpiece from the control room in the stadium.

"Jim," he said, as I continued commentary, identifying runners as they moved into place, "Jim, I can hardly believe what I'm going to tell you, but it comes from our guys at the center, so it must be true. Here's what they say happened.

"About ten minutes ago, these American athletes wandered into the lobby of Barnathan's Bungalow, just outsde Fuchs's car-dispatching office. The first heat was up on the monitor and one of the guys casually asked if we were rerunning the first round heats from this morning on tape. Somebody said no, this was live. The athletes said it couldn't be, that they were the American runners and had been told the quarterfinals were much later this afternoon.

"Everybody suddenly realized what was happening. ABC put the kids in a car and the driver busted his rear getting them over here. It was too late for Robinson and Hart. Taylor just ran from the car to the starting line."

No wonder Taylor looked nervous!

It still seemed impossible that Reynaud and Eddie had missed the greatest opportunity of their young lives as simply as a commuter missing the 8:02 train from Westport because his time table is out of date. But this was the fact.

Taylor ran a courageous, impressive race under the circumstances, qualifying handily for tomorrow's semifinals. He'll be going it alone against Borzov, Lennox Miller, and all the rest.

As the afternoon went on, more facts on the story were relayed. Stan Wright, coach of the American sprinters, took full responsibility for the unbelievable error. It was he who told the runners to go over to the stadium and warm up about 4:30 or 5:00 for a 6:15 quarterfinal. Stan said that he was working from an old schedule, a single sheet of blue paper on which all of the track and field starting times were listed. The schedule, issued about a year ago, was out of date. Changes had been made, and, of course, printed in all the new schedules.

The one I was using was in a handy, light green booklet issued to the press, called, "Who? When? Where? What? How?"

On page 119, under the heading, "31.8 Thursday" (Thursday, August 31), in very clear type, it said, "16.15 . . . 100 m. men . . . 2nd round."

In the European manner of keeping time, "16.15" means 4:15 in the afternoon. At first we thought that coach Wright might have confused 16:15 and 6:15. Many Americans do this, and had done it this week in Munich. But Stan said this wasn't the reason. He had simply used the old schedule.

In an interview in our studio with Howard Cosell, he said that the blame was all his, that he could only take full public responsibility and apologize to the boys for what had happened.

In a sense, it was more a personal tragedy for Stan than for the runners. They at least knew that they were not at fault. Stan will have to carry the memory of this day always, and there is no way to erase it or modify the results.

It was a mistake that will make the Olympics history books, along with the officials who pointed Pietri the wrong way in the marathon in 1908 and the other classic gaffes.

Many had thought that Stan might be the first black head coach of a U.S. Men's Olympic Track and Field Team in Montreal for the 1976 games. Whether today shattered that hope only the next few years will tell, but it seems likely.

It seems certain that Stan Wright will lie awake long hours in his room in the Olympic Village tonight, trying to find some rationale, some explanation for a mistake simple in its execution, but disastrous and far-reaching in its effect.

There is no explanation.

The games of the Twentieth Olympiad have their first major controversy in the storm surrounding Stan Wright's classic error.

Had ABC not been documenting the early rounds of competition, we would have missed the story, of course. More important, if we had not been covering those quarterfinals, the runners could not have seen them on the monitor at the Bungalow. Robert Taylor would have missed his heat also, since the Americans would have been strolling leisurely toward the stadium.

Robert Taylor would also have missed his heat if the ABC personnel had not put the runners into our staff car and raced them over to the stadium. In an effort to stay on top of a story, then, we have ended up right in the middle of it.

Like everyone else, we in the booth were stunned by the happening, but the events went on. Heidi Rosendahl received a tremendous ovation when she accepted her gold medal, an opening day triumph for the home team. Then there were heats in the 800 for women, and heats in the 10,000-meter run. By the time it was over, it was past seven o'clock in the evening.

The second part of my day was about to begin.

As the crowd dispersed outside the stadium, I jogged in the darkness toward the Sporthalle a few hundred yards away. I was carrying an airline bag on each shoulder, one filled with track notes, the other dedicated to gymnastics.

I had weighed them at the hotel this morning out of curiosity, and together they weigh ten kilos, or 22.2 pounds. That adds up to a lot of words, and the way things are going now, I may use them all before the Olympics are over.

I jogged and I realized how exhilarated I was feeling. The results of this day so far had not been pleasing to me as an American, but as a reporter, I had to feel an inner excitement. In my mind, it is a great privilege to have the job of reporting the events of a memorable day in the small world of sport to a viewing audience that we are beginning to hear is one of the largest ever to see sports in the United States (therefore, in the world).

The viewing audience in the early days of Wide World of Sports wasn't all that large, but the events were often memorable just the same. Jogging through the darkness this evening with the two bags of notes, I thought back to some of our earliest track and field coverage, the U.S.–Russian track meets of the early 1960s.

In 1961, our first summer on the air, ABC Sports flew twenty tons of equipment and half a hundred technicians to Moscow. Everything had to be taken, not only cameras and sound equipment, but bulky videotape machines (the Russians did not have tape at that time) and even a big generator to provide our own power, since the Soviet electrical system is not compatible with ours.

Clearance to bring in the equipment was only obtained after it had already left New York and was sitting, waiting in the Amsterdam airport.

Videotape turned out to be almost as big an attraction to the Russians as the track meet was. Underneath the stands, an informal control room was set up, in full view of anyone walking on the entrance ramps that spiraled up to the top of that part of Lenin Stadium.

When some of the crowd looked down and saw taped images playing on the control room monitors, word spread quickly, and soon, there were several thousand people watching our videotape operation instead of the live track meet.

The track meet was well worth watching, and its climax is what sticks in the mind. On a Sunday evening, all of the competition was finished, except for the high jump. Valeri Brumel, who had surprised in the Rome Olympics the year before by winning a silver medal, was about to try for a world record.

(Quiz question: If Brumel only took the silver when John Thomas was upset as the hottest favorite in the Rome games, who won the gold?

Answer: Robert Shavlakadze, another Soviet athlete, a slender man with a tiny mustache, remember?)

Brumel missed his first attempt as rain began to fall in the darkening stadium. The rain became a near-deluge as he quietly prepared for his second attempt.

He missed again, and in the control room, Roone, producing the show, began to wonder if there would be enough light for our camera to see the final attempt. Actually, the worry seemed academic, because it looked impossible for Brumel to clear the height in the pelting downpour.

The light just held as Valeri stood, moving his fingers slightly, as he always did, took that final small breath, and ran toward the bar. He cleared it, and the great crowd, sitting exposed to the rain, roared for minutes. (Our commentary position was exposed, too, but someone had brought an immense piece of clear plastic and spread it over our heads as we watched.)

It was memorable, and so it was the next year when Brumel came to Palo Alto, California, and set another world record in the U.S.–Russian meet.

In 1963, we returned to Moscow again. And again, we reached the same moment. Again, it was Sunday evening, but the weather was pleasant this time. Again, everything was finished, except for Brumel, except for another try at a world record.

In an official box, high on the rim of Lenin Stadium, Nikita Khrushchev stood, with his guest, American Ambassador-at-large and Kremlin expert Averell Harriman.

There was political significance to Khrushchev's choice of activity and guest on this day. The night before, the Soviets had concluded a long series of discussions with their allies the Chi-

nese. In retrospect, it was one final effort to preserve a crumbling relationship.

On this Sunday afternoon, the Chinese had left from the Moscow airport for home. Normally, Khrushchev would have been there with school children and flowers and protestations of Socialist solidarity.

Instead, on this particular afternoon, he decided to go to a track meet with the American who had specialized in U.S.–Soviet relations since World War II.

With the high jump bar set at seven feet, five and three-quarters inches, almost a foot and a half higher than Brumel's head, most of the crowd rose for a better look. So did Khrushchev and Harriman.

The little motion of Brumel's fingers again, the breath, the run—and again he was over, the third world record for him in three successive years of U.S.–Russian meets.

His teammates, male and female, smothered him with kisses (an old Russian custom). An old lady in a blue work dress, assigned to rake the high jump pit, enclosed Brumel in a great bear hug.

And high above the field, Khrushchev and Harriman, representing the two greatest antagonists in the world of international politics, cheered and slapped each other on the back.

Then Khrushchev hugged Harriman.

15

More Gymnastics and
More Track and Field

Now, I was walking through the press room of the Sporthalle, on my way to report on the latest chapter in the young life of another Soviet athlete, a mere tadpole suddenly playing the role of sports giant—Olga Korbut.

On Monday, she had been the unknown bursting like a star shell in the night. Last night, she had been the personification of shattered adolescent dreams—living proof that midnight always comes for Cinderella. What would tonight bring?

Doug Wilson, Gordon Maddux, Tom Maloney, and Bob Kelly were waiting for me at the commentary platform. The track events had run so late that I arrived in the gymnastics arena only forty-five minutes before the competition would get underway.

We had a brief production meeting, then I went over my

notes. Gordon Maddux and I did an on-camera introduction to the night's events on videotape. Thank heaven it was on tape, because I finally did what I had told Gordon I was sure to do at least once before the week was out: I introduced him as *Lester* Maddux.

This was the night of the women's individual event finals. This meant that a gold medal would be awarded for the vault, another for the uneven bars, another for the balance beam, and finally, one for free exercise. Four gold medal opportunities for the Russians and the East Germans, whose star is Karin Janz. She is listed in the East German information booklet as a medical student and member of the People's Police. That seems like a strange combination, but one thing is certain: she is a marvelous gymnast.

There were no Americans scheduled to perform, Cathy Rigby having failed to qualify even for her specialty, the balance beam.

For the Russians, it was a personal confrontation for their three stars, representing, in a sense, three swift generations of Soviet gymnastics. Two years ago, Ljudmila Tourischeva was in a class by herself in Russia. Last year, Tamara Lasakovitch was the sudden new star. And now, Olga Korbut.

What makes it more interesting is that Tourischeva is nineteen years old, Lasakovitch is eighteen, and Korbut is seventeen. One wonders what sixteen-year-old is lurking in the wings somewhere back in the Soviet Union.

The evening began interestingly, but not spectacularly, before the capacity crowd, when Karin Janz won the vault. The vault is not an exciting event, at best.

Then they moved to the uneven bars, where Olga Korbut had flashed to fame one night, and had embarrassed herself to tears the next time. Now, she would have a final chance. Would it be a medal of gold at the foot of the rainbow, or a lump of coal in the Christmas stocking?

It was the Olga of Monday night, smiling, confident, whipping around the bars in her special, unprecedented way. When she finished, and stood with arms upraised, smiling the bottom half of her face at the crowd, they stood and shouted and stamped like an old Judy Garland crowd. Her mark was 9.8, only .2 from perfection, but it wasn't good enough for the new-found idolators of Olga. They whistled at the mark, and booed. They refused to let the competition go on.

For at least ten minutes, they conducted their raucous lobby to raise Olga's mark. The judges, in self-defense, held a meeting, but they refused to change the mark. Olga was not the winner. The gold medal was still just beyond her short reach.

Two more events were left.

As they marched to the balance beam, I glanced around and noticed that Sean had materialized in the back corner of the commentary platform. Earlier, I had noticed that Mary was in the stands. Again, I was glad that they were around to share what was already an exciting evening. Sean had been in the stadium all day. (I must ask him tomorrow how he got in this time.)

There are six finalists in each of the individual events. They perform, not by seeding, but by a blind draw. The luck of the draw placed Olga Korbut last in the balance beam competition. The 11,000 could hardly remain patient while the other five performed. They were waiting for Olga.

In time, she walked forward, straight, serious, concentrating only on the slender four-inch beam. This is generally considered the most dangerous of the women's gymnastics events, particularly since the advent a few years ago of the aerial. It was the omission of the aerial, you will recall, that probably cost Cathy Rigby her chance to be here tonight.

Olga Korbut, being last, knew, as the crowd did, that she needed a 9.9 to win the gold medal. Her performance, in an arena populated by motionless, totally silent watchers, grew in difficulty and smoothness as it went along. The only sound was the occasional squeak of her shoes as she pivoted on the bar. She did swift-moving acrobatics and slow, graceful ballet movements.

Gordon Maddux could hardly look as she neared the end, because he knew that her final move was an aerial, followed by a forward somersault dismount. When it came, it was a masterwork of showmanship. She flipped over, off the bar, back onto it, then forward through the air, landing on the floor, arms again outstretched, the smile bursting on the crowd, which leaped to its feet, almost as if on a signal, bombarding the little girl with their tribute.

Her mark was almost a foregone conclusion. It would have taken a brave judge, indeed, to give her anything except what she got—9.9, and an Olympic gold medal.

She marched to the music now, with the others, to the final event, free exercise. This is very much like dancing, complete with musical accompaniment. She would be next to last in the women's competition in the 1972 Olympic gymnastics. Fate takes care of its friends.

The others went ahead, and they were excellent, one after the other. Tourischeva, queen of her world two years ago, gave one of the finest performances of her career. Still, the crowd waited for Olga.

When she mounted the platform, she looked like a favored grandchild about to say her piece for the old folks. Her music was Western and popular, light, rather than the classical music used by most of the girls. She flipped and pirouetted, hamming it up just the least bit. She looked like a little kid playing in the sun.

She won another gold medal, of course, although, frankly, I think Tourischeva was better in that final event. Since none of the judges was bent on suicide, though, Olga was the winner.

The victory stand was quite a picture—Olga standing on the top step, smiling and waving, living in a world where everyone was her friend. She didn't notice the girls standing next to her, the winners of the silver and bronze medals.

They were her teammates, Ljudmila Tourischeva and Tamara Lasakovitch. The impassive Ljudmila wore a face of stone, while Tamara stood, tall, blonde and straight, silent, with a tear running down the inside of her right cheek. You had the feeling that they would return to fight another day.

Olga didn't see them at that moment, and perhaps it was just as well. Everyone should have a perfect moment in his life, even if it is, in part, illusory. This was Olga's. She had seen triumph, then disaster, then total victory. In a few short days, little Olga had seen it all.

As she stood there, late tonight, waving and smiling while the crowd roared on, all that seemed to be missing was a full symphony orchestra playing "Over the Rainbow."

FRIDAY, SEPTEMBER 1 (11:00 A.M.)

Peter Dimmock, the BBC executive and sports commentator, dropped by today with the "morning line" on the Olympics track and field events. Peter displayed clippings from London newspapers advertising the wares of legal bookmakers, quoting odds, for the first time, on the Olympics.

For the record, here are some of their favorites:

Borzov is now favored to win the 100 meters, although up until yesterday's starting time foul-up, they were betting on both Eddie Hart and Reynaud Robinson to beat the Ukrainian.

Wayne Collett of the United States is a 5–4 favorite to win the 400, followed by John Smith of the United States and David Jenkins of Britain. Vince Matthews, the other American in the race, is at 12–1.

Jim Ryun is the 7–4 selection to win the 1,500, followed closely by Keino at 9–4. Pekka Vasala of Finland is third choice at 6–1.

Ladbroke's, the bookie I am quoting, thinks Lasse Viren of Finland will win both the 5,000 and 10,000 meters. They see Steve Prefontaine as no better than fourth in the 5,000.

America's Ralph Mann is picked to win the 400 hurdles.

Britain's Ron Hill is the marathon selection at 5–1. Frank Shorter of the United States is a 12–1 shot.

Oddly, neither Ladbroke's, nor Corals, nor William Hill, the other advertising bookmakers, are quoting any odds on the 800-meter race, in which the Soviet Arzhanov is favored. No one seems to know why that might be.

There are some attractive long shots in the listings, like Jim Seymour of the United States (14–1), and John Akii-Bua of Uganda (25–1) in the 400 hurdles; Shorter and Mamo Wolde of Ethiopia, both at 12–1 in the marathon.

FRIDAY, 11:00 P.M.

This was my last day of double duty on track and field and gymnastics.

Again, there was unexpected news in the qualifying aspect of competition. It came in the pole vault, which has been a matter of controversy since the opening ceremonies, and even before.

Bob Seagren, the defending gold medalist, set a world record in our Olympic Trials using a fiberglass pole of fairly recent development, manufactured in the United States. Shortly thereafter, the International Track and Field Federation said the record would not be recognized, because the pole Seagren used had not been available for at least one year to the rest of the world. It sounded suspiciously like retroactive rule-making. Furthermore, the International Federation said Seagren could not use his new pole in the Olympics. Since then, the officials have reversed themselves several times on the subject.

This morning, they came up with a totally new gimmick. According to Seagren, Kjell Isaksson, and other vaulters, they were met by an official before this morning's qualifying phase and asked to hand over their poles. The implements were taken into another room and tested on some new machine, the nature of which is not clear. Then the poles were brought back out, and each athlete was told whether his pole was acceptable or not, but with no explanation.

The poles of Seagren, Isaksson, Chris Papanicalaou (the Greek who was the first man to vault eighteen feet), and several others were declared illegal.

Seagren qualified for tomorrow's final using a different pole, but some did not make it, including Isaksson, Papanicalaou, and Steve Smith, of the U.S.

Seagren's chief competition tomorrow, then, should come from Wolfgang Nordwig of East Germany. Interestingly, Nordwig's pole was found to be legal; interesting because the original protest against Seagren's new pole was lodged by the East German federation.

Isaksson came up for an interview with me later in the day. Before the camera, he declared his disgust with the whole operation, in halting English, calling it "totally unfair." When he was finished, and we were walking out of the studio, I thanked him for coming up and said I was very sorry that this tough break had knocked him out of the games.

"Oh, well," said the young Swede, suddenly rather casual, "It doesn't really matter. I was injured anyway!"

If the officials have their secrets, the athletes have theirs, too.

Seagren is uninjured, but steaming. He thinks the whole intrigue over the poles is a brazen effort to deprive the United States of the pole vault gold medal for the first time in the history of the Olympics.

Another traditional American fiefdom went by the boards this afternoon, but the rule-makers had nothing to do with it. As Eddie Hart and Reynaud Robinson watched helplessly on the sidelines, Valeri Borzov of the Soviet Union made believers of us all when he powered his way to victory in the 100 meters. Robert Taylor was a valiant silver medalist. Lennox Miller, of Jamaica, who took the silver in Mexico, got the bronze this time.

Borzov, the pride of the Ukraine along with his teammate, Arzhanov, is quite literally, a picture-book runner. Even at this stage of his development, the twenty-two-year-old sprinter studies sequence photographs of himself and other great runners in action. He and his coach, Boris Voitas, study films at regular speed, slow motion, and stop action. Then Borzov repairs to the training track and painstakingly makes the pictures come to life.

Sprinters seldom are made. They tend to have a great natural talent, which then is honed to a fine edge. Distance runners can be made, but not sprinters.

Borzov is the exception. He started as a long jumper, was converted to sprinting at age seventeen by coach Voitas. There is a mechanical look to him when he runs, but it is one beautiful, smoothly oiled machine. And there is something else. Inside the machine is a strong, dedicated, positive-thinking human.

The combination gives the appearance of invincibility.

So, the blue-eyed, blonde-haired Borzov, born the son of an Army officer in Novaya Kachovka, Ukraine, is the successor to Thomas Burke (winner of the first 100 meters in 1896), Charley Paddock (first man dubbed "The World's Fastest Human"), little

Eddie Tolan, Jesse Owens, Bob Hayes, and Jim Hines. Add to those the names of Frank Jarvis, Archie Hahn, Ralph Craig, Harrison Dillard, Lindy Remigino and Bobby Joe Morrow and you will have a list of all the Americans who have won the 100-meters gold medal in the modern games.

The list of Russians who have won the event, or even a silver or bronze medal in the 100, for that matter, begins and ends with Valeri Borzov, the world's fastest human in 1972.

There was more bad news for the United States when Madeline Manning failed to make it through the second round of the women's 800-meter run. A gold medalist four years ago, she had made a tough comeback effort. It came up a little short.

No Americans qualified in the steeplechase, but that was no surprise.

There was a surprise on the positive side when Kathy Schmidt, an 18-year-old girl from Long Beach, California, became the first American woman to win a javelin medal since the great Mildred (Babe) Didrickson (later Zaharias), in Los Angeles, in 1932. Kathy Schmidt took the bronze today, the first chance for American cheering in the track and field aspect of these games.

Tonight, the gymnastics concluded with the men's individual competition. After last night's drama, anything would have been an anticlimax. There was slight surprise when the powerful Japanese men's team won only three of the six gold medals available. Many people thought they would sweep them all.

Still, the talk was of last night, and our booth became the center of attention for a few minutes when we brought in Olga Korbut for an interview. Tom Maloney had been talking with her earlier in the day and was surprised to find that she spoke quite acceptable English. For the interview, however, the Soviets said that she would speak in Russian, "to make a better interview," they said.

That's what they always say. Igor Ter-Ovanesian, the famous Soviet long jumper, speaks English with an American accent. Through all the years, though, he has been ordered to do his television interviews in Russian.

Interviews through an interpreter are always tough. In this case, it was especially difficult to try and capture the thoughts and vocal nuances of a seventeen-year-old through the utterances of her interpreter, who was a small, tight-lipped, unsmiling man.

Before we started the interview, I asked him if he were Russian.

"Not at all," he said, "I am very much German."

It sounded like he thought I was trying to trap him, which I wasn't.

"Oh," I said, "Good. Well, are you working as the official interpreter for the Russians?"

He shook his head. "No, indeed," he said. "I am simply host to the Soviet athletes."

"In fact," he said, "it might interest you to know that my wife is American. We met at Kansas University, and although we have since lived in the Soviet Union for a short period, I am very much a German."

I asked him what he had been studying in Kansas.

"Russian," he said.

However, Olga conquers all here in Munich, and there she stood in her blue Soviet team jacket with Russian characters on the front that look like "CCCP." She pointed to some pins she was wearing on her collar. One was an American flag. The other two were a "Wide World of Sports" pin and an "ABC, Munich" pin.

Even through the crisp, businesslike translation of the old Jayhawk from Kansas, Olga's personality emerged. She said nothing startling or revealing, just the self-conscious comments you would expect from a seventeen-year-old on national television.

When, at the end, I asked her where she would like to visit in the United States, her expression looked very much like *she* might be from a small town in Kansas.

"I would like very much to see New York," she said.

In a time when some American teen-agers think of big cities as sinks of iniquity, cesspools of corruption, filled with nothing but muggers, pollution, and people over thirty, it was somehow incongruous and refreshing to hear the little girl from Grodno say that she would most of all like to see the big town.

The gymnastics phase of the games of the Twentieth Olympiad is finished. At eleven P.M. we stand outside the mobile unit, in the dark, saying goodbye again.

We do that a lot at ABC Sports. Almost every week on Wide World, we are saying farewell to some group of people somewhere, to see them again in a year, perhaps sooner, perhaps not at all. This time it was to the German technicians who had manned our cameras and audio facilities for the gymnastics.

Doug Wilson, predictably, with the help of unit manager Charlie Baldour, had provided some champagne for the occasion.

Along with the Germans (from Radio Free Berlin) stood Doug and Charlie, Gordon Maddux and his wife, Tom Maloney, Bob Kelly, and Mary and Sean and I.

It was Mrs. Maddux, a quiet lady, who unconsciously summed up our operation. As she was handed her drink, she looked down at it, then smiled, and said, "Oh. Champagne in paper cups."

That could be the title for a history of ABC Sports. We live a great deal of our lives in tape rooms, darkened stadia, and littered control rooms, drinking out of paper cups.

But what we do is often exhilarating, such as this week in the Sporthalle, and what we drink is often champagne.

16

Track and Field

The world of a commentator gets smaller and smaller as the Olympics progress.

There are competitions in twenty sports going on all over Munich (the yachting is far away in Kiel). When I pass through the ABC center, I hear reports about boxing ("The officiating has been horrible. Five officials are going to be fired."); swimming ("Mark Spitz looks like he'll win seven golds. He may not have much charm, but he sure can swim."); wrestling ("Dan Gabel looks like a lock for a gold, and some of the other guys are surprisingly good.").

Brief reports are all I hear, though.

My world has narrowed down to our room at the Munich-Sheraton; the great Olympic Stadium, from 9:00 A.M. to 7:00 P.M.; and the ABC production center, to do commentary on the field events live during the transmission to the States from 1:00 to 4:00 A.M.

One other daily way station, and a welcome one, is the sauna and the swimming pool in the basement of the hotel. I get some heat and a swim there every morning. It really relaxes the bunched-up muscles from the previous day.

At the stadium, we have begun to feel that the crowd of 80,000 is simply there all the time, twenty-four hours a day. That isn't true, of course. In fact, the stadium is filled and emptied three times each day; for morning track, for the afternoon session, and for a soccer game at night.

The weather continues to be glorious, and the results? Well, there is tremendous variety in them. One thing is certain. The United States will not stage its traditional parade to the gold medal platform all week long, but then, that was expected before we came here. The rest of the world is catching up with us.

In the first five days of track and field, the twelve gold medals in men's events have been shared by eight countries—East Germany, West Germany, Soviet Union, United States, Czechoslovakia, Uganda, Finland, and Kenya. Winners have come from the frozen north and the steaming tropics, from Bowling Green, Ohio, and Novaya Kachovka, Ukraine.

The Russians have five men's gold medals, but including the women's events, the home team West Germans have a surprising five. The United States has only one.

It is an Olympics to interest all the world, not just the two great powers. The Olympic ideal of the individual is emphasized by the triumphs of an unorthodox hurdler from Africa and a distance-running policeman from Finland.

Chauvinists among the Americans here are disappointed and angry already, yet our country may make more friends in the world by losing some medals gracefully and winning others with dignity, than we would by sweeping the field clean with arrogance.

Consider the events of this past weekend. Consider Saturday. For the first time in history, the United States lost the pole vault gold medal. The champion is Wolfgang Nordwig of East Germany. He defeated Bob Seagren in an event filled with international politics and bad feeling.

Seagren had to compete with an unfamiliar pole, and when he missed on his last attempt in the darkness of early evening, he was an extremely bitter athlete. In full view of the crowd, he took the offensive pole and tried to hand it to Adrian Paulen of The Netherlands, an official of the International Federation (IAAF) Council, who had been the principal figure in the pole-banning incident. When Paulen tried to smile away the embarrassing moment, Seagren offered it to him again. The crowd whistled and booed. This, of course, was not the sort of graceful acceptance of defeat that is calculated to endear Americans to the rest of the world. It is understandable, however, that Seagren, who had trained long and hard, who had come back after a fairly serious accident while horseback riding, would be bitter over the high-handed manner in which his pole was taken away.

The Americans face a difficult problem in the Olympics generally, and particularly in instances where the dice seem to be loaded against them. On the one hand, it is incumbent on them not to appear sore losers in the eyes of the world. The United States has dominated the games so long in so many sports, that anything short of courtliness may be taken as bad sportsmanship. On the other hand, the Americans obviously cannot let this very situation become a weapon to be used against them.

Controversies like the pole incident must be pursued to a fair conclusion. But the United States, more than any other nation, must pursue them, in my opinion, in a dignified way, working within the framework of the rules. If the rules are wrong, work to get them changed. If the rules are being ignored, let American officials make this known, in straightforward, unequivocal statements.

Displays on the field, like Seagren's, can only hurt the cause. As I said, I understand Bob's bitterness and how he might do what he did in the deep disappointment of the moment. Still, it would have been better if he hadn't done it.

As the rest of the world closes in on us athletically, Americans are going to have to learn a new poise, a dignified demeanor that is neither arrogance, petulance, or immaturity. It is a lesson our entire nation has been in the process of learning in its relations with the rest of the world. Athletics, once again, simply reflects the general picture, but synthesizing it, compressing it, and throwing a harsh spotlight on it.

Saturday, we also lost the discus, for only the second time in fifty-two years (Adolfo Consolini of Italy won at London in 1948). Ludvik Danek of Czechoslovakia, a silver medalist in Tokyo, bronze medalist in Mexico, finally took the gold he had been seeking for fifteen years. Jay Silvester, who had performed in the shadow of Al Oerter for so long in the United States, missed his chance to capitalize on Oerter's retirement. Jay had to settle for the silver.

Ralph Mann had to settle for a silver, too, in the 400-meter hurdles. The winner was a smiling young man from Uganda, John Akii-Bua, who runs the race as if there are no barriers on the track, taking them casually with either foot as they confront him, rather than using the carefully mapped out step-pattern of the other runners.

Akii-Bua is one of forty-three children (his father had eight wives), but he looked like the only son of everyone in the stadium as he took his victory lap. His glistening black skin set off by the bright red running uniform of his country, John shook off officials who were assigned to escort him from the track, and took *two* victory laps, smiling and waving, savoring every moment of the crowd's tribute.

This was a perfect example of the individual achievement triumphing over politics. Few people in the stadium would agree with the politics of the moment in Akii-Bua's homeland, where a dictator is expelling Asians, berating Jews, and making threatening gestures toward Catholics and Englishmen. But few even thought of that in the moment of his victory. He was an appealing young man in a red suit who ran like a gazelle, not the official representative of a racist government.

Saturday was an afternoon of bitter defeats for the United States, but it was also a day of unexpected, refreshing victory.

Dave Wottle won the 800 meters.

A year ago, the slim, quiet man from Bowling Green had been thought of as a most average miler—"journeyman," they might have called him, which is a word always used to damn with faint praise. He had a history of disabling injuries (stress fracture of left ankle in fall of 1970, bursitis on right leg in winter of 1971, stress fracture of right ankle in spring of 1971).

His chief claim to fame before the Olympic Trials was a second to Marty Liquori in the 1970 NCAA Outdoor Mile Championship. Marty tells me frankly that there was no chance of Wottle catching him that day.

Since the trials, Wottle has gotten married to a Bowling Green classmate, the former Janice Pressler, against the advice of the American team coach Bill Bowerman. In Europe, he developed tendonitis in both knees and couldn't train for several weeks.

His Olympics opposition was formidable. There was Yevgeniy Arzhanov, the twenty-four-year-old Ukrainian bachelor who hadn't lost a race since the European Championships at Athens in 1969. There was Mike Boit of Kenya and Franz-Josef Kemper of West Germany.

As they hunched for the start, Wottle's mother, Wanda, sat praying in the stands. Dave looked frail. The golf cap was still in place, but his shirt tail hung out a bit, and his number, 1053, sagged around his waist, while others wore theirs as neatly as a cummerbund.

The race began and Dave immediately dropped many yards behind the entire field. "It's just the way I run," he says. The two Kenyans set the pace, with Wottle a good ten yards behind everybody. Arzhanov bided his time, in good position.

By the second turn of the second lap, the Kenyans were still running like mirror images of each other. Wottle was showing no signs of life.

With a bit more than 200 meters to go, just before the third turn, Arzhanov began to move and quickly went in front. This seemed to stir Wottle. He moved closer to the pack, then, with about 180 meters to go, he started his kick. It appeared he had waited too long.

At the head of the stretch, he kicked harder and looked strong, but he had a long way to go. The two Kenyans were still in front of him, Kemper was strong, and Arzhanov was well in front, looking like a winner. With less than fifty meters to go, Wottle closed in on the Kenyans. He caught one. Then he passed the other, Mike Boit. At that instant, you would have said to yourself, "A silver medal for Dave. Very good." But there were still a few strides left.

Two steps from the end, Wottle surged, Arzhanov ran out of gas and fell forward. Wottle won the gold medal in a finish that looks more remarkable every time we play it back in slow motion.

On the victory stand, the first Bowling Green athlete ever to make the U.S. Olympic team stood on the highest step of all. The anthem began, and I turned to Marty Liquori.

"Good Lord, Marty," I said, "He still has the golf cap on! Do you think he knows it?"

"I don't think so," Marty said.

Wottle, a very religious, patriotic young man, a staunch member of the Air Force ROTC, was certainly not known as a militant. Yet, there he stood, his hand over his heart as the anthem played, but the golf cap firmly on his head.

As soon as we could, we brought Dave up to the platform for an interview. For a gold medalist, he seemed strangely preoccupied. I asked him about the incident on the victory stand.

Wottle shook his head, very seriously. Then Dave, normally a very shy person, looked straight into the camera. "There was no excuse for what I did," he said, "and I want to apologize to the American people right here and now for leaving the cap on. I didn't know I had done it until some reporter at the press conference asked me *why* I had done it. He wanted to know if it was a protest.

"When I told him that I simply hadn't realized I had it on, this reporter (he was a European guy) said, 'Then why did you cover the letters "USA" with your hand while the anthem was playing?'

"I tried to explain to him that you are supposed to put your hand over your heart for the anthem, but he didn't seem to believe me. I'm just sick about it."

I went on with the interview, discussing the race with Dave.

He said that he was sure he was beaten at the head of the stretch, but kicked just the same. Then he thought he had a chance to catch the Kenyans.

"I thought I really might get the silver medal, but I was sure Arzhanov was going to win. But when I passed Boit, suddenly Arzhanov was there and I just ran as hard as I could."

I asked him if he could articulate his feelings on winning a gold medal.

"Frankly, it's tarnished for me by that stupid performance on the victory stand," he said. "It just kind of ruins it."

I told him that he shouldn't feel that way.

"After all, Dave, no one will even remember it a few months from now," I said.

"I will," said Dave Wottle.

Clutching the golf cap, he gave a little nod of thanks and walked away. He made me think of Charlie Brown, in the "Peanuts" comic strip. I could just see Charlie in Dave's shoes, with the words in the little balloon over his head saying, "Good grief! I won the gold medal, then left the stupid cap on."

Despite his own feelings, Dave Wottle had given the United States its first track gold medal of the games. More, he had buoyed the American spirits on a day that otherwise was depressing.

Sunday continued the run of lovely summer weather and the Germans thronged the stadium. They came to root-root-root for the home team, and on this day, Teutonic dreams of glory came true. Unexpectedly, it became Germany's greatest day of athletic triumph since the victories of Hitler Youth in Berlin, 1936.

For us, there was a great break in timing when we came on the air live, by satellite, on Sunday afternoon.

The javelin throw had been figured as the safest prediction in the field events. Janis Lusis of the Soviet Union, even at age thirty-three, was clearly the best in the world, having moved his world record distance up to an amazing 307 feet, 9 inches. He performs best under the pressure of great events. In Mexico, for example, he won the gold medal on his final throw.

Lusis looked a bit overweight when he came on the field (some said he had put on thirty pounds), but he warmed up casually. There were great cheers, though, for every move made by a bearded, stocky, twenty-six-year-old West German named Klaus Wolfermann. Wolfermann was one of the world's best, but his finest throw ever still was shorter than Lusis' world record by some 21½ feet.

The cheers were for Wolfermann because he was a member of the home team. He responded to them with the finest throwing form of his career, and on his next to last throw, he took the lead from Lusis. When the distance was posted, he ran toward the stands and leaped high in the air, throwing a phantom javelin as he let out a whoop of joy that was near disbelief.

In our control room, Chuck Howard was talking with Roone in master control and both of them were watching the sweep second hand of their clocks. Seconds before air, Lusis was getting ready to throw. If he threw before we came on, we would have it on tape and could replay it immediately. But the ideal circumstance on a live show, almost too much to hope for, would be for Lusis to be ready as we put our picture up on the screens of America.

It happened, and five seconds before air time, Chuck said, "O.K. Jim, we go live with Lusis, then replay Wolfermann's previous throw." It was great stuff, real drama.

Lusis was just about to let go when Chuck cued me. Quickly I explained that this was his last chance to retain the gold medal, that he had won on the last throw four years ago.

It was a great throw, and when it hit the turf of the stadium, it was impossible to tell whether it was short, equal, or superior to the flag marking Wolfermann's leading throw. There were the long seconds waiting for the measurement, then the electric scoreboard lit up and Wolfermann was leaping in the air again as the 80,000 shouted and waved.

Wolfermann was the winner by two centimeters, the length of a lady's little fingernail, the closest that measurements are taken in the javelin event. Lusis, a placid man, just walked away, but Bill Toomey said that he would have walked out and inspected the mark, then insisted on a remeasurement by tape.

Lusis accepted the officials' decision, and the Germans had the gold medal.

The 10,000 meters was next. The United States had some hope with Frank Shorter, but not much. Dave Bedford of Great Britain wàs the publicity saint of the occasion, having made as many headlines with his unpleasant behavior in the British training camp (he almost hit a teammate with an air rifle shot, for example) as he had by his grinding long-distance running pace. There was the veteran thirty-four-year-old Tunisian, Mohammed Gahmoudi, and Mariano Haro, of Spain, who had just become a world class runner a year ago at age thirty-one. Miruts Yifter, of Ethiopia, was a bit of a mystery threat.

And there was Lasse Viren. Viren, a Finn with an Abe Lincoln beard, had recently broken the world record for the two-mile run. He had trained all over the world in the past year, from Finland to Spain to Brazil.

In the early part of the race, Viren was running back in the middle of the pack, just ahead of Gahmoudi and Shorter. There was a sudden traffic jam ahead of him, and the Finn suddenly went down. The domino theory went into effect as Gahmoudi tripped over Viren like a line-backer being blocked out of a play, Shorter stumbled, but kept his feet and went on.

Gahmoudi sprawled into the infield and stayed there for long seconds, but Viren bounded up, limped for a few steps, then went after the racers. When they came down the final stretch Viren was not only an easy winner, but he also set a new world record.

It was a performance that kept the excited crowd, still psyched up from the Wolfermann episode, roaring.

On Viren's victory lap, there was a moment that will no doubt make all the Olympic picture books of the future.

A young man leaped across the moat surrounding the track with a huge Finnish flag. Evading the courteous security men, in their light-blue blazers and white "Ben Hogan" caps, he began to run just behind Viren, waving the mammoth flag gracefully as Viren jogged and waved to the crowd. It seemed to sum up the best aspects of individuality and nationalism in the Olympics.

It didn't have the feeling of national arrogance, but of the natural pride of a small, northern country suddenly feeling again the thrill it had so many years ago from the triumphs of Paavo Nurmi.

It was becoming quite an afternoon when the walkers came back into the stadium from their hike around town of more than thirty miles. We had been alert to the possibilities of drama in the walk ever since Mexico when Jose Pedraza came waddling into the stadium in the darkness to win Mexico's first track medal in history as he passed one Russian after they came into view of the crowd and very nearly caught the other.

Now, it happened again. As the crowd strained for a look at the tunnel where the first man would enter, the expectation was that it would be Venyamin Soldatenko of the Soviet Union. The home team, though, again had hope.

A thirty-year-old army officer named Bernd Kannenberg had come out of nowhere in the past two years. He was a former weight-lifter, of all things, who had turned to the walk at age twenty-seven. Recently, he had walked the fastest 50 kilometers of all time. But that was in a meet against Great Britain, and this was the Olympics.

It was Kannenberg, bespectacled, perspiration soaking the spread-eagle emblem of West Germany on his shirt, who came out of the tunnel first.

There were no muffled laughs about the strange-looking gait of the walkers now. This was a crowd growing accustomed to marvelous happenings, and they let out their biggest roar of the day when they saw that West Germany would win its second gold medal of the afternoon. There was satisfaction in the American camp, too, when determined Larry Young, beard, sunglasses, hat and all, came in to take his second successive bronze medal in the 50-kilometer event.

Larry holds a distinction of which he can be very proud. He is the only American ever to win a medal of any kind in either of the two Olympic walking contests.

But it still was the Germans' day, particularly when they now could contemplate another probable victory in the final race of the afternoon. Hildegarde Falck was the favorite in the women's 800 meters, and the twenty-three-year-old teacher fulfilled the crowd's faith in her by taking her country's third gold of the day.

Each day at these Olympics seems to have a different point of focus, and on Sunday it was unquestionably the flag of the Federal Republic of Germany which flew higher than the rest. The home team victories even overshadowed the memorable performance of Lasse Viren, but he will return again later in the week, to try for a double in the 5,000 meters.

Gemütlichkeit was rampant in the beer halls of Munich on Sunday night.

Today (Monday) saw the Russians make a bit of history when Borzov charged to his second gold medal, this time in the 200 meters. He was the first runner to win the 100 and 200 since Bobby Joe Morrow, sixteen years ago.

Kip Keino won the steeplechase. The thirty-two-year-old cop from Kenya is a wonder to watch. He had run the steeplechase only a few times in his life before coming to Munich, had decided to enter it only because it timed out well as far as the schedule was concerned. He couldn't double in the 1,500 and 5,000, because the finals of those races would be run on the same day. Kip wants two gold medals here, so he entered the steeple, even though he doesn't like the event.

"The steeplechase?" he said to one questioner. "The steeplechase is for animals."

He doesn't run it stylishly, at all. His hurdling is atrocious. In today's final, he seemed almost to climb up on each barrier, then jump down on the other side. But on the straightaways in between, he ran away from his field.

Kip Keino has one gold medal in his locker, and one to go. He also has a small psych going on Jim Ryun and the others waiting for the 1,500 meters. If Kip can do this in the steeplechase, what does he have in store for them in the big race next Saturday?

Viktor Saneyev won the triple jump for Russia, as expected, but he, and Keino and Borzov all were upstaged before the day was done by a sixteen-year-old girl named Ulrika Meyfarth, from Frankfurt-am-Main.

The home forces are so charged up now that they seem capable of anything, and this was the most unlikely performance so far. Ulrika had finished no better than third in this year's West German high-jump championships, yet here she was today, beating the best for a gold medal, and tying the world record in the process. Like Olga Korbut, Fraulein Meyfarth had fate on her side.

Yordanka Blagoyeva of Bulgaria was matching Meyfarth height for height until destiny intervened. On a final attempt, Blagoyeva cleared the bar, climbed out of the pit, glanced back and saw the bar in place. Then she walked away and didn't see the bar fall off, several seconds after she had cleared it. There is, of course, nothing to the old track neophyte's tale that you have made the height if you leave the pit before the bar falls off, so Blagoyeva was out.

Little Ulrika joined little Olga on cloud nine.

In room 1810 of the Munich-Sheraton, Margaret sits on the bed now, with a pillow behind her head. I am at my now-familiar post behind the littered room service table, holding a second glass of beer. We are watching the German television review of today's activities. There is no hurry about getting to sleep, because tomorrow is a day off for us, the first one since arriving in Munich sixteen days ago.

No track and field events are scheduled, so I have asked Henry Meyer to pick up Margaret and me about noon for a leisurely drive to Salzburg, Austria.

It will be the pause for a deep breath before plunging into the final days of competition, leading to the confrontation on Saturday in the 1,500 meters between Jim Ryun and Kip Keino. We will be live to the States with that one, the most eagerly awaited foot race in a long time.

The "serene Olympics" have been beautifully done to this point. Despite the pole vault unpleasantness, despite the dismissal of incompetent boxing officials, despite the strange case of the missing sprinters, the overriding impression is of the excellent job the Germans have done in organizing the games.

The citizens of Munich may be upset by the fact that the plastic umbrella-roof cost ten times more than the original estimate but it hasn't dimmed their enthusiasm as spectators. There has been an electricity at every event I have attended, and it has been a pleasant electricity, more warmth than shock. The reason is that the crowd has been watching for great human effort wherever it appears, while at the same time cheering for their fellow countrymen with hearty national pride.

Unhealthy nationalism would take the form, I think, of cheering *only* for the home team, of deep silence for the accomplishments of athletes from other countries. That hasn't been the case here.

In the sports I have been covering, some of the greatest cheers have been for Olga Korbut of the Soviet Union; Valeri Borzov, another Soviet athlete; Karin Janz, an East German; Dave Wottle, an American; John Akii-Bua of Uganda; Lasse Viren, of Finland and Kipchoge Keino of Kenya.

Naturally, the largest ovations have gone to the surprising West German track and field stars—to Heidi Rosendahl, one-centimeter winner of the long jump; to Klaus Wolfermann, two-centimeter victor in the javelin; to Bernd Kannenberg, the old weight-lifter turned walker; to Hildegard Falck, queen of the middle-distance runners; and to little Fraulein Meyfarth, the sixteen-year-old high jumper. The cheering for them was larger because they were Germans, but each is a remarkable story regardless of nationality. Their acclaim was congratulatory, not chauvinistic.

Nationalism is here, of course, in the flags, the uniforms, the politics, the arguments, and unfortunately, in some of the judging. But the overall feeling is of a great gathering of people from all over the world appreciating each individual achievement.

The Germans cheer for their own, but they are much more generous to the visitors than, let us say, the crowd in the Los Angeles Coliseum when the San Francisco 49ers are in town to play the Rams.

In his book *The Nazi Olympics*, Richard D. Mandell wrote:

. . . entranced by the Nazi Olympics [of 1936] was the world's "man of the hour." Adolf Hitler, who was entirely unathletic and was no classical scholar, became convinced that his athletes' triumphs were omens, portents whose significance was clear. The athletes, like other exceptional Germans, were to inspire the whole German *Volk*. The new master race would lead a cultural movement toward accomplishments whose glorious, though dimly divined, outlines suggested that the Germans of the future might surpass the greatest cultural creators of all time. Inspired, hardworking, unerringly led Germans would rival the classical Greeks as inventors of new beauty and joy-intoxicated styles of life.

That sense of a disturbing mysticism is not present here in Munich, 1972. If the Nazi Olympics made one think of the music of Wagner—grandiose, dark, foreboding, humorless—then these games would be best accompanied by the waltzes of Johann Strauss—schmaltzy, entertaining, romantic.

The appetite in Berlin, 1936, was for starched collars and salutes and young German maidens waiting in an Olympic grove as rewards for the winning athletes (the government took financial responsibility for any resulting pregnancies).

Here, the taste is for pigs' knuckles and beer at the Hofbrauhaus. Pursuit of maidens is strictly on a free-lance basis.

The trip to Salzburg tomorrow should be nice, if the weather holds; a day for rest, rehabilitation, and thought, with a little sight-seeing, perhaps a Sacher torte and coffee in a cafe near Mozart's birthplace, a stein of beer here and there, then back to Munich for a nice dinner downtown. It's about time we had dinner in a restaurant.

To be honest about it, though, I am inwardly already looking forward to Wednesday with some impatience. The decathlon starts then, always an Olympic classic. In the days to come, we still have such things as Rod Milburn in the hurdles, a possible American sweep in the 400 meters, the men's high jump and shot put, Steve Prefontaine against the world in the 5,000 (the world includes Lasse Viren), Frank Shorter with a chance in the marathon, and Keino vs. Ryun.

Up to here, this is the best Olympics I have ever seen.

17

Eleven Are Dead—
Tragedy at the Games

Henry Meyer called early in the morning, somewhere around eight o'clock. I had asked him to pick us up around noon, so the call confused both Margaret and me, half asleep, vaguely annoyed at the interruption of our one sleep-in morning of the games.

"What is it, Henry?" Margaret said. "I'm sorry, but I don't quite understand. Here, perhaps you'd better speak to Jim."

"Jim," he said. "It's Henry. Something fantastic has happened. The Arabs have invaded the Israeli team quarters in the village. They're holding the Israeli Olympic team as hostages and there's a report that they have already killed one man. They asked me to call you and ask you to stand by, because they are going to need you today."

I walked to the window and opened the draperies. It was another beautiful, just slightly hazy day. Straight ahead in the

200

distance was the familiar sight of the Olympic Stadium on the left, huddled under the outspread umbrella of the roof, and the Olympic Village on the right, white, angular buildings reflecting the early morning sun.

From room 1810 of the Munich-Sheraton you can see quite a way. Just in front of the hotel is a traffic circle. Street cars were making their way around it, some of them bearing a sign on top that reads, "Los Angeles? TWA. Chicago? TWA. Baltimore, TWA." Somehow, Baltimore, my old home town, seemed furthest away of all as I looked out the window. To the left of the circle is a group of modern garden-type apartments.

The only people outdoors there were a half-dozen little girls in summer dresses riding their bikes through the grass. Automobile traffic was normally heavy for the beginning of the Munich morning rush hour. In short, there was nothing at all out of the ordinary.

Then a car moved into the circle, the word "Polizei" on its side, its two-note siren (BAA-baa, BAA-baa) blaring urgently. The car threaded its way skillfully through the traffic and accelerated out the Mittlerer Ring, across John F. Kennedy Bridge, toward the Olympic grounds.

There were a few seconds more of normal traffic sounds, then another police car appeared. This one, blocked by a large trailer truck, bumped off the road onto the grass of the traffic circle, then wheeled back onto the roadway. There was no question there. This policeman was in a hurry, and he, too, was headed toward the Olympic Village.

Margaret was standing beside me.

"I guess it must be true," she said. "Imagine. It's an irony of history. Those are Germans going to the rescue of Jews."

It was the first of many ironies that struck us during the course of that day.

I don't even remember us discussing the trip to Salzburg again. We had breakfast at the window, eating good bread with fresh butter and wonderful strawberry jam, drinking German coffee that had surprised us with its fine flavor.

Standing by got to be tedious, so I went to the basement of the hotel to take a sauna. I had been doing that every day during the

Olympics and right now it seemed like a good place to think and prepare for the totally unexpected day that now lay ahead.

I was alone in the sauna.

The hot, dry air (about 195 degrees Fahrenheit) soon had me sweating in a flood; a relaxing feeling. I tried to figure out what it all might mean. If one man was already dead, this was no crazy caper by a bunch of amateur, half-joking commandoes. It was an event that would stop the clock on the Munich Games right where it was. How would they rescue the other team members? What sort of coverage would we give the event? What was happening right now in Barnathan's Bungalow?

As the questions came to my mind, the relaxation was tempered by anxiety. After the ice-cold shower, I pulled on a pair of yellow cotton bathing trunks and went out to the pool. My thought was to take a couple of laps, which is all I can manage, then wait for the call from Roone.

Instead, I reached for the telephone in back of the bar at the side of the pool and called associate producer Geoff Mason out at the ABC headquarters. It wasn't a conscious reversal of plan, just the kind of thing you do when you see a phone and have a question in the front of your mind that needs answering.

As with Henry Meyer's original call, I think I remember Geoff's words almost exactly. It is part of that permanent photoengraving process that the mind possesses, whereby certain moments of your life are retained, like how you heard about Pearl Harbor, or President Kennedy's death.

"Jesus, I'm glad you called," he said. "I've just started trying to reach you. The thing is terrible. One man is dead, they think they've killed another, and now they are threatening to kill one athlete every hour until their demands are met. We're going on the air live to the States at one o'clock (just one hour away) and Roone wants you to anchor the show. Do you have a driver there?"

I didn't think I had a driver, so I pulled my clothes on quickly and jogged upstairs to the lobby. Henry was there, waiting and ready to go.

The lobby was jammed with people. Karl-Heinz Hatzfeld, the hotel manager, stood in the middle of it. Karl-Heinz is a German who worked at the Sheraton in Dallas for eight years before returning home to open the Munich-Sheraton, and is about as much Texan as he is German.

On this morning, his German-Texan-hotel-manager smile was missing. He asked me what I knew and then admitted he was worried.

"Between you and me," he said, "we have a lot of Arab delegates and some Jews staying in the hotel. One guy from the Middle East on the nineteenth floor has had his own bodyguards outside the suite ever since he came. Now, we've asked for extra security because nobody seems to know what might happen. There are a lot of plain clothesmen here right now."

Outside, it was Munich as usual. Beautiful weather, lots of traffic.

Henry Meyer let it all hang out on the way to the village. The little BMW 1800 leaned from side to side as he weaved in and out of the casually moving ordinary traffic. It would be another of the day's ironies that Henry wrecked the little car totally later that afternoon, missing a turn in the Englischer Garten and hitting another car. Fortunately, none of the family was with him at the time. He wasn't hurt at all.

I expected to see lots of security around the television building when I arrived, but none was visible. If there was more than one stage planned in this attack on the Olympics, wouldn't it be logical that they might try to take over the television transmission, or blow up the facilities? Well, there was no security visible, aside from the sleepy young German in the blue ABC engineer's jacket who sat on a chair and watched people run in and out of our building. He was more spectator than guard.

As I recall, it was Julie Barnathan who was standing outside the ABC Center when I arrived. I asked him where the trouble was, if we could see it from there.

"Not quite," he said. "Look. It's just in back of that building the other side of the walkway. It's Building 31."

That was the first time I had heard the building number. By the end of the day, it would be written in the tragic litany of our times along with Texas School Book Depository and the kitchen of the Ambassador Hotel in Los Angeles.

Geoff Mason was sitting at his on-air post in the control room. It was behind a counter, a level above the long row of chairs where Roone and Jim Spence and Chuck Howard and Don Ohl-meyer and Larry Kamm and the necessary engineers sat during the nightly shows.

"O.K.," Geoff said. "Roone will be here in a minute. Why don't you go in the studio and put on your IFB. We're still going on live at one o'clock."

(IFB: the initials stand for Interrupted Feed Back. It is the small speaker we place in our ear, through which we can hear all elements of the program as it goes out over the air, plus any comments, instructions, or suggestions the producer may want to interrupt with, at his discretion. He interrupts by pushing a button at his control post and talking into a microphone.)

Before going to the studio, I went to the small room used as our information center during the games. It was the place where Terry dwelled, Terry being young Terry O'Neil. He had been hired out of Notre Dame a year before and put on the full-time job of assembling information for the games. Obviously, he was not prepared with data on terrorism and assassination.

I quickly went through everything that had moved on the two wire service tickers in the room, and told Terry's assistant, Bob Jenkins, a half dozen pieces of information I would like to have. Terry, himself, had been up until five A.M. on the previous night's program and was still asleep in the Sheraton, not knowing of the events that actually had started to occur even before he went to sleep.

The studio was a bare, functional room with many lights, a couple of chairs and the background used behind Chris Schenkel each night during the games. This was the first time I had sat in it, since all my assignments were on location at the stadium or the gymnastics hall.

Jacques Lesgards is a friendly Frenchman who has found excitement in the television business from his native land to Brazil and back again. Jacques is director of engineering operations for

ABC in Europe, and he was the first person with any executive authority to arrive at ABC headquarters after the siege of Building 31 began. He got there just after seven o'clock in the morning, to get things going for another day's Olympics coverage.

Jean Adami, an ABC telephone operator from New York who had been brought to the games, met him in tears. Her story was strange.

"Oh, Jacques," she said, "Something terrible is going on. They say a Russian has been killed in the Olympic Village and a shot went through the German television people's cafeteria. It's been closed down."

M. Lesgards replied with the line that men have been using since Adam.

"Now, Jean," he said. "Don't get excited."

Dave McCabe, a young American who had been hired in Munich as a general assistant, was at hand, so Jacques gave him a walkie-talkie and sent him into the village. Within minutes, Dave reported back with the terrible facts.

Lesgards told Jean Adami to alert several people, then put things in motion to get a mobile camera unit—a small one called "minicam"—fired up and ready to go into the village.

It was already apparent that they were closing up the village to press and television, so Jacques removed the ABC identification from the Volkswagen minibus that held the mobile camera. Across the road, he spotted an ice cream wagon, like a Good Humor truck, that was parked there all the time, selling ice cream to ABC personnel and athletes on their way to the village. Jacques made a deal with the ice cream man and soon the mobile unit was in its disguise, ready to move inside the gates.

Jacques then called Marvin Bader.

Marvin Bader had been bent over a basin in the barber shop of the Sheraton at 8:15 that morning when he was called to the phone. He was having a shampoo and his head was still streaming water as he listened to Jacques on the other end. The French-accented voice was telling the first bare pieces of the incredible story.

"Marvin," he said, "There's been a murder in the village, in the Israeli team headquarters. I came to open things here this morning and just found out. I must have the keys to your office to get into the village right away."

Marvin was in his car in less than two minutes, driving himself to ABC headquarters.

On the two-way radio in his car, Bader suggested to Lesgards that the minicam unit be fired up. The crash unit was originally thought of as a wandering camera to see all of Munich and to cover *anything else that might come up*. ABC Sports was aware of the need for a camera to cover the unexpected, the unforeseeable happening. Jacques told him the unit was already being set up.

When Bader arrived at ABC, two men had already gone into the village. Jim Flood, a former stage manager now in the production services area of the network, was supposed to be logistics, providing the thousands of items needed for a telecast as large as the Olympic Games. Dave McCabe, the young American, had been hired along with many others on the scene in Munich to do whatever odd jobs came up. Suddenly, these two were reporters, walkie-talkies in hand, representing ABC at the hottest news story in the world until others could reach the scene.

One of the most remarkable things about ABC's coverage that day was the way people moved into areas not properly theirs, did jobs in which they were totally inexperienced and did them well. Again, it was the outcome of the minutely detailed preplanning.

Marvin found his office already broken into by the members of his staff, which at that point consisted of Jacques; Toni Brown, a woman film director; and Gladys Deist, his secretary. They had provided Flood and McCabe with the necessary credentials.

Gladys was the lady in charge of distributing whatever tickets were available each day to members of the ABC team and their families—a thankless job at best—but suddenly she had become a member of the "Mission Impossible" squad. She had immediately, on her own initiative, called Hi Bley, head of the graphic arts department, and asked him to have his best people start making fraudulent credentials in case they were needed. She had also rounded up several athletes' sweat shirts and an Olympics hostess uniform for use as disguises. In fact, a girl working for ABC was already dressed in the hostess uniform and standing by.

Marvin called Roone at the hotel, Roone having been asleep for about two and a half hours at this point after last night's program. The orders from Arledge were to get Peter Jennings and Howard Cosell into the village, to alert Jim McKay, and to do a number of other things. From that time on, Arledge was on the telephone until he came to the center.

Mike Rebich and Dick Chalk, engineers assigned to the mini-cam unit, were found in the cafeteria and set to work.

Gary Slaughter, a young American on the temporary ABC staff, put on a sweat suit and became the lifeline into the village. Establishing himself as an athlete in the minds of the guards, and bearing an athlete's credential, he carried film and other supplies into and out of the village for long hours. Gary, black and athletic-looking, was very believable.

Not so Dave McCabe, the young fellow who went in first with Jim Flood. Dave was arrested later in the day while wearing the uniform of the Malaysian Olympic team, on the grounds that he did not appear either Malaysian or athletic.

Bader called Don Coe of ABC News at home (it was about 4:30 A.M. there) and told him Roone wanted to go live to the States at 1:00 P.M. Munich time. George Milne, of the ABC traffic department, on the scene, got to work ordering the satellite for that time.

As the morning wore on, things became better and better organized, and at about 12:30, Marvin went across from Barnathan's Bungalow to the other building where the studios, control rooms, tape rooms, and engineering facilities were located.

He ensconced himself beside Geoff Mason and directed the logistical operations by walkie-talkie.

And he made one other phone call, to Horst Hasnjaeger, a sales representative for Lufthansa Airlines who had been working closely with ABC for months on reservations. Hasnjaeger's assignment was to go out to Reim, the Munich commercial airport, and through his contacts try to find out if there were any preparations to fly terrorists and hostages out of there to another country. The answer was negative. That was an important piece of information.

First reports said that the Arabs wanted several hundred political prisoners freed by Israel or they would execute one team member every hour. Then the reports said that there was a noon deadline for execution of all the hostages. Noon passed and a new deadline was fixed—1700 Munich time, five o'clock in the afternoon, or noon New York time.

John and Holly Wilcox had been married for just over three months when the Olympics began. John, a young, good-looking ski enthusiast from Connecticut and Vermont, was production manager for the ABC film crews in Munich, a behind the scenes man. When he was aroused by Toni Brown's call on September 5 at about 8:45 A.M., he had no way of guessing that in a few hours he would be talking to a nationwide television audience on a walkie-talkie, giving reports from a spot closer to the scene than anyone else's in our organization.

Toni, his assistant, filled him in, told him that he was needed at the village. He was stunned, and just as many others, he went about the normal functions of a morning for a while before the enormity of it all sank in. In fact, he and his wife dressed, went to the dining room of the Sheraton, and were finishing their orange juice before the real nature of the emergency came to him. They left before the eggs came and drove to the bungalow.

The film crews were there, ready to go. Living in the Press Center, they had been able to get to the scene quickly. Wilcox loaded his men into a Volkswagen minibus and decided to try the main gate, gate 6, first, saving the other gate just fifty yards from ABC as a backup.

The guards at gate 6 were adamant, so they turned back, driving the minibus on the grass just outside the chain fence of the village, trying to find a place where they could see Building 31. The closest spot they found was blocked by the Canadian team building. Mrs. Wilcox stayed there with some of the crew while John went back to the bungalow.

He met Willy Schaeffler, who was working with him as a film crew supervisor. Willy's regular job is head coach of the United States Alpine ski team. Bavarian-born, he knew the country, the language, and the Olympics (in addition to skiing, he was once the first kayak champion of the United States).

John Wilcox, like the others, decided that disguises were in order. Not knowing of Gladys' efforts, he asked Willy to go get his American ski team uniform, which he had in his quarters at the press center. Shortly after Willy left, John saw another of our young supernumeraries, wearing a "NCAA Championships" T-shirt and a blue USA track jacket. Where he got them, only he knows. Wilcox didn't even know his name, nor does he now. Shirt and jacket were commandeered. The unknown young man was last seen standing in the cafeteria, stripped to the waist.

Wilcox, along with Gary Slaughter, quietly walked toward the village gate fifty yards away. Slaughter originally had worked with the U.S. track team and had gotten a team credential before he joined ABC. Wilcox's press credential was useless now so Slaughter, talking with Wilcox as to a teammate, flashed his card and Wilcox followed along. They were inside the village.

On the Plaza of the Nations, a broad area where athletes congregated for ceremonies and recreation, they found Howard Cosell and a film crew which had gotten in before the press clampdown began.

For the next several hours, Wilcox supervised film interviews done by Howard, including one with the best friend of the slain Moshe Weinberg.

Slaughter was back and forth to the bungalow, taking film and tape in and out until he literally almost dropped late in the afternoon and was relieved by Jimmy Schaeffler, Willy's son, wearing his father's U.S. ski team clothing.

After noon, Wilcox surveyed the physical situation. The spot where they were working was as close as they were allowed to the Israeli quarters. They could see nothing, because a tall dormitory building blocked the way . . . but if a man were inside that building in the right place, he could see everything.

Wilcox detached himself from his film group and walked toward the exit gate. Then he doubled back along a sidewalk to the building entrance. Carrying an athletic shoe bag that was bulging with camera equipment and a walkie-talkie and must have weighed forty pounds, he told the building guard that he was a U.S. boxer and had to meet his coach inside the building. He had left his credential in his room, he said, but it was a very important meeting concerning his bout that night. He got in.

Quickly, he made for the elevator, and pushed the button for the third floor. Why the third? He has no idea. It was just a button.

At the third floor, Wilcox got out and turned to the left, again on impulse. He entered a suite of several rooms. They were empty, beds unmade, the water running in a bathroom basin.

He walked to the balcony that fronted the suite. Looking straight across to another building no more than fifty feet away, he saw the face of a man leaning out the window of the room directly opposite him. The man was holding a submachine gun in his hand. No one had to tell Wilcox that it was the lookout for the terrorists.

The two men stared at each other for just a few seconds. Then John Wilcox turned around, and as calmly as he could, went back inside the room.

Fred Schuhmann is a huge, hearty man, vice-president in charge of television facilities and services for ABC. His job is as large as he is. It consists of providing all of the engineering facilities (control rooms, tape machines, the whole thing) and all production facilities and services. The latter includes studios and sets, graphic arts, offices, and a myriad of functions right down to the cleaning of the floors.

On this Tuesday, Schuhmann ended up as stage manager, standing in the studio next to the camera with a headset on, giving me cues and keeping the studio area under control.

It was a volunteer effort on his part (the regular stage manager was assigned elsewhere and wasn't due back until later in the evening).

Marty Pompadur was another volunteer. He is a corporate vice-president, right-hand man to President Elton Rule. On this day, he stood quietly by in the control room, ready to do whatever seemed helpful. At times, this consisted of bringing me coffee and chicken soup from the cafeteria.

"Stand by, please, Jim," Freddy Schuhmann said, "Roone says will you please put your IFB on. Quiet in the studio, please."

In the moment before we went on the air, we were not aware, of course, that we would finally leave the studio almost fifteen hours later, after one of the most emotionally draining days of our lives.

Our basic coverage team was in place. In the control room, Roone Arledge would run the show, give the orders, feed me information and suggestions, and occasionally, just try to encourage me. Chuck Howard stood behind Roone. Behind him, at the table on the higher level, were Geoff Mason and Marvin Bader, both on walkie-talkies to our people around the Olympic grounds and the village.

Julie Barnathan prowled the control room, ad-libbing engineering impossibilities as Roone requested them.

Fred Schuhmann and the cameraman were with me in the studio. Young Bob Jenkins was running copy from the wire service machines and getting me other facts I needed.

Peter Jennings had worked his way into the Italian team headquarters in the village and was standing by, using the room telephone as his mike. Julie's men had linked the telephone line right into our audio system, somehow getting excellent sound quality from it.

It was another of the day's ironies that Peter Jennings had welcomed the assignment to Munich as a break from his regular job for ABC News—reporting from the Middle East on Arab–Israeli tensions.

Somewhere in the course of the long day, someone asked me how it had felt to suddenly switch from sports to news when we went on the air. The honest answer is that the thought didn't come to my mind. Reporting, I think, is simply the communication to someone not on the scene of a given event, a happening. The reporter's job is to tell as clearly and accurately as he can the facts of the situation and, in the case of television, to explain the meaning of the visual image on the screen. More subtly, I think the reporter must communicate the mood of the moment. What is the inner emotional reaction to the scene, in the words of one who is there?

There is the largest of gaps between careful reporting of emotions and sensationalist reporting, or worse still, reporting calculated to trigger ugly emotions, thoughts—possibly even actions— by the viewer. The proper function is responsible communication, not rabble-rousing. Ideally, it is the difference between a painting that captures the fact and feeling of a scene, and a campaign poster that stirs the beholder to partisan action. The measured, mid-Western, unemotional tones of Elmer Davis were perfect to present the inflammatory daily reports of World War II on the radio. Conversely, it was also good reporting when Arthur Godfrey was moved to honest tears while reporting FDR's funeral, and when Walter Cronkite uttered an involuntary, "Go, baby, go," as America's first spacecraft slowly began to rise from earth.

Assuming a fairly wide range of interests on the part of the reporter, it does not really matter whether the subject matter is sports or news. If the event is given its proper perspective, if the facts and the feelings are reported accurately and promptly, then the reporter is doing his job.

It would be impossible and tedious to detail everything we did and said after Roone cued me to talk on our first live transmission, but certain sights and thoughts do float to the surface of my mind.

I am sure I will never forget the heads of the terrorists, popping out of windows and doors regularly like some sort of dreadful puppet show, turning from side to side, alertly spotting their adversaries; the man in the mask, the man in the white hat.

The door leading from our studio to the street was opened at one point, and outside I saw a line of military trucks, their engines idling. This was the very spot where athletes had walked on their way to and from the opening ceremonies. Where the men of 120 nations had walked in peace, the trucks of the *Bundesgrenzschutz* (West German Border Police) now stood.

Chuck Howard noticed it, too.

"I walked back from the stadium that day alongside the athletes," he said. "Who could have thought we'd see this?"

The border guards, in uniform, with submachine guns in their hands, were unloading from the trucks. The incongruity that linked sport with terror, though, was the sight of other border guards, holding guns but dressed in athletic sweat suits of red and blue, disguises for a planned assault on the terrorists. Uniform of the day—sweat suits and submachine guns.

I remember going to the offices of Israeli television after our first transmission, looking for their producer–reporter, who had been inside the village and was now semi-official spokesman for the team. It was not a pleasant walk to the office. I expected to find women weeping and men cursing.

What I found was different. The Israelis seemed less *surprised* by the tragedy than anyone else I had seen. As they moved quietly and competently about the offices, there was great sadness and bitterness in their eyes, but I also sensed a determination and a preparedness; not resignation, but an acceptance of reality.

One man explained it to me as I waited.

"We live with this every day of our lives," he said. "Every citizen of Israel knows that an implied condition of his citizenship is the possibility of ambush and death. We do not accept its inevitability. We do not plan to let it continue. But we accept the fact that it exists as of this moment."

The producer–reporter arrived. Although obviously exhausted, he was courteous and cooperative. He came to our studio for an interview, in which he told me all he knew of the day's events, from the knock on the door in the middle of the night to his own expulsion from the village because he only had a press credential (another of the day's small ironies—an Israeli being ejected from the Olympic Village while the Arabs stayed inside). He gave me the reportorial facts—the number of men who escaped, the number still inside. Ten were still in there, Weinberg's body having been removed, but it was believed that another man was dead and still lying in one of the rooms.

Aside from a camera on top of the television tower, which had been commandeered and was being directed by the Munich police, our lone live camera, on a sidewalk just outside the village fence, peering some seventy-five yards away at the Israeli apartments and the terrorist lookouts, was the world's window on the incredible afternoon.

We saw the terrorists, but we never saw the Israelis. It was a Burmese soccer coach who told us at one point, through John Wilcox, that he was able to see the men, that they were standing back to back in a circle, hands bound to each other, eyes blindfolded.

Time after time, I summed up the facts on the air and read again the ultimatum issued earlier by the killers. Here is the way the wire service transmitted it at 1:23 P.M. Munich time:

Munich leadall intruders

The terrorists tossed a paper out of a window of the Israeli quarters. It bore the title, "Communique," and listed five points of their ultimatum:

1. West Germany must declare itself prepared to bring the Israeli hostages to a place to be specified by the "revolutionary forces" inside the Olympic Village.

2. West Germany must provide the guerillas with three airplanes. The Israelis would be divided into three groups and placed aboard each of the planes. After the first plane left, the other would in succession leave as soon as word was received that the previous one had reached the as-yet undisclosed destination.

3. Any attempt to interfere with the operation would result in the liquidation of the hostages. West Germany would bear full responsibility.

4. The ultimatum deadline would run out within three hours. [It was extended.]

5. In the event the ultimatum is not heeded, orders would be

given "to carry out revolutionary and just force in order to give the war chiefs of the Israeli war machine a hard lesson."

The communique ended with the appeal: "Revolutionaries of the world, unite."

West German Chancellor Willy Brandt was in Munich now. Secret negotiations were under way.

I interviewed a survivor, a man I am sure I will never forget. His name was Tuvia Sokolsky, coach of the Israeli weight-lifting team. He spoke no English, but what he said and meant was crystal-clear, through the words of his interpreter and the expressions on his face.

Mr. Sokolsky is a small, muscular man, apparently in his late forties. He is balding and wears a small mustache. You could imagine him as a neighborhood tailor in New York, or a delicatessen owner in Los Angeles.

As he sat, slumped in his chair in the studio, his hands folded in front of him, perspiration beading his forehead under the hot lights, his face showed the weariness of centuries-old persecution, the sorrow of a brother at a graveside, the potential wrath of an Old Testament Jehovah.

Patiently, in Hebrew, speaking softly, wearily, he went through the description of the morning that now was like a dirge being sung in different voices.

Then I asked him the question that I thought I must, the question that was in the front of the minds of hundreds of millions of people watching around the world.

"Mr. Sokolsky," I said, "If you were standing right now at the side of the German directing the rescue forces, what would be your suggestion, what would you tell him to do?"

After the translation of the question, the small man sat and thought for a moment. He moved in his chair. He spoke, and as he did, I saw his eyes mist up, heard his speech falter. As he finished, his mouth turned far down at both corners and he lowered his head.

The translator spoke.

"What Mr. Sokolsky said is difficult to translate and it is more moving to me in Hebrew than I can make it in English. I will try. He says that he has always vowed to himself that he would never give in to cowardly terror, to these men who will not fight us hand to hand and face to face, but only when they are armed and we are not. He says this is a principle most important to him, one that he has told himself he will never betray. And yet, he says, he must be honest and tell you what is in his mind now, that the only thing he cares about is to see his friends alive and free, at whatever the cost."

The dilemma of Tuvia Sokolsky was the dilemma of the world, but particularly of Willy Brandt and Golda Meir. The hostages themselves would have no say in the decision.

We continued to watch the Arab lookouts, and through the control room window I could see events taking place on the monitors from other venues that now seemed insanely irrelevant —a volleyball game, the genteel "dressage" horsemanship event at the Nymphenburg Palace, American heavyweight Duane Bobick being mauled by the Cuban, Teofilo Stevenson.

What had been important and exciting yesterday, seemed almost blasphemy today. Why were the games still going on? The question was being asked all over Munich, and in time it was announced that they would stop, temporarily, but not until this afternoon's competitions were completed. We wondered if Avery Brundage and the other IOC members could have listened to Tuvia Sokolsky and still permitted "Olympics as usual."

Another announcement came. There would be a memorial service in the Olympic Stadium at 10:00 tomorrow morning for the slain Moshe Weinberg and the other man presumed dead inside the suite of rooms.

The hours from four to six in the afternoon grew increasingly tense. The deadline was five o'clock, the terrorists had said, and shortly after four, it appeared that an assault would be made, an attempt to free the prisoners by force.

The border guards in athletic suits began to spread out around Building 31. Our camera followed one man on the roof, a submachine gun dangling from his hand almost as casually, it seemed, as a golfer carrying a putter. Certainly, I thought, I must look tenser sitting here in the studio staring at the monitor, than he does, leaning against a wall on the rooftop, fifty feet from potential death.

Down below, a woman security guard stood in full view of the people inside the rooms. She was there for most of the day. One report said that it was felt the terrorists might be less likely to shoot at a woman.

The man in the white hat conferred with a negotiator for the Germans. He was the Bavarian minister of the interior. Later, I was told that the gunman grew apprehensive during one of the meetings.

"You are going to do one of two things," he said to the German. "Either you are going to kill me or try to take me as a counter-hostage. In either event, I think you should know that you are going with me."

From behind his back, he produced a hand grenade, its pin already pulled halfway out.

At another moment, the minister went upstairs to the balcony and pounded on the door of one of the rooms. It was an urgent pounding, accompanied by shouts that we could not hear. Another negotiator was inside the room, talking to the Arabs, and apparently, there was concern for his safety. After a few minutes, the other man came out, quickly, and they left.

Five o'clock came and went. It became evident that the deadline had been extended, either formally or informally.

During this period, Jennings was giving his reports from one angle and I from another. John Wilcox was brought in by walkie-talkie. He, remember, was closest to the scene. Actually, he had changed rooms, and instead of the rumpled suite, he was now in the Burmese soccer team's office, a floor below, with just as good a view.

John had stayed in his original position until a nervous Burmese had returned to the rooms and insisted that he leave. He had tried the doors on all the floors above, found them locked, and finally found refuge in the soccer team's office.

The team manager was very friendly and at one point got John a steak from the building cafeteria. But another Burmese was less helpful. He appeared to be drunk and wanted to throw a whiskey bottle at the Arab lookout. The manager dissuaded him.

Wilcox had no thought of being an on-the-air reporter. In fact, he had been on the air for an hour or more, intermittently, before he realized it.

The communications setup among the commentators was this: I could hear Jennings and he could hear me, through a telephone, the mouthpiece of which was being held to a speaker in the control room. Jennings could not hear Roone. Wilcox could hear Jennings, because each of them had a walkie-talkie on the same circuit. Wilcox could not hear Roone or me.

Everyone, including viewers all over America, could hear Wilcox, because Jennings was holding his walkie-talkie speaker to the mouthpiece of his telephone. It was the most tenuous of communications links—John Wilcox speaking into the tiny mouthpiece of a walkie-talkie; his words coming out the small speaker of Jennings' walkie-talkie and into the mouthpiece of Peter's telephone; the telephone line being fed into the master audio output of ABC, then shot to a tiny satellite, 22,500 miles in the sky; then down to a ground station in the United States, into New York master control, then around the nation through cables and microwave links.

There was one problem. Wilcox was working too close to his microphone and his words were coming out distorted.

Roone spoke in my earpiece.

"Jim," he said, "This will be the world's most public instruction in microphone technique. Will you please tell Peter, on the air, to tell John to work a little further back from his mike. His words are distorting."

We did it, as the country learned not to speak too close to a walkie-talkie mike. It was the only small smile of a terrible day.

It was almost six o'clock. Since there was no word of an official extension of the deadline, we had to presume that it might have been moved back to six o'clock.

A few minutes before that hour, Roone came on again with unexpected instructions.

"Jim, we have a problem," he said. "CBS has exclusive use of the satellite starting at six o'clock and they simply will not share it with us. Tell the stations around the country that it looks like we will have to leave the air at six, but that you and Peter will continue your commentary on radio. It isn't definite, but alert them. It probably will happen."

There had been long conversations in the control room with CBS and with ABC News in New York. Apparently, early in the day, someone not in a major executive position at ABC had refused to share our picture with CBS. They had grown intransigent and now wouldn't share the satellite, whether we shared the picture or not.

It came at the most critical of moments. At six o'clock, just as the assault on the Israeli rooms might have taken place, the American people stopped seeing pictures of the scene. We continued our description, though, on more than a thousand radio stations.

Later, when we left the air for a while, Wilcox called Geoff Mason on the walkie-talkie.

"Hey, Geoff," he said. "Was I on the air?"

"Yes," said Mason. "Nice job."

"Well, thanks a lot for telling me," said Wilcox. We will never know whether John, who had never been on the air before, would have done a better or worse job if he had known that he was talking to millions of people, not just Peter Jennings. The job he did was just fine.

As I said, various small episodes float to my mind as I think back over the long day. Somewhere around 7:30 in the evening, we heard that Willy Brandt was making a statement on German television. Jim Spence, vice-president in charge of sports planning, went with me through the labyrinthine corridors of the world television center to try and persuade the chancellor to do an interview for us.

Jim spent most of the Olympics with Roone, assisting him in the production of the nightly telecasts to the States. Since he was pretty much locked to the control room, he often forgot his credential. On this evening, he had no credential, nor was he wearing his ABC jacket.

The chancellor of West Germany emerged, grim-faced, from the German studio and moved quickly down the corridor. He was going, we were told, to the studio of Israeli television. There, he would make a statement in English, for the Israelis and the English-speaking world.

We still had hope of getting him for an exclusive interview, so Spence and I followed along, walking quickly a pace or two behind the chancellor. We went down a long, narrow corridor, with no windows or doors, just wallboard on the sides and overhead. Suddenly, and with a literal chill, the scene reminded me of pictures I had seen of the path Bobby Kennedy had taken to the kitchen of the Ambassador Hotel.

I realized that Jim, at my side, had no credential. Here, then, at one of the most critical and dangerous moments in the history of the West German Republic, a man totally unknown to the security people was within touching distance of the country's leader. It was a classic example of the impossibility of total security for a public figure.

I stood in the Israeli control room, making notes as Brandt spoke. The man who interviewed him was the same man I had talked to earlier in the day.

We failed in our attempt to interview Brandt personally, and for a good reason. We followed him until he went into the office of Robert Lembke, head of DOZ, the German television consortium, which was coordinating the worldwide broadcasts of the games.

We found that the chancellor was on the telephone, that he was attempting some delicate negotiation to save the hostages. It may have been during this period that the Germans agreed to provide a bus and helicopters for the terrorists to make their attempted getaway.

Later, I walked into the control room just in time to see a bus pulling away from Building 31. It was the departure of the killers and their hostages.

Over in a corner, I noticed our son, Sean, leaning on the counter, staring at the scene on the monitor. Apparently, he had been there most of the day. Sean had come to Munich for fun, and he had found it; seeing the ceremonies, the gymnastics, the track and field; listening to a strange language; wandering the Marienplatz in the late evening with new friends, indoctrinating himself in the wonders of Bavarian beer.

Now, the experience had deepened, changed from an escapade into a learning process. On the screen, he saw the fact of cold madness, the reality of violence, the simple look of bravery ("grace under pressure," Hemingway said).

Around him in the control room, he saw the men who had befriended him as he grew up in the world of ABC Sports. Before, he had seen them laughing as they worked, on golf tournaments or swimming championships or ski races. He had observed their professionalism, but now he saw it in a new dimension. It was no ball game now. It was the biggest news story in the world, one that struck at the emotions as it tested the men's skills.

Sean saw the men of ABC Sports retaining their poise, adjusting the skills of the stadium to an arena where the outcome would not be victory or defeat, but life or death.

Have you ever dropped something into a pond and watched it float away from you, maddening close to your reach? "So near and yet so far," is the cliché. That was what it was like when the helicopters went up at about 10:30 P.M., rising from the Olympic Village in the night, their red lights blinking, observing standard safety procedures as they moved out toward their unknown destination.

Our daughter, Mary, was standing outside, beside the ABC camera, when the choppers slowly flew overhead.

"Dad," she said later, "It was so terrible, so frustrating. There they were, so close you felt you could almost touch them. But nobody in the whole world could help. It made you feel angry and sad at the same time."

The news came that the helicopters had gone to an air base at Fürstenfeldbruck.

Then, a report that we could scarcely believe moved on the wire service ticker. It said that all of the terrorists had been killed at the airport, and all of the hostages had been saved.

Just a couple of minutes after the report came over, I did an interview with Konrad Ahlers, official spokesman for the West

German government. Herr Ahlers is something more than a presidential press secretary. He has an official post, speaking for the nation, not just the chancellor. He, too, had just heard the news from the airport. Speaking carefully, the slender, dignified Herr Ahlers said that, *if the reports were true*, he was most gratified. The German government had been under tremendous pressure, he said, and of course, felt particularly sensitive because Jews were involved. "A bad outcome might reopen old wounds," he said.

He told of attempted negotiations with Egypt earlier in the day, when the terrorists had demanded that they be flown to Cairo. For a diplomat, he used strong language, saying that President Sadat had refused to speak to Chancellor Brandt on a technicality of protocol, and that the premier of Egypt had been totally uncooperative. Certainly, he said, it would affect future relations between the countries.

The mood began to change in the studio and control room as we waited for definite confirmation of the news. Roone started planning a rundown for our principal transmission of the night.

People began to tell each other of some of their experiences during the day, to laugh at some of the silly things they had done under the pressure of the moment.

The confirmation of the freeing of the hostages didn't come. Instead, at 12:34 A.M., this moved on the Associated Press wire:

> Bulletin
> battle
> Munich (AP)—An airport battle between German police and Arab commandoes Tuesday night, in an attempt to free Israeli hostages, left one policeman dead and several injured, with one terrorist a suicide victim and three others killed.
> An Olympic spokesman, giving this information, said the fate of the hostages was not known and that several terrorists escaped in the battle. (more)
> 1bs1234cetsept6-72

"The fate of the hostages not known?" This was a very different story. If they knew of the fate of the Arabs, why did they not know the fate of the hostages? Was something being held back?

One minute later, the wire came to life again:

Bulletin matter
Munich—battle 2
The Olympic official, giving brief details of the airport battle prefaced his remarks with the words, "We are afraid the information given so far is too optimistic."
Earlier reports had said that all the hostages were safe and uninjured, and made no mention of police casualties. (more)
1bso035cetsept6-72

If the previous information was "too optimistic," then they must know that *some* of the hostages are not safe, or at least have been wounded.

Six minutes later came the most concrete information we would have for a long time:

urgent
Munich-battle 3
The spokesman said contact with police had been difficult but that the following unofficial information had been gathered after an airport battle reported to have lasted up to two hours:
One policeman was dead, and several—perhaps three—have been wounded.
Three Arabs have been killed in the shootout, and one committed suicide with a grenade.
An undetermined number of terrorists escaped, and are being pursued.
"We have no definite word on the hostages, whether they are safe or not," the official said. (more)
ibso041cetsept6-72

The earlier story, then, on the freeing of the hostages, had been completely irresponsible and untrue. And if the spokesman had no "definite" word on the hostages, what was the *indefinite word*? No one was saying, and that was a suspicious circumstance.

By the time Chris Schenkel and I went on the air, live again to the States, Fred Schuhmann, a stage manager all day, had left for the BBC studio to try and find Herr Schreiber, the Munich chief of police, for an interview.

The stage manager who cued us to begin now was Jim Flood,

Schuhmann's assistant, and one of the first two men to go into the village the morning before. Like everyone else, Flood was hanging in until the end, doing what had to be done.

Chris and I summed up the events of the long day, including the sports events which had taken place before the Olympics were halted. There was no word as to whether, or when, the games would be resumed.

On a commercial break, I went into the control room and found out that a press conference was scheduled soon at the press center. We had no camera there, but Marvin Bader had gone over with a walkie-talkie. If there was any word before we had to leave the air, Roone told me, he would give it to me instantly in the earpiece. Everyone's mood was even darker than it had been hours earlier. You had to feel that something was wrong.

Shortly before we were scheduled to go off the air, at 2:30 A.M. Munich time, Roone said,

"This is important, Jim. Tell the stations that we will take a 33-second station break, then come back and wait for the announcement from the press conference of what happened to the hostages."

I did.

On his arrival at the press center about one o'clock, Marvin had found what seemed to be thousands of people thronging the area.

He had gone immediately into the office of Hans (Jonny) Klein, the press chief. There was small talk for a few minutes, then Marvin had been asked to leave. They had to have a private meeting, he was told, and then there would be a press conference at which the ministers of the interior for Bavaria and West Germany would give the word on what happened.

The meeting seemed endless.

Roone, through Geoff Mason on the walkie-talkie, was putting more and more pressure on Bader to get some solid information. We had to go off the air at 2:30, Marvin was told, and we had to have some word.

"What the hell is going on?" Geoff shouted, "We're going off the air!"

At this point, Roone was telling me that we would stay on, but Geoff hadn't heard it yet.

At 2:23, the meeting broke up. Marvin went to Otto Kentsch, assistant to Klein. Kentsch and Bader, a German and a Jew, had become good friends during the several years of preparation for the games.

"Otto's the kind of guy who cares. You know, Jimmy?" Marvin said later on. "Just a hell of a nice man."

Geoff was still calling in the walkie-talkie when Marvin asked Kentsch, earnestly, looking straight into his eyes, "Otto, what the hell happened out there?"

Kentsch looked deeply sad. His eyes were watery.

"I can't tell you, Marvin," he said.

Marvin pulled him aside from the group that was about to begin the press conference. He explained that we were about to go off the air, that he knew Kentsch couldn't make the official statement, but that we had to have some idea, something to base our summary on.

The two men continued to stare into each other's eyes.

Then Kentsch said, "They're all dead, Marvin."

"What are you talking about? All the hostages?"

"Yes, Marvin, all the hostages."

Marvin Bader had given up cigarettes for forty-six days until that moment. It wasn't until a half hour later that he realized he had lit one after hearing the terrible news.

After the station break, Roone filled me in. I said on the air that we had reason to believe the news would be very bad. We did not say categorically that they were all dead, because this was privileged information from Otto to Marvin and it was not official. It seemed that the official word would be given by the interior minister any minute, because the conference was under way. After all, the family of David Berger, for example, was probably watching in Ohio, waiting to hear if he was alive or dead. We had to be as cautious of Kentsch's report as we had been of the earlier cruelly erroneous bulletin.

If you were watching on television, you probably remember the next agonizing hour. Peter Jennings had joined Chris and me. So had Lou Cioffi, ABC News' Bonn correspondent. Lou had come to Munich for a holiday, to see the Olympics with his wife, and now was in the midst of the story. It was another irony.

While Jennings covers the Arab–Israeli story from the Arab side, Cioffi normally covers the Israelis. By pure coincidence, then, the network's two top experts on the people involved were on the scene in Munich at the right time.

We talked and waited. The interior minister was describing all of the day's events chronologically, instead of telling immediately what had happened to the hostages.

At one point, Roone said that we now had a radio line out of the press conference. We did, and we put it on the air. First, we heard a long passage of the interior minister talking in German. Then, as the English translation began, the voices of two German commentators came in and drowned it out. Naturally, they were beginning to discuss on German radio the remarks that they already understood. The radio line, then, was useless.

The tension was as thick as I have ever felt in a studio. My recollection of what we talked about is dim at this moment. But I remember Roone telling me that it was official, that they were all dead, and I remember summarizing the day's events.

I remember saying, "This morning at ten o'clock, in a little more than six and a half hours, the athletes and the people of Munich will gather in the great Olympic Stadium for a memorial service. They will pay tribute to the slain Israelis, then try to find some hope and solace for themselves and for this poor old world."

I finished with the three words that, I thought, summarized everything that had happened, everything that had been said in the twenty-three hours since the assassins scaled the fence of the village.

"They're all gone," I said.

Margaret had half-awakened when I turned the key in the lock of room 1810.

"What happened, Jim?" she asked. "Someone said they were all saved."

"They're all dead, Margaret," I answered.

Now I stand in the dark getting undressed, clad at the moment, ridiculously, in my bathing trunks, which I had put on to take that swim almost twenty hours ago.

The wonderful games of the Twentieth Olympiad lie in ruins after the events of yesterday and early this morning. The people of the nations gathered here have retired to their beds in deep despair. The city is silent. The cheering has stopped.

In the past decade, politicians and statesmen have learned to live with the possibility of their own sudden and violent death. Assassinations have shaken the structure of the world's greatest stronghold of representative government. Still, what happened at the Fürstenfeldbruck air base near Munich a couple of hours ago was different, and even more of an outrage against humanity than the other killings. The murdered Israelis were not representatives of their government. They were sportsmen, some of them wrestlers and weight-lifters, men who had dedicated themselves to the cultivation of their bodies so that they could best another man in an equal contest, under the rules.

The fanatics of the Black September Movement violated the sanctuary of the Olympic Village, tied the hands and blindfolded the eyes of these men whose physical capabilities were their reason for being here. In time, under the pressure of ambush from German police snipers at the airport, they fulfilled the terrible threat they had made many hours before. Having not had their way, they destroyed their captives.

At this moment, it appears that the games are over, that the preparations of many years were in vain, that the fragile concept of the "serene Olympics" was a farce or a foolish dream.

No Jew needs to be told that a pounding on the door in the middle of the night means terrible danger is at hand. For too many centuries in too many lands, it has meant that persecution, terror, and brutality have come again to visit the once-Chosen People. It was almost reflex action, then, for wrestling coach Moshe Weinberg to leap from his bed at the first alarm at 4:30 yesterday morning, to fling his strong body against the door as a human barricade, and to shout to his colleagues to flee, quickly, by whatever means they could find.

They ran, in their night clothes, to windows and balconies. Some jumped from the second floor, like weight-lifting coach Tuvia Sokolsky.

While they were still frantically trying to escape, Moshe Weinberg was dead, first victim of the assassins' bullets. His body was flung outside the door, later recovered by the German police and taken to a hospital morgue, where it was identified by his mother. Ironically, she is one of the few Jews still a resident of Munich.

These are the others who now lie dead:

Mark Slavin, an eighteen-year-old Greco-Roman wrestler, had emigrated from the Soviet Union to Israel only three months ago. He had told friends that his long-held ambition was to participate in the Olympics for his country, by which he meant Israel. Mark spoke only Russian, and so was only able to understand the last day of his life by the testimony of his eyes. He was to have started competition in the games on the day that ended in his death.

Yosef Romano, thirty-one-year-old employee of a paint firm, was a fifteen-year veteran weight-lifter, the champion of Israel in his class. He had taken a six-month leave of absence to prepare for the games. Mr. Romano was the father of three children.

Zeev Friedman finished twelfth in bantamweight weight-lifting in these games. He was a twenty-four-year-old physical education teacher, who came to Haifa from Poland.

Yacov Springer was another former Pole, who had coached the Israeli fencing team until his resignation last year. The fifty-two-year-old physical education teacher from Tel Aviv was at the Olympics as a fencing referee.

Kehat Shur, forty-five, was coach of the shooting team.

Eliezer Halfin was a nineteen-year-old lightweight weight-lifter and a soldier in the Israeli Army. He emigrated from Russia a year ago.

Amitzur Shapiro, forty-three, was an outstanding track coach, handling the Israeli girl's team here, including the world-class sprinter, Esther Shahamorov. (The Israeli girls, incidently, escaped death because they were lodged in a different building.)

Yosef Gottfreund, forty-eight, was a wrestling referee.

David Berger was a brilliant young man from Shaker Heights, Ohio, who had emigrated from the United States to Israel just a year ago. At age twenty-eight, he was a weight-lifter, and a man with a considerable future ahead of him. He studied pre-law at Tulane University and psychology at Columbia. His father is still a doctor in Shaker Heights.

Andrei Spitzer, a graduate of the Dutch Fencing Academy, came from Rumania, and was the new coach of the fencing team, as well as head of a school for all the fencing coaches of Israel. At age thirty, he was the father of a two-month-old child.

All these men died at the hands of the killers.

It is five o'clock in the morning. At 7:30, I must get up and prepare for the memorial service.

Will the games be restarted?

Before we left Roone's office after the telecast, word had come that Willi Daume, chairman of the Olympic Organizing Committee, had said that he didn't see how he could recommend a resumption of the games. The way I feel at this minute, I have to agree. I simply can't imagine talking about sports on the air soon again.

"The thrill of victory and the agony of defeat, the human drama of athletic competition," seem like trivial words from another world, overwhelmed by the obscenity that was concluded in the early hours of this morning, when the shots rang out, and the helicopter exploded, and all those men died, at Fürstenfeld-bruck, the air base twenty-eight miles from Munich.

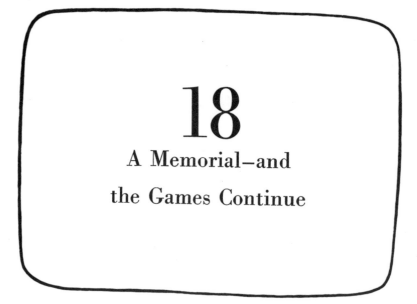

18

A Memorial—and

the Games Continue

There has never been a gathering like this. Eighty thousand people from 120 nations are in the Olympic Stadium in Munich. The flags fly at half-staff, including the Olympic banner itself. At a time when there should be cheering for the men running and jumping in the decathlon (that was this morning's scheduled event here), the Munich Philharmonic Orchestra is playing funeral music by Beethoven.

Many of the people here came to attend a memorial for two men, having gone to bed last night after the false report on German television that the rest of the hostages had been freed. The full force of the horror has just reached them.

The teams of the nations are gathered in the infield, some seated, others standing on the grass along the homestretch. This was where they had stood after marching in on that lovely opening day of the games. It is a similar day as far as the weather is concerned—sunny, perhaps hotter and hazier. But the mood is as different as life and death. On the opening day of the ceremonies, everyone felt as young as the children greeting the athletes with their handmade garlands. Today, everyone is old.

Daybreak brought no rays of hope with it. Seventeen men are dead—the eleven hostages, five of the killers, and a Munich policeman. Three Arabs are in prison.

Most of the teams are dressed in their parade uniforms and seated in blocks, chunks of color; some red, others blue or green. The Americans came informally, on their own initiative, and are scattered among the other countries. There is a report that the Soviets stayed away, but looking through my binoculars, I can't be certain of that. They may be scattered through the crowd, too.

The games will go on, apparently within a matter of hours. Avery Brundage said so, in his embarrassingly inappropriate remarks a few minutes ago. He talked not about the slain men for whom the memorial was being conducted, but about the Olympics. He seemed more angry at the interruption of the games than grieved at the death of the men.

He pointed out that the bigger the Olympics became, the more they seemed subject to commercialism, politics, and now to criminals. And then he linked the political maneuvering that had excluded Rhodesia from the games with the murders. In the Rhodesian case, he said, "we gave in to naked political blackmail," and now we have murders.

It seemed so insensitive to equate a political controversy with wanton murder, particularly here, as the pitiful survivors of the team of Israel sat in the front row, wearing their yarmulkes and grieving for their brothers.

When Brundage announced, in ringing tones, that the games would go on, the applause that greeted his words also seemed terribly out of place, like cheering in a church.

The remarks of West German President Gustav Heinemann had been more in keeping with the occasion. Such a short time ago, he had opened the games by speaking the fourteen words prescribed by Olympic regulations: "I declare open the Olympic

Games, celebrating the Twentieth Olympiad of the modern era."

It occurs to me that in the days of the ancient games, although it is not true that wars were stopped for the Olympics, it is a fact that soldiers were given safe conduct through enemy lines to participate in them. Last night, that tradition was broken, for the first time in all the long centuries since the first games in Greece. Even within the confines of the Olympic Village, safe conduct is no longer guaranteed.

Dr. Heinemann spoke to the occasion today, saying that here there is "no division of North, South, East, or West, just the division between decent people who want peace and those who would destroy the world by violence."

There were remarks by the Israeli ambassador and their *chef de mission*. The lesson was as obvious as a medieval morality play. Two men in yarmulkes spoke without bitterness, thanking their hosts for trying to save the hostages, even though, in the end, it could not have turned out worse.

When last the Olympics were held in this country, men in yarmulkes were being beaten and thrown into concentration camps. Now, they stood like mankind's conscience, reminders of the past as they were symbols of the terrible present.

Never before, never in man's history, have so many people of so many nations stood together for one grieving hour, to contemplate the sickness of their race—the race of man—and, hopefully, to think more seriously than ever before how they might be a friend to their neighbor, to the man standing next to them today in the Munich stadium, to all the 80,000 here from around the world, to the one billion solemnly watching television sets in every nation.

I am sitting on the stool in front of the monitor, at the same station where I watched Dave Wottle and John Akii-Bua and Kip Keino and Larry Young.

Helping me, as spotter, is Marty Pompadur. He was here when I arrived this morning. Chuck and Andy are in the control room, Roone is again back at master control. And tomorrow, we must return to this spot for the beginning of the decathlon. It will begin just twenty-four hours late.

I know it will be hard for us to find an appropriate attitude toward the competition. I wonder if the athletes, themselves, will find it difficult to bring their enthusiasm and effort back to its peak.

WEDNESDAY, SEPTEMBER 6 (10:00 P.M.)

We have finally eaten dinner in a restaurant.

Roone Arledge, whose two oldest daughters, Betsy and Suzy, are here with him for the games, asked Margaret, Mary, Sean, and me to join them and Chris Schenkel for dinner at a very good Austrian restaurant. We just had time for it, between an interview I did with Willi Daume, president of the Olympics Organizing Committee, and our preparation for tonight's transmission to the States.

We were all exhausted, but the dinner was a most welcome break, just the same. Betsy Arledge showed us a leather pocketbook a friend had made for her, Sean talked to Chris about sports, Mary, Margaret, Roone, and I talked about things other than the tragedy. The dinner had not been planned. In fact, I hadn't planned on working tonight at all.

After the memorial service, I had returned to the hotel and slept until five in the afternoon. This evening, Henry Meyer, the young student–driver, had invited the family to a party at the fencing fraternity to which he belongs. The invitation had been given before the events of yesterday, but they were going to have some sort of gathering, anyway.

Margaret was wondering aloud whether we should go or just stay in the hotel and have a decent dinner, when the phone rang. It was exactly 6:00 P.M. Geoff Mason was on the other end.

"Jimmy," he said, "I'm really sorry to drag you out again, but Willi Daume is coming for an interview and Roone wants you to do it. O.K.?"

The interview was to be at 6:30, so I took off quickly. Later, Roone had the idea for dinner, so things turned out well.

Now, we must go back to the studio and get ready for tonight's 1:00 to 4:00 A.M. transmission. I'll be reporting on the memorial service and later developments.

Apparently, there is to be no letup in the tension. Just before coming to the restaurant, I tore a piece off the wire saying that the Bavarian government had instituted a manhunt for fifteen other terrorists, believed to be plotting bombings somewhere in the area. I didn't mention it during dinner.

Our kids will return to the States tomorrow on an early morning flight. School will be starting soon, so Mary must return to college for her sophomore year and Sean must begin his senior year in prep school.

Such normal events seem very far away tonight, and they must to the kids, too.

We'll miss them. Since Margaret and I are going to take a motor trip through the wine country of France after the games, we won't see them for about twelve days.

Despite her aversion to farewells and airports, Margaret has volunteered to take them to the plane in the morning, so that I can sleep until it is time to go to the stadium.

Mary has friends to say goodbye to, the Canadian swimmers among them, I presume.

Sean is coming out to the ABC center.

"I just want to take one more look around, Dad," he said.

THURSDAY, SEPTEMBER 7 (11:00 P.M.)

Mary and Sean flew home this morning.

The Olympic Games resumed, with everything set back exactly twenty-four hours. From the results of today's competitions, the athletes appeared to be as sharp as before. Everything looked the same—80,000 people in the stadium, television cameras in place. You had to look closely to see the one small detail that was different from the earlier days of competition. Far across the stadium from our position, not far from the Olympic flame, the flag of Israel was still flying at half-staff. The flags of all the other nations had already been moved back to the top of their poles.

The spirit of the games is gone. The serenity has been shattered; the childlike feeling of excitement and fun has disappeared.

Is the resumption of the games a desecration, a blasphemy on the memories of the men who died? Or is it a small statement from mankind that life on the planet will go on, despite all, that the only hope for the people of earth is to endure, and to gather together, to try to find that most elusive of goals—some way to become one community?

There was an air of unreality to the earlier mood of light-hearted *Gemütlichkeit*. Perhaps the confusion and uncertainty of today's resumption can be fused into a far more serious, but eventually positive, mood. Maybe the people gathered here can understand that, although we are not floating on cloud nine with little Olga and little Ulrike, we are all in the same leaky boat, and the time is at hand to patch it up or sink.

My thoughts all day today were more of these things, quite frankly, than of what I saw on the field below me. To put it more accurately, it was as if my mind had two separate compartments —one concentrating on the serious, the other attuned to the competition I was reporting on.

Somehow, the one event that suffered most today from the change of mood was the decathlon. Normally, that exhausting endurance contest is one of the most serious parts of the Olympics, symbolizing the triumph of staying the course over the brief explosion of energy.

I think it is *because* of the decathlon's usual symbolism that it suffered today. After the true test of emotional endurance that the people of the world have been through these past forty-eight hours, the symbolic test seems only another sports competition. Nothing less, but nothing more.

Rodney Milburn, Jr., won his gold medal in the 110-meter high hurdles this afternoon. After his summer of discontent and financial problems, the Southern University student proved that he is truly dominant in his event, that *Track and Field News* was correct last winter in naming him the world track and field athlete of the year.

There was another positive occurrence for the United States when Kathy Hammond, running against a strong field in the women's 400 meters, won the bronze medal. The twenty-year-old blonde from Carmichael, California, finished only half a second behind the winner, East Germany's powerful Monika Zehrt.

The conflicts that divide men intruded again on what should have been a happy American occasion. In the men's 400 meters, Vince Matthews and Wayne Collett finished first and second. The United States might have gotten all three medals if John Smith hadn't pulled up with an injured leg in the first 100 meters of the race.

On the victory stand, Matthews and Collett didn't look like happy winners. They didn't look unhappy, either. They just looked like they didn't care.

Vince, who had made such a great comeback from retirement to Olympic victory, did pull Wayne up to the top level of the rostrum with him, but then, as the anthem played, the two of them talked to each other, turned around and glanced at the stands and the sky, and generally seemed in a hurry to leave.

As they walked off the field, there was whistling and booing. Matthews responded by twirling his Olympic gold medal on its ribbon, like a kid playing with a Yo-Yo.

Later, in an interview with Howard back in the studio, Wayne said that their attitude had reflected the way white Americans feel about black—casual and uncaring. Matthews said that the twirling of the medal had been an act of impulse. He said that it didn't have to do with racial protest, but was to show the people who had thought he was finished that he was, in fact, the gold medalist.

The behavior of the two athletes certainly was not a positive protest, like the Black Power salute given in Mexico City by Tommie Smith and John Carlos four years ago. Smith and Carlos made a planned, positive statement, one they obviously felt deeply. Matthews and Collett showed casual disrespect. It seemed more an unplanned, negative act than a positive statement of belief.

The United States will not win the decathlon this time, although little Jeff Bennett, five feet, seven inches tall, is giving a fine account of himself and could get a medal in tomorrow's final events.

Renate Stecher of East Germany put her name in the record books by winning the women's 200 meters. Having already taken the 100, she became the first girl since Wilma Rudolph at Rome in 1960 to sweep the sprints.

In the first round heats for the 5,000 meters, there was a happening that brought back memories of Eddie Hart and Reynaud Robinson. Miruts Yifter of Ethiopia, one of the favorites in the 5,000 (Steve Prefontaine told me the other night that he feared Yifter most of all), reported to the wrong gate of the stadium. The guard steadfastly refused to let him in, and eventually the race went off without him. When he realized what had happened, that he was out of the Olympics, Yifter collapsed, crying, in his coach's arms.

There seem to be so many sad things about the games of Munich.

FRIDAY, SEPTEMBER 8 (8:30 P.M.)

More sadness. A few minutes ago, in the darkness outside the ABC studios, I saw Jim Ryun and his wife, talking softly with friends. I gave Jim my sympathy. He said that there will be a protest, and he seemed sincere when he said that he has real hope of running in tomorrow's semifinals. His hope almost certainly will be in vain. Jim Ryun, as of this moment, is out of the Olympics. It is the latest incredible moment of Munich.

Today was merely the first round of qualifying heats for the 1,500 meters, the first necessary formal step, leading toward the great confrontation on Sunday between Ryun and Kip Keino.

The crowd found it intriguing that Ryun and Keino were in the same heat today through a coincidence of the draw. (Some people are claiming tonight that this was an error, that their previous times should have seeded them into different heats.)

It wasn't necessary for either of them to win, of course, just to finish comfortably among the leaders to move on to the semifinals.

The race developed as expected, Ryun and Keino running easily at the back of the pack, while less famous men took their moment in the sun and led the race.

As they reached turn three of the third lap, Keino decided to go to the front. Shifting gears smoothly, he went around the outside of the pack, and by turn four, was leading the race. Ryun did not move with him. Instead, Jim stayed at the back, in traffic.

Marty Liquori and I made note of this in our commentary, and unconsciously, I made a sadly prophetic remark. Pointing out Ryun's position as they were between turns three and four, I said, "There was a time when it didn't bother us at all when Jim hung back. But in the past few years, we have learned to hold our breath until he makes his move. So many strange things have happened. Sometimes the kick hasn't come at all."

It couldn't have been three or four seconds later that the impossible thing happened. Jim Ryun, in a flash, wasn't running. He was lying flat on his back, up against the inside rail, motionless for long moments. Down with him was Billy Fordjour, a Texas college student from Ghana.

Then Ryun was up, limping. He began to pick up speed, then was in full stride again. But the other runners were already in turn two of the final lap as Ryun crossed the finish line on lap three. It was obvious that he would not, could not, make it.

When the others reached the finish, Keino was leading. He glanced to his right and left just before the tape. Crossing the line, he looked around again. He was looking for Ryun, who, he assumed, would be right behind him.

When Kip saw Jim, far down the stretch, laboring and straining, he clapped his hand to his head in disbelief. He waited until Jim finished, then went over and put his arm around the shoulders of the stricken Kansan.

The great race would not take place on Sunday. Four years of defeat, then retirement, then comeback and occasional victory, interspersed with inexplicable bad performances, had led to the final ignominy for Jim Ryun—exit from his final Olympics, not in valiant defeat, head-to-head with his old rival, but flat on his back at the head of the stretch. The fastest miler of all time would never win an Olympic gold medal.

Ryun and his personal coach, Bob Timmons, think they have grounds for protest. As late as turn three, the race had been led by a runner from Pakistan, but as Keino began to move, the Pakistani faded quickly. He was totally out of gas. As they entered turn four, he was still fading, on the rail. Then he drifted out a bit, in front of Ryun. There was a jam, Fordjour ran into Ryun as Jim slowed down, and they fell.

Was it a foul? Certainly not on Fordjour's part. Possibly, but only possibly, on the part of the Pakistani. Most of the experts feel that it was no worse than normal race jostling, and that the protest is a mere formality.

Jim Ryun has always had an inner ear problem which affects his balance. For that reason, he traditionally has stayed away from other runners, as far as possible under race conditions. Today, he was in the one place that proved most dangerous, yet he says tonight that he was where he wanted to be, that his race schedule was perfect to the moment of the fall.

The Russians finished one–two in the decathlon today. Jeff Bennett gave it a good try, but finished fourth.

Vince Matthews and Wayne Collett were banned for life from the Olympic movement by the IOC for their actions on the victory stand yesterday. The USOC has protested, claiming that it should be a disciplinary problem for the Americans, not the International Committee.

It almost certainly is a ruling that will cause future problems. When an athlete moves around on the victory stand, who will say whether it is a gesture of protest, or an unconscious act? Already tonight, someone mentioned that an American girl's swimming relay team had moved around and giggled during the playing of the anthem after their victory.

I didn't see that moment. Apparently they were only behaving self-consciously, as teen-age girls often do. But who is to interpret the *meaning* of athletes' behavior from now on?

Another depressing day.

SUNDAY, SEPTEMBER 10 (9:30 A.M.)

Henry Meyer has been driving more carefully since he totaled the little BMW 1800. Right now, we are cruising slowly across

John F. Kennedy Bridge on the Mittlerer Ring, bound for the stadium for the final day of competition in the games of the Twentieth Olympiad.

The track and field events don't begin until 2:30 this afternoon, but I have to view some videotape at the ABC center for an Olympics highlights show that will be on later tonight. I have a good deal of the script and commentary to take care of.

Right now, I am distracted. As I came down in the elevator just a few minutes ago, a stranger asked me what I thought about the basketball game. I told him that I didn't know anything about the basketball game, that I had been very tired last night, and went to bed early.

"You don't know that the Russians beat the Americans?" he asked.

For a moment, I didn't believe him. The Americans had never lost a *game*, let alone a gold medal, since basketball formally entered the Olympics, at Berlin, 1936. How could it have happened?

Apparently, the Soviets played very well, the Americans played rather badly, and then there had been as chaotic an ending as the Olympics have yet seen. The game seemed to have ended as the clock ran out, with the Americans the winners. They began their celebration on the court, but the horn sounded urgently from the scorer's table. For some reason, it was declared that the game was not over, that there were three seconds left.

The Russians threw the ball the length of the court in the extra three seconds, scored, and won the game. Or did they? The Americans have protested, the members of the team have voted unanimously not to accept a silver medal, and all is bitterness and confusion.

Well, I suppose I should have known that something of an unbelievable nature would have to happen before yesterday ended. It had been too normal an afternoon, too free of the incredible.

To be sure, the result of the shot put had been closer than any in Olympic history. The winner was Wladyslaw Komar, a Pole who has been knocking around the European track and field circuit for more than a decade, with indifferent success. Between him and Hans Peter Gies, of East Germany, who finished fourth, was a difference of only one and three-quarters inches!

George Woods, of the United States, won the silver medal, losing out to Komar by half an inch. Hartmut Briesenick, of East Germany, took third by a quarter of an inch, over his teammate, Gies.

There were those who wanted to start another international incident over the manner of Woods' loss. On his final throw, a do-or-die effort, George hit the tiny flag indicating Komar's new Olympic record (how many improbable incidents like that have there now been in these games?).

The angrier Americans immediately claimed that Woods must have beaten Komar. How could he hit the tiny metal flagstick, yet not have thrown further than Komar? To me, and to a good many others, it appeared that the shot imbedded itself at the *base* of the flagstick, making the slender wire bend over, but leaving the nearer rim of the shot's impression short.

The argument was softened by the post-race statement of the gently spoken, 300-pound Woods. "I would have liked to take another throw," said George, "but I think the ruling will stand."

It did.

There was American disappointment, but not incredulity, when Dave Wottle and Bob Wheeler were both eliminated in the 1,500-meter semifinals. Ryun had been the big hope in this one, despite Wottle's amazing performance in winning the 800. Jim, hoping against hope, worked out yesterday, and was at the stadium in uniform, ready to go, in case there was a surprise reversal of his elimination. It never came.

The jinx that has followed the United States in the 1,500 since 1908 continues, then. No American has won the race—not Joey Ray, or Glenn Cunningham, or Jim Ryun, or any of the other great American milers—since Mel Sheppard triumphed in London sixty-four years ago.

Wottle nearly made it into the final, but he kicked a bit too late, by his own admission, and just lost out. His comment was typically direct. "I started too late," he said. "I relied on my kick. I made a mistake."

Wheeler is still a boy among men at this stage, but could

certainly have a shot at the gold medal four years from now in Montreal.

Repercussions of the Matthews–Collett incident were still being felt.

No American team appeared for the heats of the 4 × 400 relay, an event that had been conceded to the United States before the games began. The reason was simple. With John Smith injured and Matthews and Collett barred, there simply were not enough runners left to field a team. It meant that Lee Evans, gold medalist in the 400 at Mexico, had made the trip in vain. He had qualified only for the relay in the trials in Oregon.

Randy Williams, an appealing nineteen-year-old sophomore at the University of Southern California, saved some glory for the United States by winning the long jump. Randy's winning jump was more than two *feet* short of Bob Beamon's leap to immortality in Mexico, but it was a good jump, all the same (twenty-seven feet, one-half inch), and better than Hans Baumgartner of West Germany by two and a half inches. Arnie Robinson took the bronze medal for the United States.

Williams made quite a picture after his victory. He stood waving and smiling at the crowd, proudly wearing his gold medal—and holding his teddy bear.

And now, the final day of competition. It is a big one, with the 1,500, the 5,000, the high jump, the marathon, and men's and women's relays, all yet to be decided.

Now, what in the world of an impossible nature can happen today?

SUNDAY, SEPTEMBER 10 (11:45 P.M.)

The reports of shooting in the Olympic Village appear to be false now, but the past hour has been one to further shred the emotions of the tired people working here in the ABC center.

We have been putting together an Olympics highlights show, to go on the air on tonight's 1:00 A.M. transmission to America. It's been a hard job, at the end of a long and exciting day. Still, all was proceeding on schedule until the reports began to circulate through the tape rooms—from wire service reports and by rumor—that there was renewed violence in the village and there might be bombs planted right here in the television center.

First reports said that there was shooting in the Olympic compound and that three Russians were reported dead. Peter Jennings and John Wilcox went into the village in search of the facts. Unquestionably, there were sirens to be heard outside our building as police cars arrived. There were policemen searching the television building.

Then came another wire service report. An Austrian youth had fallen to his death about a half mile from here while trying to climb one of the flagpoles. This was confirmed, but apparently was unconnected with the other reports.

A few minutes ago, our two AP wires moved conflicting stories simultaneously. One quoted a Munich police spokesman as saying that a man had been seen on a spiral staircase in the quarters of the Moroccan team, firing three or four shots. The spokesman did not know of any casualties, and said that the mystery man had been seen fleeing toward the fence of the village.

At the same time, the other wire was typing out a statement from press chief Hans (Jonny) Klein. There was nothing to any of the shooting reports, Jonny said. "It is a macabre piece of nonsense," he declared.

Now, Jennings and Wilcox have reported back. Klein is right, they say. There is nothing to any of it, except for the boy falling to his death. He was probably in search of a souvenir flag when he died, in the words of the police report, "of the sort of injuries one suffers when falling from a great height."

Let's review the events of the day now, because the final afternoon of track and field competition was exciting and, of course, productive of the unexpected.

First to appear on the track were the marathoners. Beside me in the booth, Erich Segal was leaning forward like a greyhound on a leash. He looked like he would have liked to run the race himself. Probably, he would.

This was the event in which Erich had predicted victory for Frank Shorter, his former student. Frank was down there with the rest of the huge field, looking calmer than Erich, but just as confident. His hair was neatly in place, his small mustache trimmed, his track suit as smoothly fitted as if it had just emerged from the Brooks Brothers tailoring department.

The marathoners went off, circled the stadium, then left to a great cheer from the crowd. There was a change of mood among the 80,000 today, it seemed. For the first time since the tragedy, they seemed ready for an afternoon of excitement. This was their last chance to regain at least some vestige of the wonderful feeling that had prevailed earlier. They were setting sorrow aside, for a few short hours at least.

Just after the marathoners left, the 5,000-meter field took to the track. Many thought it was the strongest in any of the track events. There was Lasse Viren, already winner of the 10,000; Emiel Puttemans, the Belgian gardener; Harald Norpath, the storklike runner from West Germany; Mohammed Gahmoudi, the defending gold medalist from Tunisia; Ian Stewart, the pride of Scotland; and, of course, Steve Profontaine. This was the time for Pre to prove that a youngster could come from comparative isolation in his native Oregon and beat the canniest veterans in the world, men tested in years of international competition.

Before the race, as we commented live, Erich made a statement that he can stand on tonight. "Steve Prefontaine," he said, "will win the Olympic gold medal in the 5,000 meters. But he will not win it here today. It will happen in Montreal, four years from now, in 1976."

Certainly, the first part of his forecast was true. Pre ran himself to exhaustion today, staying with the leaders until the final steps, when he stumbled and fell across the finish line, much as Arzhanov had when Wottle caught him in the 800. It was Viren an easy winner for his second gold medal. He is the first man since Vladimir Kuts of the Soviet Union, in 1956, to win both the five and the ten. Gahmoudi was second, and Ian Stewart closed in a rush to take third from Prefontaine. Pre held onto fourth.

Then came the 1,500. Even as they came on the track, there was a feeling of anticlimax. With Ryun out, it was Keino against the world, and the world did not look too strong. Yet, when it was over, Keino had lost. It was another gold medal for Finland. Pekka Vasala crossed the line first. With his rather long, curly hair and Van Dyck beard, his arms outstretched and his toes neatly pointed on the victory lap, Vasala looked like a figure from some old Nordic folk tale.

Certainly, the long, dark northern winters will be brightened for years to come by grandfathers telling small boys of that day when Viren and Vasala brought double Olympic glory to Finland in the course of one-half hour.

The finish of the marathon returned these games to their accustomed state—the realm of the impossible. Periodically, as the other races came and went, we had cut to the cameras placed around town to observe the long distance specialists on their tour of the city. As the race reached its final stages, sure enough, it was Frank Shorter leading the pack, running through the streets of his old home town. Well, at least, the place where he was born. Frank actually resided in Munich for only a few months after his birth, which occurred while his father was an Army doctor here.

Frank was a strong leader, solidifying his position as the runners neared the Olympic Stadium. Erich and I were observing him on a monitor, watching through the lens of a camera mounted on an electrically powered truck. The truck cruised ahead of the leader, documenting his progress for the world.

At last, it was almost time for him to come into the stadium itself. The crowd milled, leaning out for a better look at the marathon gate, waiting for the figure of Shorter to appear.

I was splitting my visual attention between the image of the American on the monitor and my live view of the gate when, for a brief moment, I thought that we had made a terrible mistake. A figure was entering the stadium, but it was not Frank Shorter! It was a blond runner in a blue and yellow track suit, wearing number 72. Shorter was number 1014.

Quickly, I scanned the list of entrants in front of me. As I did, Erich was already shouting, "That's not Frank. That's an imposter. He's a fake! Throw him out of the stadium! This sort of thing used to happen in the Boston Marathon."

Thank heaven, there was no number 72 on the entry list. After all, it was always possible that the camera truck might have let a runner slip past it far back in the early stages of the race, that somehow the information we had received was in error.

The imposter was already on the backstretch, acknowledging the cheers of the crowd, when Shorter came through the marathon gate. By now, the more expert of the spectators realized what had happened and were beginning to whistle and boo at the stranger.

Frank, of course, couldn't imagine what was going on. Here, after all the long years of effort and training, he had achieved his exhausting goal. But where were the cheers? Why the whistling? What had he done wrong?

It was a prank, but it was also a very dirty trick on Frank Shorter. He is an authentic amateur, a lover of his sport. A part of his reward certainly should have been a crowd on its feet, cheering his accomplishment to the skies. Instead, there was confusion.

By now, we were conjecturing why in the world anyone would do something so ridiculous, so cheap.

"I hope the man's name will be found out," I said, "so it can be recorded for a bit of athletic infamy."

Erich was furious. "I hope his name will not be known," he said.

"Pay no attention to him, Frank!" Erich called out. "You're the winner!"

In our tiny earpieces, Chuck Howard, from the control room, said, "Erich, Frank can't hear you."

I thought Professor Segal's comments were well-suited to the occasion. The novelist in him recognized the moment to let an honest expression of emotion take over from the precise comments of a track expert.

He was a teacher standing up for his student; a part-time marathoner identifying with his friend, the gold medalist; the author of *Love Story* knowing a romantic moment when he saw one.

The imposter, we later found out, is a West German youth who has been living in the youth camp here. The number "72" had been cut from a Coca-Cola poster reading, in part, "Munich, '72." It was a prank, nothing more, and there will be no prosecution, the Germans say.

This last day of track and field turned out to be the best day for the United States. Shorter's victory set the tone.

There was a fine silver medal performance by the American girls in the 4 × 400 relay. As her coach, Fred Thompson, proudly smiled and commented at my side, Cheryl Toussaint, of the Brooklyn Atoms, ran her entire lap of the stadium with one track shoe. The other one had come off when she collided with another runner during the baton handoffs.

Cheryl's lap was amazingly good, under the circumstances, and Kathy Hammond's was excellent on the anchor leg. Only the world-record performance of the East Germans beat out the American girls.

There was Dwight Stones. The youngest member of the American men's track team was in the fourth grade in 1962 when he saw Valeri Brumel set a world high jump record during ABC's telecast of the U.S.–Russian track meet. Then and there, Dwight tells us, he decided to be a high jumper. He built himself a set of high jump uprights and used a mattress for a landing pad.

He is tall and skinny (6'5", 165 pounds), tow-headed, and boiling with enthusiasm as he competes. He could pose for a picture called, "The Old College Try," or something like that. This is appropriate for the eighteen-year-old grandson of the man who wrote "Fight On!" the football song of USC. What is not appropriate is that the grandson attends USC's cross-town rival school, UCLA.

That came about only because Dwight was able to get an athletic scholarship to UCLA after USC turned him down.

He surprised everyone in the Olympic Trials by winning, and he surprised everyone again today. The crowd soon took to his cheerleader attitude. Each time he makes a height, Dwight unconsciously sticks out his tongue and shakes his head in disbelief, at the same time shaking his fist in triumph. Then, hearing the crowd cheer, he turns to them and shakes both fists, as if it is something he and the crowd are accomplishing together.

This afternoon, he and the crowd accomplished a bronze

medal with a leap of 7'3", only three-quarters of an inch lower than the winning jump of Russia's Yuri Tarmak.

Finally, there was Eddie Hart. How fitting it was that the United States' final moment of victory at these Olympic Games should go to Eddie. Given enough time, the occurrences of life tend to come full cycle, and so it was here. Hart had been forced to stand on the sidelines, helplessly, and watch Valeri Borzov win the 100 meters gold medal. Often since then, in the night, he must have relived that moment when he ran wildly down the tunnel to the stadium, trying desperately to make that quarter final heat, only to hear the gun go off when he was within yards of the starting line.

Now, there was one more chance. In the 4 × 100 relay, Hart would run the anchor leg and so would Borzov. And there were other stories. Legs one and three for the United States would be run by Larry Black and Gerald Tinker. Their mothers, who are sisters, sat in the stands. Mrs. Black would be watching her son in action for the first time; Mrs. Tinker would be watching Gerald run for the second time. Running the second leg for the United States would be Robert Taylor, who had shouldered the burden all alone in the 100 meters, and had won the silver medal.

The Russians figured to be strong on the first leg with the explosive little Korneliuk, weak in the two middle legs, and, of course, ultimately powerful on the anchor with Borzov.

Larry Black, a 200-meter man, but an expert on running the curve, stayed with Korneliuk very well. Then Taylor took over and ran a terrific straightaway. Things looked good, but the pass from Taylor to Tinker would be crucial. In earlier heats, their pass had been sloppy, and the wolves were standing poised to leap on Coach Stan Wright again. Wright, the goat of the wrong starting time incident, has also been under fire for the passing technique he insists the team use. It is considered obsolete by many, and dangerous. Put as simply as possible, the technique requires each runner to transfer the stick from one of his hands to the other, thereby giving him an opportunity to drop it. Historically, the United States has been very bad in Olympic baton-passing.

A good many breaths were held as Taylor approached Tinker, but the fears were groundless. The pass was perfect, and Gerald flew around the curve on the inside, as Eddie Hart danced impatiently, waiting for his moment. Again, there was a perfect pass. Unexpectedly, the Russians, now trailing by several strides, made a sloppy transfer.

Borzov took off after Hart, the world's fastest human chasing the only man who might have been able to challenge him for that title. It took Valeri about ten meters to pick up momentum after the uncertain pass, but then, it appeared to me, he began to gain on Hart.

The race was on. Soon, it became apparent that even Borzov's charge wouldn't be enough, and then, Hart seemed to pull away again, in the closing strides.

Who had won the confrontation? Well, the Americans had won the race, that was certain. Head to head, I thought that Hart and Borzov were just about even over that final 100 meters, but in fairness, it should be remembered that Borzov's start was stumbling, while Eddie's was smooth.

It was a moment of explosive exuberance to end the United States participation in track and field here. Black, Taylor, Tinker, and Hart hugged each other and waved to the crowd. They started a victory lap, smiling like kids who had gotten just what they wanted for Christmas. It was a moment to let off steam, to release tension and frustration for every American on the scene, and so they did, roaring their congratulations to the four young black men jogging and laughing down on the track.

It had started poorly for the country in track and field those long days ago. All through, there had been defeat and controversy mixed with victory. All told, there were only half as many American gold medals in the men's events as there had been in Mexico (six this time, twelve four years ago). But the United States had won more medals overall than anyone else (nineteen versus thirteen for the USSR). They had tied for most gold medals with the Russians.

Have the Americans slipped? I don't think so, not at all. They missed the shot put gold medal by a centimeter. Disqualification ruled them out of the 4 × 400 relay, which would have been almost an automatic gold. There was the pole vault controversy.

More important is the fact that the rest of the world is catching up. The Russians are always tough. Finland is back as a major track power. The Kenyans are here to stay. Other nations are on the move, the two Germanys, for example, and little countries like Uganda.

Olympic track and field is a more exciting contest for the change. It is a spectacle with something for everybody—East and West, every continent, many countries.

What will it be like four years from now? Probably closer than ever, with at least one important new factor on the scene. It seems inevitable that the Communist Chinese will be in the games at Montreal.

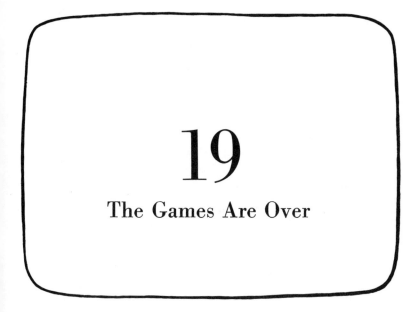

19

The Games Are Over

The closing ceremonies of the games of Munich took place at night on Monday. The crowd was the same as always, 80,000, but the temperature had changed. The beautiful summer weather had moved out overnight. It was crisp, even chilly, as the crowd moved into the stands, some carrying blankets.

The scene looked more like a night football game than anything else. Still, it seemed appropriate that the seasons would change, almost on cue, as the games ended.

It was time for those who had come here to start picking up the threads of their own individual lives again; to think about home, and work, and the autumn months ahead.

First, though, there would be the closing. It had been planned as a great, explosive celebration, complete with fireworks against the cool, black sky. The fireworks had been canceled, partly out of respect to the slain Israelis, partly as a security measure. All of us would be glad when this final evening was over, actually, because there were disturbing reports of possible disruption, even violence, at the stadium. The next morning, the security officials would admit that they had been seriously guarding against a possible air raid, by a single bandit plane, on the stadium itself. Almost anything was possible.

When the athletes walked in, waving, in loose ranks, not according to nations this time, it was immediately evident that neither they, nor the crowd, were quite certain how to act. After the unprecedented happenings of Munich, should there be laughter and nostalgia, or silence and grieving?

The ceremonies eventually reflected both. There was a certain amount of snake-dancing by some of the athletes; principally the British, led by hurdler David Hemery, and Mexico, led by their 1968 gold medalist, swimmer Felipe Munoz. But that came toward the end, when most of the other competitors were leaving the stadium.

The moments that will linger in the mind are the serious ones. The extinction of the Olympic flame always signifies an ending, and endings, like good-byes, are sad. But this time there was more. In tribute to the Israeli Olympians, men in old Bavarian costume stood on the hill of rubble that had been transformed into lovely parkland and fired volleys from ancient blunderbusses.

Somewhere beneath the grass they stood on were the remains of buildings and bodies, remnants of the wrath dropped on Munich by allied bombers. Millions of Jews had died at the hands of Germans before the bombers finally brought the slaughter to a halt. Now, the volleys rang out in tribute, the riflemen on the hill in full view of most of the crowd in the stadium.

The avowed aim of the games of Munich had been to demonstrate that the people of Germany wanted, more than anything, to be part of the family of man. They were sensitive, most of all, to the memory of what had been done to the Jews.

Now, at the end, we have the final irony. On the very land where Chamberlain took off, bearing, he thought, "peace in our time"; on top of a hill built from the result of the later holocaust; in full view of the people from 120 nations; at a time when they had hoped to be revelling in the "serene Olympics," celebrating and looking to the future with the blackboard rubbed clean of the past; the Germans, instead, were mourning the Jews with this memorial volley.

"We wish it hadn't happened," they were saying. "We wish it had turned out better. We're sorry."

The death of the young is always tragic, and the death of an athlete has its own special pathos. The English poet A. E. Housman put the feeling into the lines he entitled, "To an Athlete Dying Young." As the Olympic flag was lowered, it seemed appropriate to me to read some verses from the poem as our tribute to the heroes of Building 31:

> The time you won your town the race
> We chaired you through the market-place;
> Man and boy stood cheering by,
> And home we brought you shoulder-high.
>
> To-day, the road all runners come,
> Shoulder-high we bring you home,
> And set you at your threshold down,
> Townsman of a stiller town.
>
> Smart lad, to slip betimes away
> From fields where glory does not stay,
> And early though the laurel grows
> It withers quicker than the rose.
>
> Eyes the shady night has shut
> Cannot see the record cut,
> And silence sounds no worse than cheers
> After earth has stopped the ears:
>
> Now you will not swell the rout
> Of lads that wore their honours out,
> Runners whom renown outran
> And the name died before the man . . .

The poem had moved me many years before, in a high school English class. Who could ever guess that it would one day be an appropriate ending to the Olympic Games?

The Olympic flag, a symbol of continuity, was borne from the stadium by the eight West German rowers who had won a gold medal in Mexico. It would return to the stadium in Montreal four years from now.

A man-made rainbow was illuminated over a corner of the stadium. Made in Minneapolis of something called Stratofilm and inflated with helium, the rainbow was 1,500 feet long and 600 feet high, arching from a man-made lake in front of the Schwimmhalle to the top of the hill of rubble. The rainbow was in the Olympic colors and it moved in the light, cool breeze. Its sinuous motion was awesomely beautiful, and its symbolism more important than ever. Long before the games, the rainbow's designer had said that he wanted it to symbolize "peace and understanding among nations."

Each spectator had been given a tiny electric torch when he entered the stadium, and in time, the signal was given to light them, then wave them in farewell to the athletes. The stadium lights were out. What looked like 80,000 gracefully moving fireflies flickered in the blackness.

I had been almost alone in the commentary booth when the ceremonies began, but now I happened to glance around and said, on the air, involuntarily, "Hey, I just looked up and all the guys are here."

Behind me stood Erich Segal and Marty Liquori, Fred Thompson, Jim Dunaway and Fred Baer and Dick Ebersol, all the men who had shared the stadium experience with me. (Bill Toomey had to leave early to join his wife, Mary, in London.)

They were all just standing there, still sharing the final minutes of the experience, and they all smiled at my surprise. It had been an entirely happy booth all through the games. The personalities of the group were varied, but we worked well together and I hope we will again.

The band was playing "My Sweet Lord" as the athletes filed out, still waving. I did my wrap-up of the games of the Twentieth Olympiad:

The games are over. Looking back, "games" seems such a frivolous word to describe an experience that evoked every human emotion; seventeen days that certainly mirrored the world, with its beauty, its spirit, its people, its troubles, end even the terrible sickness of mind that has become so familiar in our time.

Were they seventeen days that changed the world?

Probably not. If all the wars and all the churches, all the heroes and all the villains of history have not changed the basic ways of man, then certainly the seventeen days of Munich won't do it.

This time that so many millions of us have shared together has, however, turned a glaring spotlight on the good and the bad, the strengths and the weaknesses. From what we have seen, each man can make his own judgment.

Because of the games of the Twentieth Olympiad, all of us should know something more about the earth and its people than we did before.

It seemed like the moment for a personal reaction, and I said that the only positive lesson I could find was that "neither madness nor violence nor unspeakable atrocities can stop the spirit of man to keep living; to try to make something out of the world as it is."

After the ceremonies, in the control room down below, Chuck Howard had provided champagne, with the logistical assistance of unit manager Marshall Lopez (who even found glasses, rather than paper cups).

Amid the crowded litter of the past weeks, among the monitors and the wires and the old rundowns, we stood—Chuck and Andy; associate director Lou Frederick, who has traveled half the world with Chuck and me; associate producer Terry Jastrow; technical director Walt Kubilus; and our British crew. There was champagne and "so long" from the Americans, "cheerio" from the British. Then there was more champagne and many "*auf wiedersehens*" as the German crew from down the hall insisted that we join in their farewell.

It all lasted only about ten minutes, then it was back to ABC for one last transmission to the States at 1:00 A.M. (the ceremonies had been videotaped). I had to stay around for the first hour of that transmission. I would have liked to have seen the very end, but I was just too tired. In addition, Margaret and I were getting up early in the morning to start our post-Olympics drive through Europe.

As I was leaving, Roone was still behind the console, running everything as he had since he acquired the rights to these games years ago.

I lifted one earpiece of his headset as he stared at the monitors.

"Everything you've built for twelve years came together on this one," I said. "Congratulations."

I walked out into the darkness. It was colder, and a few athletes were huddled into their warm-up jackets as they made their way back to the village for the last time. The lights were out in most of the dormitories.

Someone had laid a wreath in front of Building 31.

The next morning, Margaret and I took off in a little orange BMW 1800 rental car. We drove, on a beautiful day, through Bavaria, Margaret finding a nice old Meissen pitcher in a shop in Kempten.

That night in Zurich, we checked into the new Hotel Atlantis in the dark, and were confused in the morning to awake to a strange cacophonous sound, like some sort of discordant temple bells. We were surprised, on looking out the window, to see that it was a herd of Swiss dairy cows, slowly making its way out into the fields, each with a different-sized bell around its neck. Observing the scene was a little Swiss girl, with her finger in her mouth.

Margaret said that she thought she would read the child's book *Heidi* as soon as she got home.

From Zurich, we drove through Switzerland to Geneva, then on over the Jura Mountains to Lyon, in France. Outside that gastronomic capital, in the town of Collonges-au-Mont-d'Or, we ate at the restaurant of Paul Bocuse, perhaps the best in the world. The next day, carefully following a map prepared for us by our European representative, Georges Croses, we took our time cruising through the vineyards of the Beaujolais country.

Georges Croses is a Frenchman who loves his wife, Regine, his homeland, its language, its food, and its wine in approximately that order, and he had meticulously chosen for us the most beautiful route possible. We stopped in the village of Fleury at the equivalent of a neighborhood bar. We ate cheese and sipped the ordinary table wine, the best Beaujolais I had ever tasted.

Margaret said she thought the view out the old wooden casement window past the windowbox of geraniums to the narrow village street outside was one of the prettiest she had seen, particularly the way the rays of the afternoon sun were slanting through the panes onto the crumbly cheese and the glasses of clear red wine in front of us.

And now, at midnight, we are in our room at the Hostellerie de la Poste, in the village of Avallon. We're at the top of a winding old stairway. Outside, under a single light, the rounded cobblestones of the small courtyard are shining, softly.

The summer of 1972 is over now. It has taken me from Pebble Beach to Prestwick, from the Beverly Hills Hotel to the Esso Motor Inn, from Indy to Eugene to Hayward to Munich.

We have seen beauty in sport—the one-iron of Jack Nicklaus drilling that ball into the wind off Carmel Bay, nearly flying it into the hole as he wrapped up the U.S. Open; Olga Korbut flying around the uneven parallel bars, somersaulting on the narrow, four-inch balance beam, dancing and pirouetting in the free exercises; Mark Donohue delicately taking his car through the turns at Indy, handling 900 horsepower at 200 miles an hour with the skill of a surgeon making an incision; Eddie Hart surging down the stretch in front of Borzov, smiling as he hit the tape, making up for so many things that had gone wrong.

We have seen great disappointments—Hart and Robinson missing the start; Jim Ryun flat on his back, writhing in misery and defeat; the American basketball team furious at the strange ruling which had turned their victory to dust; Jerry Grant watching Donohue fly past in the closing laps, just when it appeared that Grant might work a miracle at Indy; Nicklaus again, standing behind the eighteenth green at Muirfield, watching his grand slam campaign come to an end as Lee Trevino chipped into the hole.

We have seen death—Jim Malloy smashing into the wall out of turn three that morning in Indianapolis; the massacre at Munich.

The summer is over.

As it began, it looked much like the schedules of the eleven previous summers, at least of the other Olympic years. Now, at the end, looking back, it is as if all the other summers had been magnified and slightly distorted into a dream-like appearance.

It was a summer of the incredible.

It is over, though, and we now look to the future. There will be a future, I am convinced, for the Olympics as for all sports.

I thought of that about an hour ago, as Margaret and I were taking a walk before bedtime through the little village of Avallon. On a side street, the light was dim, but we saw two figures coming toward us.

An old man and a young boy were walking together. As they walked, the youngster—wearing those extra-short shorts that little French boys wear—would pause and bend over, work one of his feet into a crack in the sidewalk, put his knuckles down on the cement, then mutter, "Allez!" and begin to run.

He was practicing starts.

Epilogue

A coincidence of the schedule brings me back to the Olympic grounds in Munich on the last day of the year. I am on my way to Garmisch-Partenkirchen for an international ski-jumping championship tomorrow, but the road leads directly past the Oberwiesenfeld. Jacques Lesgards, Doug Wilson, and I have stopped for a brief look around.

The Hill of Rubble is dusted lightly with snow on this clear, very cold day. A dozen people stand on its summit surveying the grounds. Tourists are much in evidence, strolling through the silent venues.

The great stadium looks much the same. Only our wooden platform has been removed. The plastic roof still spreads over the scene, but with a bit of snow encrusted on it, it looks dusty and dull.

"Holiday on Ice" is playing in the Sporthalle where Olga Korbut dazzled the world.

The man-made lake, from which rose the immense, man-made rainbow at the closing ceremonies, is frozen solid. Perhaps two hundred people are ice skating on it. A few couples on skates slowly push baby carriages across the ice.

Two kids are chasing each other across the lake on bicycles.

Barnathan's Bungalow still stands, but soon will be moved to a factory somewhere in Germany, there to take up an anonymous life as just another windowless warehouse.

The television center is in the process of demolition. We walk through the remains of our studio and control room. The walls have been crushed into a mess of white fiberboard. One chunk of it still bears a piece of paper on which is written in flow-pen, "TODAY'S EVENTS."

The Olympic Village looks cold and impersonal. Only a very few of the high-rise apartments are occupied so far (by students). Walking through it, you realize that its warmth last summer came from the athletes themselves, and the color from their uniforms. The only color visible now is a pair of yellow winter underwear bottoms hanging out a window.

We stand now in front of Building 31. Looking through the window on the first floor, we see two empty rooms. On the floor lie two plastic shopping bags. That's all.

To the side of the front door, where the man in the white hat stood, smoking a cigarette as he bargained with the mediator, is a marble tablet, five feet wide, standing on steel legs about five feet high. Carved on it, in German on the left side, Hebrew on the right, are the stark facts:

"In this building lived, during the games of the XXth Olympiad, the team of the nation of Israel, from the 21st of August until the fifth of September, 1972 . . ."

It bears the names of the Israelis who died, and at the bottom says,

"Think of them."

A single green wreath sits atop the tablet. On the blue and white ribbon adorning it is the name of the lady who placed it there:

"From Frau Emmy Pinter of Würzburg to the dead of the fifth of September".

Tomorrow, a new year begins.

Picture Credits

Index